EDUCATION AND RACE FROM EMPIRE TO MULTIRACIAL BRITAIN

Second Edition

Sally Tomlinson

First edition published in Great Britain in 2019
Second edition published in Great Britain in 2026 by

Policy Press, an imprint of
Bristol University Press
University of Bristol
1–9 Old Park Hill
Bristol
BS2 8BB
UK
t: +44 (0)117 374 6645
e: bup-info@bristol.ac.uk

Details of international sales and distribution partners are available at policy.bristoluniversitypress.co.uk

© Bristol University Press 2026

DOI: 10.51952/9781447378327

British Library Cataloguing in Publication Data
A catalogue record for this book is available from the British Library

ISBN 978-1-4473-7829-7 hardcover
ISBN 978-1-4473-7830-3 paperback
ISBN 978-1-4473-7831-0 ePub
ISBN 978-1-4473-7832-7 ePdf

The right of Sally Tomlinson to be identified as author of this work has been asserted by her in accordance with the Copyright, Designs and Patents Act 1988.

All rights reserved: no part of this publication may be reproduced, stored in a retrieval system, or transmitted in any form or by any means, electronic, mechanical, photocopying, recording, or otherwise without the prior permission of Bristol University Press.

Every reasonable effort has been made to obtain permission to reproduce copyrighted material. If, however, anyone knows of an oversight, please contact the publisher.

The statements and opinions contained within this publication are solely those of the author and not of the University of Bristol or Bristol University Press. The University of Bristol and Bristol University Press disclaim responsibility for any injury to persons or property resulting from any material published in this publication.

Bristol University Press and Policy Press work to counter discrimination on grounds of gender, race, disability, age and sexuality.

Cover design: Robin Hawes
Front cover image: iStock

Contents

Acknowledgements		iv
List of abbreviations		v
Introduction		1
1	Empire and ethnocentric education	16
2	Internal colonialism and its effects	33
3	Ending Empire: education for ignorance, 1945–60s	44
4	Post-imperial anxieties and conflicts, 1970–90	61
5	Inequalities and education markets, 1990–97	81
6	New Labour: wars, race and education, 1997–2005	100
7	Not so New Labour: race and education, 2005–10	113
8	A divided society: race, class and education, 2010–16	125
9	A dog's breakfast: Brexit, 2016–19	143
10	Boris, COVID and educational chaos, 2019–22	159
11	Multiracial Britain, Brexit and the end of Empire, 2022–25	172
Conclusion		187
Notes		191
References		197
Index		222

Acknowledgements

This book uses work from social and imperial history, politics, educational policy and the politics of race, ethnicity and education. So many thanks to all colleagues with whom over the years I have been able to discuss and argue over the issues and learn from them. Special thanks to Tahir Abbas, Kalwant Bhopal, Linda Akomaning, Sue Caudron, Danny Dorling, Dave Gillborn, Carol Vincent, Geoffrey Walford, Paul Warmington and Brian Tomlinson for the tech stuff. Thanks to Jo-Anne Baird and Victoria Murphy, heads of department, for the hospitality of the Department of Education, University of Oxford, while this book was written and re-written. The book is (still) dedicated to the late Professor John Rex, who made it his intellectual life's work to destroy racism in all its forms, and to Baroness Doreen Lawrence who fought murderous racism.

List of abbreviations

AP	alternative provision
APPG	All Political Party Group
CATE	Council for the Accreditation of Teacher Education
CEA	Conservative Education Association
CERD	Commission for Ethnic and Racial Disparity
CNNA	Council for National Academic Awards
CRC	Community Relations Commission
CRE	Commission for Racial Equality
CRED	Commission on Race and Ethnic Disparities
CRT	Critical Race Theory
DCFS	Department for Children School and Families
DES	Department to Education and Science
DfE	Department for Education
DIUS	Department for Innovation Universities and Skills
DUP	Democratic Unionist party
EBD	Emotionally and Behaviourally Disturbed
ECHR	European Court of Human Rights
ECJ	European Court of Justice
EEC	European Economic Community
EHCP	Education and Health Care Plan
ESN	Educational Subnormality
EU	European Union
FBV	Fundamental British Values
FE	Further Education
GCSE	General Certificate of Secondary Education
GM	Grant Maintained
HEFC	Higher Education Funding Body
HMI	Her Majesty's Inspectors
LEA	Local Education Authority
NEU	National Education Union
NODM	National Organisation for Deported Migrants
NUT	National Union of Teachers
Ofsted	Office for Standards in Education
ONS	Office for National Statistics
PISA	Programme for International Student Assessment
SAGE	Scientific Advisory Group Emergencies
SEMH	social emotional and mental health
SEND	Special Educational Needs and Disability
SMSC	Spiritual, Moral, Social and Cultural
TTA	Teacher Training Agency

UK	United Kingdom
UKIP	United Kingdom Independence Party
WTO	World Trade Organization

Introduction

> The years between 2016 and 2024 were the most sustained period of domestic political drama since the second World War and arguably far longer than that ... Differences of class, race, education and origin all became refracted through the prism of Brexit.
>
> Shipman 2024: 881, 885

This book is a second edition of *Education and Race from Empire to Brexit* (2019), which took readers through the period from the height of the British Empire around 1870 to late 2018 when then Prime Minister Theresa May was negotiating the terms of exit from the European Union (EU). What followed was six years of a roller coaster ride of events in the politics of Brexit, Empire, race and education. The exit process was not completed until three Conservative prime ministers later – Boris Johnson, Liz Truss and Rishi Sunak. Rishi led what were to be final leaving negotiations in January 2023. This was rapidly followed months later by the newly re-elected Labour Prime Minister Keir Starmer, suggesting renewing closer relationships with the EU, while at the same time attempting to placate newly elected President Trump whose ambitions included the expansion of an American Empire. The British Empire continued towards a final disintegration, with the new government agreeing to give back the Chagos Archipelago – islands in the Indian Ocean taken from the French Empire in 1814, to independent Mauritius. Meanwhile, Trump suggested in early 2025 that the USA could take over Canada, one of the largest Dominions in the former British Empire. The Canadians were outraged, its then President Trudeau suggesting that this idea and the imposition of higher trade tariffs (taxes) on Canada were a 'very dumb thing to do'. But President Trump, elected for a second time, had begun to change a global order in which the USA was no longer a permanent friend to Europe, Britain or its former Empire. The book title had to change, as the years beyond Brexit were, as journalist Zoe Williams pointed out, a 'nightmarish phase' when it was 'impossible to believe that people so unprepared, so thoughtless and histrionic were steering the ship' (Williams 2024). The book leaves the original Chapters 1 to 9 more or less as in the 2019 edition, and then adds two more chapters covering the period 2019–22 and 2022–25, with a short, concluding chapter.

The current title is a reminder that the country is actually multiracial, multicultural and multifaith, and whatever the hostile views and beliefs of some politicians and a minority of the public will remain so.[1] Having lived through and studied the transformation of the society over the past 50 years, it is sad that there are still people yearning for an imperial white country minus all immigrants but a socio-historical view is the approach adopted here. While some of the activities and behaviour recorded may seem banal or even amusing, it should be remembered that people defending what they think of as their nation, ethnicity, religion or culture are often prepared to kill and die for their beliefs. This is one reason why education is so important to combat ignorance and despair. The chapters describe what happened in what is still the United Kingdom, but global information and comparisons are noted. Major world issues over these years were and remain continued conflict in what in imperial days was described as the Middle East, with a Palestinian–Israeli slaughter in Gaza which exacerbated racism, islamophobia and anti-Semitism in Britain, and the invasion of the Ukraine nation by President Putin of Russia who is dedicated to expanding a Russian Empire. Post-Second World War, successive USA governments encouraged European countries to decolonise but were compliant in 'regime change' in many areas of the world. A major shock to the world by 2025 was the abdication of the USA from global democratic leadership under the imperially minded former property developer President Trump and his billionaire friends.[2]

The first edition of the book noted that the vote to leave the EU had increased hostilities towards racial and minoritised groups and individuals, and also towards immigration of all kinds. Popular newspapers and other media especially denigrated the migration of refugees, asylum seekers and economic migrants arriving in small boats across the 'English' Channel (the French simply call it Le Channel), legal methods of migration having diminished over the years. Over the recent years the politics of race, ethnicity, culture and identity have mostly continued along familiar negative and often patronising lines, with even one of Queen Elizabeth's ladies in waiting forcing the 'where do you really come from' conversation on a British-born subject who happened to have a darker skin tone at a Buckingham Palace reception in 2022 (BBC News 2022). There continued to be contradictions between the unpleasant lived reality of racism for most of those living in the UK with racial or religious labels and the appointments of a few 'successful' minority people, including a Black female leader of the Conservative Party in 2024.

An understanding that there is actually a Global Majority in the world who are 'not white' has begun to percolate, although this has in some cases supported old lies that 'they' are taking over the country (Gillborn 2024). The book attempts to cover something of the politics and ideologies of Empire. It covers the arrival of immigrants from the former colonial countries, links with Europe and free movement of labour, the arrival of refugees and asylum seekers from global conflicts, growing hostility to the EU, often helped on by misinformation and lies, and the post Brexit years when disillusion with the Leave decision became apparent but a popular anti-immigrant nationalism became more obvious. The failures of an education system which in the 21st century had become a divisive, competitive, market enterprise largely retaining an ethnocentric curriculum are discussed. In the UK we have more successful 'schooling' in terms of testing and exam passing, but we do not have successful education. We continue to manufacture ignorance of the past in a divided and divisive education system in which neither the present nor the future can be clearly understood.

The added chapters of the book cover some of the major issues and controversies that have dominated politics and policies in Britain over the past six years to 2025, a major issue in the post-Brexit period being the COVID-19 virus pandemic, which led to an overrepresentation of death and illness for Black and Asian people, and a source of educational disruption for a generation of young people. A second major issue was the murder of a Black man, George Floyd, by a white police officer, in Minneapolis, USA, on 25 May 2020, provoking international horror and protest, and energising both a Black Lives matter movement and also conservative political and cultural discoveries of 'woke' practices.[3] A third continuing issue has been the rise of far right political parties both in Britain and other European countries. The small but violent 1970s British National Front turned into a UK Independence Party, which morphed into a Reform Party, which by 2025 had five MPs in Parliament. Right-wing populism and its political representation became a force to be taken more seriously, especially as closer ties developed both to the American Trump presidency and to European far-right groups. Trump and his appointees appeared to be living a back to the future scenario in February 2025, when the foreign secretaries of the USA and the Russian Federation met in 'imperial mood' (Borger 2025) in Saudi Arabia. They were there to discuss the invasion of Ukraine by Vladimir Putin's Russian army in 2022 and a possible carve-up of that country. Historians remembered a cartoon drawn in 1805 'The plum pudding in danger', which showed English Prime Minister William Pitt and French General Napolean Bonaparte carving up the world as a plum pudding, and also the 1939 meeting in Munich between Herr Hitler and the Italian Leader Mussolini, meeting to discuss the carve-up of Czechoslovakia, which helped lead to the Second World War.

It is important to ask what schools and the wider education system were doing over these troubled years to prepare young people for their changing world, especially given that much information and disinformation was increasingly passed over via social media and digital means. Most British people, including the supposedly well-educated, have learned little about any of the world's empires, possibly apart from the Roman Empire, endlessly romanticised in film and literature. They know little about the British Empire their grandparents were born into, which after the Second World War and with some brutal conflict turned into a Commonwealth of some 53 nations,

31 of them with fewer than 3 million people. This included some 14 overseas territories that provide offshore financial centres and 'tax havens' for rich individuals and global companies (Dorling and Tomlinson 2020). They knew little about the processes of decolonisation, the arrival of immigrants from the Caribbean, the Asian sub-continent and other post-colonial countries. The incorporation of settled citizens and their descendants into the British class structure while recognising differences continues to be regarded as a problem, especially for Muslim citizens. It was only in 2018 that the full story of the deliberate creation of a 'hostile environment' towards migrants created by the Home Office, with Theresa May then the home secretary, began to emerge. This policy, defended in a subsequent book (May 2023) led to some of the early Caribbean migrants, the 'Windrush generation', being deported despite working for some 70 years in Britain. Over the years there has been deliberate confusion between economic and family migration encouraged from post-colonial countries, with refugees and asylum seekers fleeing conflicts overseas, and with European workers who arrived under EU rules of freedom of movement of labour. Populist politicians encouraged those who think of themselves as victims of globalisation that has outsourced jobs overseas, or taken by migrants in the country, to feel dispossessed. Many who regard themselves as rightful residents turn on those regarded as 'not British' and make them scapegoats, with racial and migrant hatreds intensifying. These views have not diminished much over the years since the Brexit vote in 2016 despite polls indicating that a majority of people in the UK by 2024 viewed the decision to leave the EU as a mistake, and there being a distinct shortage of former European workers in crucial sectors of the economy. British citizens, ignorant of their own history, have found it difficult to understand that a future world of superpowers may no longer include Britain as a major influence, although the country may ally again more firmly with the rest of Europe.

Education and delusions of Empire

Age was important in the Brexit decision, with 60 per cent of those over 65 voting to leave the EU. Older people had experienced in various forms an ethnocentric jingoistic curriculum still resonant with late 19th- and 20th-century consciousness of Empire. This book covers a period when popular imperialism was at its height, which coincided with a time when mass education was developing. A value system based on military patriotism, xenophobia and a nationalism that excluded racial minorities, colonial and foreigners was filtering down from the upper class public schools to the middle class grammar schools and the elementary schools attended by the working classes. In 1902 a history textbook recommended by the Board of Education extolled *Men of Renown* who had conquered and plundered countries inhabited by 'savage crowds eager to slay Englishman' (Finnemore 1902: 254). In early juvenile literature the noble Tarzan was forever fighting in jungles against wicked Black men, a new Tarzan film being released in 2016. In 1948 an *Empire Youth Annual* included an article on an exciting train journey from Delhi to Lahore without a mention of the horrors of the previous year when the partition of India led to millions slaughtered (Faucett 1948). Eventually, even Ian Flemings's favourite secret service agent James Bond needed a makeover 70 years after the first novels depicted him making racist, sexist and homophobic remarks.

Schools and textbooks for over a hundred years were places of myth-making and evasions about Empire. Until the 1960s, maps of the world still had large sections coloured pink because the countries 'belonged to us' and a curriculum tacitly supporting the merits of Empire and silent on exploitation and cruelty was the norm. Race and Empire shaped the concept of national citizenship and resentment of immigration shaped the view of who should belong and who should be excluded. In 2016 at the time of the referendum a YouGov poll reported that over 40 per cent of respondents thought the British Empire was a 'Good thing' and 'an unwillingness to engage with the warts and all of imperial history makes Britian particularly blind to how governments and people of other countries view British society' (Owen 2016). In social class-conscious Britain, racism and xenophobia have no bounds. In 2017 the 4th Viscount St Davids was jailed for racially abusing Gina Miller, a business woman who had won a legal challenge over the government on voting. He described her as' a boat jumper ... if this is what we expect from immigrants, send them back to their stinking jungles' and offered money to anyone 'who will accidentally run over this bloody troublesome immigrant' (Rawlinson 2017). The comments of Boris Johnson both before and after he was appointed foreign secretary by Theresa May in 2017 suggested that the colonial mentality that characterised the British State survived even in Eton-educated men. He had claimed that 'The African continent is a blot, but it is not a blot on our conscience. The problem is not that we were once in charge, but that we are not in charge any more' (Msimang 2016), and when foreign secretary, informed a United Nations meeting that 'of the 193 present members of the UN we have conquered or invaded at least 90% of them' (see Brown 2017: 27). Despite being forced to resign as prime minister in 2022 after many transgressions with the truth, Boris Johnson was contemplating a return to politics in 2025.

The long and continuous political discussions over the terms of Brexit and global trade demonstrated a reluctance to engage with 21st-century realities. Initially, there seemed to be an idea that 'the UK could bring all its former colonies back into a warm free trading family based on delusions about empire' (Kappal 2017). There was much discussion about embracing world trade rules and new alliances, and about trade with Northern Ireland which now had a border with the Irish Republic and thus with the EU. The public were treated to endless political and media speculation about an Irish 'backstop' which sounded to many like a plumbing problem rather than a trade arrangement. There was a manufacture of ignorance about globalisation, as governments spread the belief that they cannot control economic cooperation between countries, the movement of labour round the world as transnational businesses look for cheaper labourers or the disappearance of local, regional and national industries and jobs. There was an increase in precarious forms of work, lower wages and widening inequalities, with rising unemployment and greater social and economic insecurities. Former prime minister Gordon Brown wrote in his autobiography that the end of Empire and free market beliefs had led to more poverty and joblessness (Brown 2017). Danny Dorling has described in detail the rising inequalities in Britain over four decades and the ways in which the rich live apart from the poor, especially those who keep their money in the 14 small overseas territories remaining in the British Commonwealth. In 2023 he suggested that the nation was on the way to becoming a 'Failing State' through ever widening inequalities (Dorling 2018, 2023). In the USA Democrat Senator Bernie Saunders described in detail some of the appalling inequalities in the USA that made it 'OK to be angry about capitalism' (Saunders 2023). But even he could not have envisaged a re-energised President Trump taking a second term of office and recruiting his billionaire friend Elon Musk to help run the USA.

Although in Britain politicians of all parties had supported longstanding myths that immigrants into the country were a major cause of social and economic problems, Richard Sennet (2006) among others drew attention to the consequences of the insecurities generated by inequalities as whole populations became frightened and project their anxieties onto migrants, foreign workers and refugee and asylum seekers. The right-wing media had always colluded in this. Out of 144,779 newspaper and magazine articles published in the ten weeks up to the Brexit referendum almost all included negative comment on immigration. In the years following there had been constant negative coverage and pernicious linkage of refugees and asylum seekers with crime. Lies that recently arrived asylum seekers were involved in the terrible murders of three small girls in Southport, England, in 2024 led to refugees and asylum seekers housed in a hotel in Rotherham, Yorkshire, being threatened with being burnt alive by an English rioting mob, the sort of event people thought had been relegated to medieval times (Brown and Al-Othman 2025 and see Chapter 11).

Empire and the long goodbye

The start of what is referred to as the 'First British Empire' is debatable. The actual take-over of land is usually claimed to be the island of Bermuda, following a British shipwreck there in 1609. Ironically, the island is now a tax haven for wealthy people and multinational companies. Collingham has claimed that earlier 'The British empire was born on Newfoundland's stony beaches', as by 1540s fishermen were sailing past Iceland to catch cod to feed the expanding Royal navy (Collingham 2017: 13). Eventually, through conquest and exploitation, looting the land and labour of other countries, Britain emerged as a major sea power and trading nation. The East India Company, a forerunner of the imperial conquest of India was given a Royal charter in 1600, and began sending those precious spices to brighten up boring British food. By the 18th century half the imported goods into Britain were foodstuffs, especially sugar produced by slave labour in the Caribbean. The East India Company was a corporation with a standing army and by 1765 had taken over the State of Bengal from the Mughal emperors, sending out Lieutenant-General Robert Clive, a supposed military genius, but later described as 'an unstable sociopath' (Dalrymple 2015: 25) to run the company, take over the grain market and create a famine in which 10,000 people died, while enriching himself and company shareholders. A Mughal official complained that 'he had to take orders from (English) traders who had not yet learned to wash their bottoms' and Dalrymple concluded in 2015 that 'For all the power wielded today by the world's largest corporations – Exxon, Mobil, Walmart, Google – they are tame beasts compared with the ravening territorial appetite of the militarised East India company' (Dalrymple 2015: 27). Clive was one of the *Men of Renown* included in the 1902 history textbook through which several generations of British children learned about Empire (Finnemore 1902).

Over the 19th century the full 'second' British Empire was created as more and more territories were added. From those early claims to Bengal a British Empire ruling a quarter of the globe had been created under Queen Victoria – by 1880 crowned Empress of India. In 1849 *The Times* newspaper proudly recoded the annexation of the Punjab by which the area was now to be part of the British Empire of India, the local Maharaja having to hand his province over to the British at gun point and 'solicit clemency from the British government' (*The Times* 1849). By the mid-19th century, Britain had embraced an industrial revolution and described itself as a workshop of the world, with much of this revolution depending on slave and indentured labour overseas, importing the raw materials, the food, the gold and even those ostrich feathers for ladies hats from colonised lands. British imperialists pursued 'free trade' and attempted to break down protectionism – how countries protect the import and export of their goods and services – to open up markets for British goods and economic control. The rail network the British built in India was mainly to transport goods for export and by 1900 a fifth of wheat imports came from India. Collingham recorded that between 1875 and 1914 some 16 million Indians died in famines and a colonial government did little to alleviate this, insisting that it was 'nature's way of keeping a check on the Indian population' (Collingham 2017: 221). It was in India that the British government, military, missionaries and others perfected the doctrine of racial, cultural and moral superiority of a white Britain over what they described as 'corrupt and barbarian societies' with imperial conquest bringing, as Lord Macauley later told parliament 'a triumph of reason over barbarianism … the imperishable empire of our arts, our morals, our literature and our laws' (Elkins 2022: 45).

As this book covers the period from the late 19th century, it is worth noting that the high point of imperialism in the 1920s and 1930s was a period when successive governments were abandoning notions of free trade and introducing 'imperial preference'. The 1924 Empire Exhibition aimed to persuade people to buy goods from imperial countries, a major item of interest being a life-size model of the then Prince of Wales on horseback made entirely out of butter (Paxman 2012: 247). It melted quicker than his brief kingship in 1936. In 1926 the government set up an Empire marketing board, which produced 72 reports in ten years. A report on *Why Every Woman Should Buy British and Empire* included a recipe for an Empire Christmas pudding with ingredients to be sourced from all corners of the Empire. A filmed ceremony in December 1926 in the London Overseas League included turbaned Indian servants carrying the required sultanas, currents and candied fruit, and even Irish eggs and Cypriot brandy. As a symbol of national and imperial pride, the Royal family were induced to eat the pudding at Christmas. The official caterer for the Indian Pavilion at this exhibition was Mr Veeraswamy who later opened the first Indian restaurant in Regent Street, London, noted for serving Balti (bucket) food. The restaurant became popular with fashionable society and later 'Indian' food became a staple of the British diet.

The long goodbye of Empire has its own war of words, as historians, politicians, journalists and fiction writers debate and continue to add to a voluminous literature and argue over whether the British Empire was good for the world or not. The Victorian educated classes were fond of Edward Gibbon's *The Decline and Fall of the Roman Empire* (1781). Emulating Gibbon, Piers Brendon produced *The Decline and Fall of the British Empire* (2007) in which he covered the loss of the American colonies in 1781 to the handing over of Hong Kong to China in 1997, concluding that while there was violence and exploitation, on balance 'the lust for conquest is part of the human condition and the spirit of imperialism is not dead' (Brendon 207: 656), a view which imperially minded leaders in the 21st century might agree with. Historian Niall Ferguson, whose *Empire: How Britian Made the Modern World* (Ferguson 2004) extolled the benefits brought to the world by the British Empire, criticised those who pointed out the exploitative nature of Empire as Marxists and was taken on as an advisor to Conservative

Education Secretary Michael Gove helping to rewrite the English history curriculum. Bruce Gilley in 2017 made a case for Britian to recolonise and even create new Western colonies (Gilley 2017). His article led to demands that his paper be retracted, but Nigel Biggar, Professor of Moral and Pastoral Theology at Oxford University, supported Gilley as having 'intellectual integrity and moral courage' (Biggar 2023: xiii). Biggar created an 'Ethics and Empire' seminar series in 2017, objected to students and fellow academics supporting the removal of a statue of colonialist Cecil Rhodes from the front of an Oxford College and complained that academic 'post-colonialists' in his own university were a 'disparate bunch' (Biggar 2023: 5). His own defence of imperialism was published in 2023 as *Colonialism: A Moral Reckoning*, in which he argued that the Empire was not particularly racist, violent or exploitative. He was nominated for a peerage in 2025 by a Conservative prime minister and in his maiden speech in the House of Lords complained about those wanting to 'decolonise' the curriculum.

In contrast, John Newsinger documented the atrocities of Empire in *The Blood Never Dried: A People's History of the British Empire* (Newsinger 2006). Jeremy Paxman wrote amusingly but pointedly about decolonisation and a long irreversible decline of Empire, in which the 'sound chaps' who ruled and their Home Counties wives enjoyed sundowners on the veranda and suet puddings had long since retired. He pointed out that even the imperial sport of cricket, once governed by the Marylebone Cricket Club (MCC) is now run by and international committee in Dubai. Paxman suggested that the native British had been cushioned from reality for so long because the Empire gave such comforting illusions about their place in the world and 'the stupid sense that they were born to rule' (Paxman 2012: 285). Porter noted that the notion of a British Empire conjured up images of domination and pride, assisted by those pink bits on the maps on school walls, which using the Mercator projection actually exaggerates the areas of colonial lands and dominions (Porter 2015). But the most horrific account to date of the cruelties and violence perpetrated as countries and their peoples were taken over is probably by Caroline Elkins, Professor at Harvard, USA, who offered a different account of the Empire in *Legacy of Violence: A History of the British Empire* (Elkins 2022). She wrote in detail about the unremitting violence and the racialised views that secured British interests as they took over other lands. Closer to home, British historian David Olusoga, experiencing considerable racist violence while growing up in England, wrote on *Black and British: A Forgotten History* (Olusoga 2016) and in literature and TV programmes endeavoured to show the linkages between people over several hundred years between colonial countries and the imperial centre and the import of beliefs in the inferiority of those from former colonised countries. One reaction to critics of Empire is to point out that other European countries had empires and were forced to decolonise in often violent ways. David Van

Rebrouk produced a large volume in 2024 describing the way the often violent Dutch decolonisation in Indonesia had led the way to a 'modern world', although he also noted that American imperialism was expanding from the 1950s (Van Rebrouk 2024: 517). One positive of a global media is that knowledge of the histories and consequences of empire building and ending can be shared worldwide through digital means even if schools do not provide much information.

Brexit after Empire

Legends of imperial triumph and conquests formed the basis for the widespread belief in a superior white British heritage and the pervasive notion, shared across all social classes, that the British had economic, moral and intellectual superiority over previously colonised people, and indeed over all 'foreigners'. This was perhaps the most damaging legacy of the long goodbye of Empire. In the often violent decolonisation in the 1950s and 1960s, Britain abandoned the protection of post imperial goods, although instigating a lucrative and sometimes illegal arms trade. The British Empire was finally considered to be dying after 1956 and the debacle of trying to retain the Suez canal in Egypt after its President Nasser nationalised the high road to India for shipping (Lloyd 1984). In 1972 the country joined the European Economic Community (EEC), which was finally voted for in a referendum in 1975. Conservative politicians, as veteran Tory MP Kenneth Clark recorded, were eager to join the European trading block, although many Labour MPs were opposed. Twenty-one years later Margaret Thatcher signed the 1986 Act which created a single market for European trading. Six years after that, in 1992 another Tory prime minister, John Major, signed the treaty bringing the European Union into existence despite Eurosceptics and anti-EU supporters claiming the country had lost an opportunity to renew imperial trade.

The British public were asked in 2016 in a referendum promised by Prime Minister David Cameron whether to leave the EU and close ties with the rest of the now 28 member states. The UKIP Party claimed that 'Outside the EU the world is our oyster' and envisaged closer ties with what had become a Commonwealth of former imperial countries. If schooling from the 19th century had presented the British Empire as a romanticised and seemingly permanent entity that was mainly a force for good, no such romanticism had ever been attached to the EU. Few British leaders had ever been enthusiastic for a European Project. Despite the Maastricht Treaty to join what was now the EU, right-wing groups, including a self-styled European Research group, kept up permanent opposition and yearned for a return of British blue passports instead of the EU scarlet ones. Criticism from UKIP and its member in the European Parliament, then led by Nigel Farage, drowned out any positive measures membership of the EU brought and in 2016 a 'Leave' campaign, organised by Dominic Cummings, later an advisor to Boris Johnson (see Chapter 10) voted to leave the Union, 17.4 million voting out and 16.3 remain, with 28 per cent of the electorate not voting at all. Leavers finally got their blue passports back, which were actually made in France. There followed an outpouring of literature debating who voted in or out and why but Moore and Ramsey demonstrated just how much money various rich men had contributed to influencing the vote, especially through digital advertising (Moore and Ramsey 2017). Former *Sunday Times* editor Tim Shipman, who had devoted himself over six years to documenting progress after Brexit, was able to produce a 926-page book *Out: How Brexit Got Done and the Tories Were Undone* (Shipman 2024). It was ironic that while Shipman ended his book in early 2024 with a comment that 'Brexit was a brutal process that churned up and spat out careers broke friendships and strained peoples sanity' (Shipman 2024: 905), a year later friendships were being renewed and old alliances made, in response to threats and hostilities from those other great imperialists Russia and the USA.

Structure of the book

There is a large and still growing literature on the British Empire, the Commonwealth, the incorporation of post-colonial people and on the education history, policy and practices as the education system grudgingly responded to the incorporation of children who over the years were variously labelled in policy documents as New Commonwealth, ethnic minority, Black and minority ethnic (BAME) and other labels. Much of the recent literature, both academic, policy oriented, biographical or fiction, is now produced by Black and minority scholars and writers, documenting the past and present experiences of those for who the British Empire and its aftermath were not 'Great'. This present book, as every socio-historical text, is necessarily selective of significant events.

Chapter 1 notes that explanations for the 2016 Brexit vote, trade wars and past and current race and migrant hostilities and hatreds, must start with the British Empire, especially from the 19th century when power, wealth and dominance became concentrated in a white world. Racial arrogance and assumptions have continued into the 21st century. The chapter discusses the development of education in England over the late 19th and early 20th century, as well as events associated with imperialism and its beliefs. It records the way British values and invented traditions, imbued with nationalism, militarism and racial arrogance, were filtered down from elite 'public' schools to state secondary and elementary schools, and comments on the teaching, textbooks and youth literature. Chapter 2 suggests that by the 21st century the whole notion of a United Kingdom – the Union with Scotland, Northern

Ireland and Wales – was debatable. These countries had been internally colonised by the English in much the same ways that the British Empire's overseas colonies had been created. It offers a brief overview of the way the subjects of these Celtic countries were taken over, their languages and culture denigrated while they were dominated politically and exploited for labour. It notes that the English working class from the 19th century were encouraged to regard Irish and Black people as inferior and until the 1960s landladies could legally put up notices in their windows refusing Black or Irish renters.

Chapter 3 covers the period from 1945 to the 1960s, as former colonies fought for or gained their independence, often with brutal resistance from British troops and government. While Labour Prime Minister Attlee agreed to Indian independence in 1945, former Prime Minister Winston Churchill was loudly opposed to decolonisation and independence, and when back in power considered using the slogan 'Keep Britian White' in the 1955 general election. Although immigrant labour was desperately needed, immigration control acts were passed in the 1960s and discussion of the brutalities of decolonisation were missing from public discourse as well as the school and university curriculum. Schools did little to inform young people about the realities of decolonisation and why Black and Asian and other minorities had arrived in the country. Politicians and schools regarded immigrant children as problems and the response to the children was largely negative. All social classes were, to some extent, united in hostility to the arrival of former colonial migrants. By the end of the 1960s Conservative and Empire supporter Enoch Powell MP claimed that a sense of being a persecuted minority was growing among the working classes (Powell 1968), socialist notions of the brotherhood of man were disappearing and middle class Conservative Associations were firmly against immigration. Chapter 4 documents the ways in which former colonised subjects with a variety of backgrounds, languages and religions were openly regarded as a threat to British identity. Policies included more immigration control, campaigns for repatriation and politicians claiming the country was being 'swamped' by immigration, and the early 1980s saw violent clashes between the police and young minorities. The chapter records changing education policies as moves towards comprehensive education increased, with anxiety that young people were not prepared for the world of work. Minorities were subsumed under the label of 'disadvantage' with worries about their lower school achievements and placements in an expanding special education sector. There was little curriculum change in schools despite a Green paper in 1977 which asserted that 'The curriculum appropriate for the imperial past cannot meet the requirements of modern Britain' (DES 1977), and attempts by teachers, local authorities and academics to change policies in a multicultural and anti-racist direction were met with hostility.

Chapter 5 suggests that over the 1990s more tensions emerged over immigration after the Maastricht Treaty in 1992 which guaranteed free movement of capital, services and people in EU countries. The 1991 Census was the first to introduce an 'ethnic' question and the geographical spread of minorities became clearer, with settled minorities embracing a British or English identity as well as ethnic identities. There was an increase in numbers of non-Europeans to take professional and service jobs and an increase in refugees and asylum seekers from global conflicts. False beliefs that the 'white' majority were missing out in housing, health and other social services increased and the first Gulf war against Saddam Hussein's Iraq in 1990 led to more racism directed at Islam. Neo-Nazi parties continued to recruit young whites and the murder of Black student Stephen Lawrence in 1993 focused attention on racial hostility. The chapter documents educational legislation from 1988 to 1996, which turned schooling into a market place, stressing parental 'choice' and competition between schools. Teacher preparation and university courses on race and education disappeared and multiculturalism was derided. John Major left office claiming that policy should be colour blind and must just stress disadvantage. Chapters 6 and 7 describe how the New Labour government came to power in 1997 asserting a commitment to social and racial justice with initially some equitable policies – a Human Rights Act, state funding for Muslim schools alongside other state-funded religious schools, an inquiry into the murder of Stephen Lawrence and an Ethnic Minority Achievement grant. But the Blair government continued the Conservative education policies of choice and competition that exacerbated social and racial segregation. Rioting in northern towns led to further assertions that 'multiculturalism has failed' and a report on the *Future of Multiethnic Britain* commissioned by Home Secretary Jack Straw was attacked in the right wing media and disowned by the government. As Prime Minister Tony Blair supported seven wars, the invasions of Afghanistan in 2000 and Iraq in 2003 helped radicalise a small number of young Muslims and the ending of restrictions on free movement of Eastern European people led to more antagonism to economic migration. Before leaving power in 2010, the Labour government passed both an Equalities Act targeting all kinds of discrimination and a Borders, Citizenship and Immigration Act to deter migrants. It also set up a review into university fees, which resulted in their being raised to £9,000 a year by the incoming Conservative/Lib Dem government and generations of young people being landed with life-time debt.

Chapter 8 covers the period of a coalition government and a period of austerity which negatively affected all working class people, including minorities and those with disabilities. Austerity was justified by blaming the Labour government, unions, immigrants and the poor for claiming benefits. The country was no longer able to exploit an Empire and was becoming more divided into rich and poor areas, 'school choice' making this worse. Riots and conflict in 2011 in London and other cities after a police shooting of a young Black man led to more hostility to minorities and the demonisation of Muslims and Islam reached a peak with a hysterical reaction to lies about a supposed 'Trojan Horse' infiltration of schools by Islamists. British values, which turned out to be those of democratic value globally, were to be taught in schools while the whole system became more undemocratic. Curriculum reforms ensured a narrowing of the curriculum and more competitive testing. Chapter 9 covers the period 2016 to 2019, perhaps one of most turbulent in British political history as the vote to leave the EU resulted in political parties, individuals, groups and the EU slugging out to arrive at some kind of Brexit. Those tasked with an exit from the EU appeared at first to have little understanding of their task, with civil servants joking that an 'Empire 2.00' could be created, and there were often vicious arguments between the 'hard Brexiteers' who wanted nothing more to do with an EU and trade to be carried on under world trade rules and more moderate politicians of all parties. Prime Minister Thereas May produced several schemes for a softer Brexit which were rejected by her party and her Foreign Secretary Boris Johnson resigned his post with an eye on the leadership. Despite a series of scandals in her government and the tragedy of a fire in Grenfell Tower which killed 72 mainly minority people, May soldiered on and held a general election in June 2017 supposedly to consolidate her position. The Conservatives lost seats, May shed tears when she announced her resignation in May 2019 and Boris Johnson was elected as prime minister in July, promising to 'get Brexit done' by October.

Chapter 10 takes up the story of another turbulent three years to 2022 as Johnson began with an illegal attempt to prorogue Parliament so that there would be no parliamentary discussion of his attempts to finalise leaving the EU. While preoccupied with this and a second divorce, he decided too late to lock down the country when the full horror of a global pandemic (COVID-19) struck in early 2020. The chapter includes more on his unruly government and the scandals of 'Partygate' over the years. It covers the progress of the pandemic including educational chaos under two education secretaries, Gavin Williamson and Nadhim Zahawi. It discusses hostile political reactions to the murder of George Floyd in the USA in May 2020 and the 'Black Lives Matter' movement, the 'woke' agenda and guidance to schools on British values and 'extremists', and the publication of a report by a Commission on *Racial and Ethnic Disparities* (Commission on Race and Ethnic Disparities 2021) which minimised the extent of racial hostilities and the continuation of a hostile environment for migrants.

Chapter 11 continues the dismal story to 2025 as Johnson resigned over lying to Parliament to be replaced for only 49 days as prime minister by Liz Truss and then Rishi Sunak until the Conservative Party was defeated in a general election in July 2024 when Keir Starmer and Labour took over. A churn of another five education secretaries of state over these years (one, Michelle Donelan, lasting only two days in post) attempted to deal with the effects of the pandemic which had left a generation of partly schooled children, many with claimed mental health issues. The emphasis on an 'academic' curriculum and behavioural programmes, a supposedly 'broken' system for children with special educational needs and disabilities, the rise in school exclusion and an alternative provision system, an inspection system which led to the suicide of a head teacher and the continued reluctance to create an inclusive, less ethnocentric education system for all young people are some issues discussed. A newly elected Labour government with Education Secretary Bridget Phillipson was initially faced with the murders of three girls in Southport in August 2024 by a boy whose Christian parents were immigrants from Rwanda. The question remains as to how far the education system can compensate for continuing racial hostilities in a post-imperial society where migrants and minorities have long been blamed for social and economic ills.

A brief conclusion to the book draws the themes of the book together as a new era in global imperial history develops. The UK under Labour Prime Minister Starmer took the first hesitant steps towards a reset of relations with the EU, not quite reversing Brexit. Power blocks in the world will more likely be American, Chinese and Russian. There will be no comeback for Old European Empires and the British Empire will not be making a comeback, although those island tax havens for the rich may be even more in demand. There is some evidence that schools and higher education are slowly changing the content of learning to come to terms with a post-imperial role, although there is still much ignorance of the past. The country is slowly accepting that it is multiracial, multicultural and multifaith, and despite problems will not be going back to an old imperial mode.

1

Empire and ethnocentric education

> What is Empire but the predominance of Race ... do we not hail in this, less than the energy and fortune of a race, than in the supreme direction of the Almighty.
>
> Lord Rosebery 1900

The race Lord Rosebery referred to in his inaugural address as Rector of the University of Glasgow in 1900 was a white race, Social Darwinists having by that time decided that 'Mankind is usually divided into three primary races'. These were the Caucasian or white race, the Mongolian or Yellow race, and the Negro race, with a note for the 'Red Indians' of America telling them they were part of the Mongolian race (Stembridge 1951). Jasper Stembridge, whose geography textbooks were used in schools into the 1980s in England, was a worthy man, explaining that geography should help boys and girls 'see social and political problems in a truer perspective and give them a sympathetic understanding of other peoples' (Stembridge 1951: iii). But the treatment of 'other peoples' met largely through the expansion of the British Empire, and through wars and violence, was certainly not sympathetic. Trying to explain the British Empire to most young people, unless they have specifically 'done a module' on some aspect, is to invite incomprehension. Even older people, schooled during decolonisation, have little knowledge about empire, commonwealth or recent global migrations, although regrets for a lost empire still linger. How Britain became and will remain a multiracial country, still baffles and upsets many, with hostility and fear that a 'white race' may not be predominant at all.

But explaining the 2016 Brexit vote, trade wars, and race and migrant antagonisms must start with the British Empire, specifically in the later 19th century when power, wealth and trade dominance were concentrated a predominantly white world. Any early 19th century humanitarian notions, which had influenced legislation ending slavery, gave way, as more countries were added to the empire, to beliefs that 'black and brown subjects were natural inferiors' (Lloyd 1984: 180). Beliefs that God was in favour of white supremacy and imperial expansion were widely embraced, Queen Victoria was proclaimed Empress of India in 1877 and there was a 'scramble' for imperial control of African countries by major European powers in 1884.

American historian Goldberg wrote that by the late 19th century race 'had assumed throughout the European orbit a sense of naturalness ... a more or less taken for granted marking of social arrangements ... an assumed givenness and inevitability in the ascription of superiority and inferiority' (Goldberg 2009: 3). Science and literature, scripture and law, culture and political rhetoric were co-opted to establish assumptions of white superiority. Although in 1771 Prime Minister William Pitt and French Napoleon were famously lampooned via a cartoon of a plum pudding representing the globe for dividing the world up between them, the 1880s to the 1930s was the high point of imperial conquests and trade which benefited Britain. Imperial expansion by this time was dedicated to capturing markets and claiming natural resources in colonised countries for exploitation. An ignorance of the actual territories comprising the British Empire continued into the 20th century, some people being confused in 1982 when the Argentineans invaded the Falkland islands, which many thought were Scottish islands. Imperial arrogance was evident during this war, naval officer David Tinker writing that 'The navy felt that we were British and they (the Argentineans) were wogs, and that made all the difference' (Tinker 1982: 178). David was killed aged 26, in the war.

But it was Victorian beliefs in racial superiority, underpinned by pseudo-scientific rationalisations for political and economic take-overs and exploitation of other countries, plus renewed militarism and notions of patriotism, that survive to the present day. Enoch Powell, Conservative MP, claimed in a speech in 1961 that 'the unbroken life of the British nation' was something unique in history and the continuity of the nation's existence was unbroken when the connections linking England to 'distant continents and strange races fell away' (Powell 1961). He referred to these places and races even while colonies in the continents were fighting for independence and Britain was becoming more multiracial, multicultural and multireligious. His appeal was as a major advocate of an imperialist ideology and a populist nationalism which in the 21st century has found expression in right-wing politics in and out of parliaments, and in a resurgence of white supremacist activities in Europe and the USA. The aim of this chapter is to link some significant events in the development of education in England in the 19th and 20th century with imperial events and ideologies. This was a period when, as Hoque noted, a rhetoric of coloniser versus the colonised, powerful versus powerless, civilised versus uncivilised, modern versus backward, educated versus uneducated, helped shape and institutionalise race, class and gender relations between white people and those from the 'dark continents' of Africa and Asia (Hoque 2015). The chapter indicates the way in which 'British Values' imbued with nationalism, militarism and racial arrogance were filtered down from public schools to secondary and elementary schools through an imperially oriented curriculum, textbooks and juvenile literature which reflected and entrenched beliefs in the superiority of white people and a distrust of foreigners.

Education and empire

In Andrea's Levy's novel *Small Island*, the child Queenie is taken by her father to the Empire Exhibition in 1924. Watching a Black woman skilfully weaving cloth, she was told that 'we've got machines to do that' and 'They're not civilised, they only understand drums' (Levy 2004: 5). At this time an African American classical pianist Florence Price was composing her Symphony No. 1 in E minor, in which she incorporated drumming, drums being forbidden under slave regimes in case secret messages were transmitted. Price's symphony was premiered by the Chicago Symphony orchestra in 1932, and in 2018 featured in a concert by the Cheltenham Philharmonic Orchestra in England. There has always been more interest in how the Empire influenced education in colonised countries than how schools taught about empire to the children of the imperialists in Britain (see McCulloch 2009). Lord Macaulay did his best by asserting that he had not found one Orientalist 'who could deny that a single shelf of a good European library was worth the whole literature of India and Arabia' (Moorhouse 1984: 77). The arrogant beliefs that imbued imperialists from the high point of empire to eventual decline made it hard for educators at all levels to overcome the xenophobia and ignorance that continued to be demonstrated even in negotiations to leave the European Union (EU) after 2016.

The 1880s through to the 1930s was a time when, after vast areas of Africa and Asia were taken over – the Empire was at its height and a range of invented imperial traditions were developing. The period coincided with the expansion of a social class-based expansion of mass education in England. Historians of education agreed that the struggle to deliver education to the working classes over the 19th century mirrored a hierarchical social structure which placed their schooling firmly within the lower layers of the social class pyramid. Brian Simon, in his studies of education from the 18th to the 20th century, noted that after universal secondary education developed, class and interest group conflicts persisted, but what was actually taught in schools was always influenced by the public (non-state private) schools attended by the upper class young. The values underpinning schooling filtered down from public to grammar to elementary schooling (Simon 1960, 1990). With some prescience he noted that from the later 19th century the role of examinations became more important especially in these public schools. As one maths textbook of 1892 pointed out, 'many persons who are supposed to have received the best education the country affords, are in matters of numerical information ignorant and helpless, in a manner which places them far below members of the middle classes' (Colenso 1892; introduction). Future engineers and merchants of the Empire needed to be able to work out the gross annual receipts and dividends to British shareholders who invested in railways, especially in India where money needed to be converted to and from rupees, and they needed to be examined on their knowledge.[1] While upper class boys were being trained to run the Empire, the imperial subjects were not so lucky. Some elite schools in colonial countries, set up along the lines of English public schools, were educating colonial elites, but the masses had little or no schooling. When the British finally did leave India the illiteracy rate was 80–85 per cent across the country.

Significant events

1864	Report of the Clarendon Commission on English public schools.
1868	Schools Enquiry Commission.
1869	Francis Galton (*Hereditary Genius*) and the rise of Social Darwinism.
1870	Education (Elementary) Act.
1885–89	Edgerton Report on defective children.
1899–02	Boer War and concern over (white) racial deterioration.
1902	Education Act.
1905	Aliens Act.
1906	Labour Party formed.
1914	First World War.
1916	Sykes–Picot Agreement.
1917	Balfour Declaration.
1919	Scheme to distribute land in Kenya to white European officers.
1919	Jallianwala Bagh massacre. Indian Independence movement.
1922	Labour party Manifesto on *Education for All* (school leaving age 14).
1924	Empire Day and Empire Exhibition at Wembley.
1926	Empire Marketing Board set up.
1931	Mahatma Ghandi visits Lancashire.
1930s	42 million British subjects. 500 million imperial subjects.
1939–45	Second World War.

In 1864 The Clarendon Commission reported on the top nine public schools. It was chaired by the Earl of Clarendon, whose family owned land in Jamaica and had been connected to slavery and the sugar trade. A culture of athleticism was encouraged, and the schools encouraged belief in the superior moral virtue of the upper class boys they were educating. Cheltenham school claimed it was a training place for defenders of the Empire; Haileybury and Marlborough were praised as places where those going out to rule the Empire 'lived and died as officers and gentlemen' (Simon 1960: 328). Commissions and reports on the then existing grammar schools for the middle classes and on elementary education, led to the conclusion that 'the different classes of society ... require different teaching' (Schools Inquiry Commission 1868: 63). Although public schools retained their emphasis on the classics, their schools and those for the middle classes were to have a grounding in maths, science, English, history and geography.

An 1870 Education Act created mass elementary education for the working classes, concentrating on literacy, numeracy. moral and manual training, although it was not until 1876 that schooling to age 12 was made compulsory. A Moral Instruction League was influential enough for a syllabus for moral teaching to be placed into the 1906 code of regulations for elementary schools. There were similar intentions behind sending missionaries out to moralise to the colonised and teaching the working-class to be well behaved and moral. Francis Galton, a cousin of Charles Darwin, via his writings on *Hereditary Genius* (1869), helped to popularise Social Darwinism and eugenic theories, through which it was eventually suggested that low ability, mental defect, delinquency, crime, prostitution, illegitimacy and even unemployment were inherited tendencies in the lower social classes (RCCCFM 1908). A Royal Commission was set up in 1885 to report on the education of those considered physically and mentally defective, chaired by Lord Egerton, whose family had also become wealthy by interests in the West Indian sugar trade (Egerton Report 1889). Eugenic theories underpinned beliefs in the inferior intellect of the lower classes and of the colonised.

Passion for the classification of supposed races along biological lines developed around the same time as eugenic theories were spreading. The stereotypes of the defective, ignorant and idle lower working classes in England was similar to the stereotypes of lazy and stupid 'natives' overseas. Assumptions of biological and cultural deficiencies in the lower classes and in other supposed races persisted into the 20th and 21st centuries. In 1899 the British government became concerned about a 'degenerate' working class, while recruiting for the Boer war against Dutch settlers in South Africa. Army recruits were discovered to be weak and malnourished, and in the final wars of imperial expansion, demonstrated to an Edwardian elite a deterioration of what was termed the (white) 'British race'. Efforts were made to improve the health of school children – a schools medical service being set up in 1907. Baden Powell created his Boy Scout movement in 1908 with the intention of transforming 'pale narrow-chested miserable specimens who smoked, loafed and practised self-abuse' into a healthy race (Brendon 2007: 226).

Despite the First World War being won with the help of recruits from the Empire, especially from India and African countries, and with labourers from China, in 1918 the government set up a scheme to distribute some of the best land in Kenya to white Europeans who had fought for 'King and Country' (Best 1979). In 2018 the artist William Kentridge set up a project in the Tate Modern Turbine Hall in London, to illustrate that the spread of the World War cost millions of African lives, as many people were conscripted by force to join and the British were eager to take over the German colonies in East Africa. Ironically, some Africans joined the war thinking that if they took part alongside white soldiers, they would be regarded as equals and given rights afterwards (Kentridge in Aspden 2018). Meanwhile, in 1916 the Sykes-Picot Agreement, named after the British and French diplomats who signed it, carved up the Middle East territories between these countries, setting the stage for a perpetuation of conflicts into the 21st century. The 1917 Balfour Declaration concerning Palestine and a Jewish Homeland similarly set up future conflicts over land. Hostility to immigrants and a closing of free movement from Europe was evident via the 1905 Aliens Act. This gave the Home Office responsibility for immigration, and it was introduced to control the numbers of Jewish settlers arriving from Easter Europe and Russia, who settled in the poor areas in London's East End. This Act was partly in response to claims that 7 million immigrants would swamp British shores. In 1900 a British Brotherhood League collected 45,000 signatures on a petition to against immigration and to 'stop Britain being a dumping ground for the scum of Europe' (Benewick 1969: intro). This League was subsequently overtaken by an Immigrant Reform Association and Oswald Mosley's National Union of Fascists.

Labour and education, 1900–39

By the early 1900s there were signs that Western European imperialism might be faltering. Lawton, in his study of the Labour Party and Education from 1900 wrote that the Boer war indicated to Ghandi that the British were not invincible and could be opposed in India (Lawton 2005: 18). The Russian revolution, First World War and the ending of the Hapsburg Empire suggested that empires and their colonies could not last for ever. But English education, dominated by a public school-educated aristocracy and civil service, persisted in its role of propping up the social structure and the imperial overtones. In the 1890s only around 2.5 per cent of young people, largely upper and middle class, received a secondary education. Some elementary schools had developed a higher elementary education for working class children with grants from local schools Boards. A legal judgement put a stop to this in 1900, and local School Boards were abolished in 1902. The Duke of Devonshire, one of the country's richest landowners, had, along with other aristocrats, worried that local school boards and trade unions were demanding a secondary education for all children rather than a narrow selection of 'scholarship' children. Another rich Irish landowner, the Marquis of Londonderry, appointed as president of the national Board of Education in August 1902, oversaw the 1902 (Balfour) Education Act. This was largely the work of civil servant Robert Morant 'whose views on education were essentially based on upper class assumptions of social stability' (Lawton 2005: 12). The Act ensured that only those working class children with what was considered to be of exceptional ability, could join children whose parents could pay secondary school fees.

The Labour Party, formed in 1906, led the movement for secondary education for all, with the school-leaving age raised to 14 in 1922, although another Lord to Chair the Board of Education, Lord Eustace Percy from the Duke of Northumberland's wealthy family, suggested that secondary education ought to remain exclusive. The Hadow Committee reported on *The Education of the Adolescent* in 1926, and recommended selection by 'differentiation' – a secondary modern school would have a four year course 'with a realistic and practical trend' (Hadow 1926: 95) while grammar schools would pursue a literary and scientific curriculum. Technical and trade schools should develop to cater for the needs of local industry. Any possibility of comprehensive schooling disappeared for some years and by 1939 and the start of the Second World War, 88 per cent of young people had left school by 14. Secondary modern schools were for children who 'would not need any measure of technical skills or knowledge' (Ministry of Education 1946: 13).

While the Empire was beginning to decline, the 1919 Jallianwala massacre in Amritsar in India, when troops fired on an unarmed crowd gathered in response to Mahatma Ghandi's campaign for passive resistance to British rule, created unease among the working class in England. In 1931, when Ghandi visited Britain, he was welcomed ecstatically by mill workers in Lancashire, who recognised a connection between imperial rule and their class position. During the 1920s and 1930s trade with the Empire, encouraged by protectionism and 'imperial preference' at least ensured the working classes were fed, and there were attempts to boost patriotism through Empire Days and the Empire Exhibition at Wembley that the child Queenie visited. Despite the Empire Christmas pudding that the Royal family were induced to eat, enthusiasm for the Empire needed nourishing, and imperial propaganda and education served this purpose.

History, values and curriculum

What constitutes a curriculum at all levels in education is a product of the values and decisions of the dominant social and political groups of the time.

What developed as 'the curriculum' in English state schools continued to be influenced by a period of imperial enthusiasm and a final expansion of the British Empire, and certainly excluded discussion of the more unpleasant realities of British rule. It was during this period that many aspects of what is regarded as 'British culture and values' came to be reflected in the curriculum. What was acceptable curriculum knowledge would now be regarded as ideological manipulation, as the selection of what passes for curriculum knowledge at any one time depends on the values of controlling elites and their views and interests. It is not surprising that imperial values permeated education and curricula for so long. Keith Joseph, leaving office as Secretary of State for Education in 1985, reiterated a mythologised view of British values. Referring to a government policy for an ethnically mixed society, he wrote that: 'British history and cultural traditions are, or will become, part of the cultural heritage of all who live in this country ... schools should be responsible for trying to transmit British culture, enriched as it has been by so many traditions' (Joseph 1986: 8).

The problem remains that many of the traditions and values were and are highly questionable in terms of democracy, tolerance and justice, with imperial contacts largely taking the form of military conquest, appropriation of land and wealth, slavery, forced labour and denial of human rights. Just 20 years before Joseph wrote, in the early 1960s during African opposition to a white-dominated Central African Federation, captured African fighters had heavy stones tied to their penises for hours (Williams 2011), presumably not something Joseph would have wished school children to know about.

The 19th- and early 20th-century view of the world was not traditional at all but spread by education and imperial propaganda into popular consciousness. Propaganda took many forms; a major visual effort to impress visiting dignitaries to the London Foreign Office was the commissioning of a series of grand murals, the final one depicting 'Britannia' – intended to demonstrate a victorious Britain upholding peace. Imperial subjects and the colonised may have had different views of British peace-keeping, but these did not figure in the English school curriculum and alternative views continued to be resisted. Teachers in schools and increasingly in universities, have during the 20th and into the 21st century been subject to more political direction and control, and the ethnocentric nature of schooling has only changed slowly. School pupils may now be less likely to enquire of Zimbabwean actors, visiting Gloucestershire schools in 1988, whether they were cannibals (Dorras and Walker 1988).

Public school influence

The social and political values of the upper classes in England in the 19th century came to influence mass education in England via the public schools, and the world views implicit in the curriculum in these schools filtered into the developing state elementary and secondary schools in the early 20th century. In a 2018 analysis of the privileges that still come with a public school education, Robert Verkaik pointed out that 'Public schools have helped to write British history. They have been cheerleaders for colonialism and controlled the narrative of Empire' (Verkaik 2018: 45). A clear illustration of this was provided by Lawson-Walton, an exponent of the duties of government to Empire, who wrote in *The Contemporary Review* in 1899 that 'since the energies of the British race had given them their empire' and as 'British rule of every race brought within its sphere has the incalculable benefits of just law, free trade and considerate government' it was the duty of public schools to provide competent rulers (Lawson-Walton 1899: 306). In his studies of images of Empire in Victorian and Edwardian public schools Mangan (1980, 1986) concluded that the British Empire was run by public schoolboys and the values imbibed by public school boys eventually influenced all school pupils. An awareness of Empire among public schoolboys, allied to themes of militarism and patriotic self-sacrifice, were instilled by public school headteachers and staff, most of whom were committed imperialists.

W.H. Moss, Head of Shrewsbury School from 1872 to 1908, believed that God had entrusted England with the task of creating a Christian Empire held together by military means, and he set up one of the first Cadet Corps with competitions in shooting and drill and serving generals invited to review the boys. He also recommended training army officers so that 'boys with brains and character would be would be available for the preservation of English dominions in times of war', and their public school ideals would permeate down the ranks of soldiers (Mangan 1986: 119). J.E.C. Weldon, Head of Harrow School, was another enthusiastic proponent of Empire. He read a paper to the Royal Colonial Institute in 1895 on 'The Imperial aspects of education' arguing that 'The boys of today are the statesmen and administrators of the future, in their hands is the future of the British Empire.' He believed in the moral superiority of white people to govern their 'racial inferiors' and to demand 'instinctive obedience' from imperial subjects, and on one occasion approved of a boy beating up an Egyptian fellow students who had 'said something bad about the British race' (Mangan 1986: 121). One of his pupils, Winston Churchill, was some 60 years later, to suggest that 'Keep Britain White' might be a slogan in the 1955 general election campaign.

In Scotland, H.H. Almond, Head of Loretto School in Edinburgh from 1962 to 1903, also reflected the values of imperial government, militarism, moral and religious superiority over imperial subjects and the healthy discipline acquired on the games field. He delivered an annual lecture on 'The divine governance of nations', in which he asserted that God's purpose for the British was to guide world history, and the major purpose of a public schools was to create neo-imperial warriors. In the school magazines of Eton, Haileybury and Cheltenham, the public school boy was defined as a warrior patriot, a role enthusiastically embraced by Fettes – the Scottish public school opened in 1870. From 1966 to 1971, Anthony Charles Lynton Blair, later the British prime minister, attended this school, and although he was reportedly more interested in rock music than militarism, actually led the country into seven wars during his ministerial tenure. The school magazine *The Fettesian*, with a first edition in 1878, excelled in 'strident jingoism' (Mangan 1986).

The public schools 'traditions' of military self-sacrifice and imperial patriotic duty gave rise to a host of organisations with these values. These included the Boy Scouts, the Boys Brigade, The Empire Youth Movement, the Navy League, the League of Empire, the Girls' Patriotic League and many others. The 'traditions' were especially promoted by Eton-educated Reginald Brabazon, 12th Earl of Meath, who was associated with a variety of patriotic organisations, including a Duty and Discipline Movement and a Lads Drill Association – intended to prepare a fit and healthy working class. His series of papers on *Essays in Duty and Discipline* included some eminent contributions from the Archbishop of Canterbury, Winston Churchill, Baden Powell and others, and he was severe on the moral deterioration of women whom he thought were failing in their marital and child-rearing duties (Lord Meath 1910).

Eugenics and motherhood came together in movements aimed at women, with the Labour-supporting Fabian Society being keen to educate British girls in motherhood, and the 1904 Board of Education regulations placing needlework, laundry and cooking for girls in the elementary curriculum. For boys, a National Service League was formed in 1899, which proposed compulsory military service and eventually incorporated the Lads Drill Association, school cadet corps and rifle clubs. The League intended to include working-class boys and its programmes were 'designed to improve national physique and instil a sense of citizenship among the young as well as cleanliness, punctuality, order and discipline in order to improve the industrial and commercial efficiency of nation and Empire' (Mackenzie 1984:155). In 1912 it held a conference of Teacher Associations, set up an Imperial Union of Teachers and prepared a series of textbooks and atlases of the British Empire. A more political organisation was the British Empire Union (BEU) funded in 1915 'to increase knowledge of Empire … and make our people increasingly empire-minded' (Mackenzie 1984: 157). This organisation linked Empire to capitalism and conservatism, attacked socialism and communism and survived until 1959, arguing against de-colonisation, and for protected Commonwealth trade. The BEU, as were many of the imperial organisations, was supported by a public school-educated aristocracy and also over the years by industrial and commercial firms. Verkaik (2018) pointed out that minor public schools also trained many of the middle classes who were to become the 'bureaucratic workhorses' of the Empire, administering large tracts of imperial lands but still imbued with the sense of racial and class superiority.

Imperial values, education and social class

Historians of the left and right have argued over how far imperial values affected the working class, but in the early 20th century it was becoming clearer that the emergence of new nationalisms created a need for new rituals and invented traditions to solidify working class support for the state. There was a need for more justification for colonial wars, expansion and conquests than was catered for by Social Darwinist ideologies of racial superiority. Glorification of Empire found expression in pageantry, school textbooks and juvenile literature, and a filtering down of the imperial values from public schools. It was due to Lord Meath that an Empire Day came about, a Court Journal in 1910 explaining that Meath's self-sacrificing devotion to Empire was a noble idea to be instilled into the minds of the young (Guest 1910). Empire Weeks included patriotic plays, pageants, songs poems, flags and speeches, and Empire Day persisted until 1958 when it became Commonwealth Day. To a young Robert Roberts, brought up in a Salford slum in the early 20th century, school was a 'gaunt, blackened building, made exciting by learning that there were five oceans and five continents … most of which seemed to belong to us' (Roberts 1971:140). The teachers were fed on patriotism helped along by the popular imperialistic book *The Expansion of England* (Seeley 1883) and especially the heroic works of Rudyard Kipling.[2] The children welcomed Empire Day and the flag waving, processions, bands, uniforms, free mugs and chocolate that accompanied royal visits. Roberts detailed the way state school teachers copied their public school 'superiors' in fostering an ethnocentric view of imperial greatness and racial superiority. The public school ethos, distorted by myth, set standards and ideals for slum boys.

In a further study of early 20th-century working-class youth, Humphries (1981) noted that the ideologies of imperialism had a direct appeal to working class boys, as it reflected any number of their cultural traditions – fighting, gang warfare over street territory, superiority over foreigners and assertion of masculinity. Upper-class beliefs in the social inferiority of the working class and the racial inferiority of the colonised came together, in a language of 'slum monkey' 'brute savages' and 'aping' others. Later in the century Willis (1977) documented the ways in which fighting, racism and sexism were still part of the values espoused by working class boys, although these values were similar for upper and lower class boys. The major importance of the cultural values which were disseminated from the upper to the working class was that through the influence of imperial propaganda and a distorted school education, the 'lower classes' were encouraged to believe in their economic, political, social and racial superiority over the rest of the Empire. The domestic underclass could become the imperial overclass and all classes could unite in a comforting, national patriotic solidarity. This white class solidarity has demonstrably persisted into the 21st century and goes some way towards explaining the xenophobia and racism still part of the British heritage and British 'values'.

The influence of textbooks

Justification for imperial expansion, colonial wars and conquests and the continued dominance over colonised people was reproduced on a large scale in late Victorian and Edwardian textbooks and juvenile literature, with an Education Code of 1892 recommending ways of teaching about British colonies.[3] The Geographical Society proposed the study of Empire geography for secondary schools in 1896 and school geography, history, English and religion all became vehicles for imperial propaganda. This stressed heroic military adventures, great voyages, missionary activity and the subjugation of those Rudyard Kipling eloquently described as 'lesser breeds without the law' (Kipling 1949: 46). Oxford Professor Herbertson, a prolific writer of geography textbooks, his *Junior Geography* selling over a third of a million copies, urged teachers to make use of geographical manuals and even daily newspapers. His series on *Commercial Geography* was intended for students of Empire and of 'non-British civilised lands'. Higher and complex economic civilisations could induce the colonised to produce goods where the inhabitants previously only needed to supply themselves. Thus:

> the intervention of a higher economic civilisation can be seen in parts of Africa ... here the native is not displaced, for he alone can healthily perform the necessary manual labour, but his work is organised by the Europeans, who also ensure the peace without which sound economic progress is impossible. (Herbertson 1906: 56)

Even in a 1971 textbook, British children were still being taught that opening up areas of Africa could only be done under European guidance. Academics Honeybone and Robertson wrote that 'The mineral resources of West Africa are clearly very important and have been developed under British and French initiative. Railways have been built, roads constructed, and ports developed under European guidance' (Honeybone and Robertson 1971: 72). Contact and opening up actually meant that the land and labour of people in Africa was being looted and cultures and institutions destroyed.

History, introduced into the public school curriculum by Matthew Arnold at Rugby, did not become compulsory in senior and elementary schools until 1900. This was a time when a single ideological slant was introduced into school texts (MacKenzie 1984: 177). The slant was a convergence of ideas of military conquests, patriotic support for imperial dominance and racial superiority. The past was skewed to fit current ideals. In textbooks the American Civil War and slavery were glossed over, and moral responsibility for conflict shifted to the colonial countries. Omissions, half-truths and lies encouraged pupils to believe that the territorial and commercial wars fought were ultimately for the benefit of the colonised.

The popular history book recommended by the Board of Education in 1902 suggested that *Men of Renown* (the book included three women – all queens) was a suitable way to teach history to higher elementary classes (Finnemore 1902). In this text the presentation of 'natives' who fought to resist imperial rule as possessed by evil ill-feeling towards their benevolent rulers was a persistent theme, and their cruelty towards women and children was stressed. Sir Henry Havelock and Lord Lucknow were described as suppressing the Indian Mutiny of 1857 (known in India as the First War of Independence) in which 'English women and children were called upon to suffer horrors and torture to which one cannot give a name' (Finnemore 1902: 237). The emotive language of this book, the 'pluck, endurance and heroic bravery' of British troops, was contrasted with the 'fiends incarnate' who were resisting British rule.

The Thrill of History (Magraw 1919) which went into seven editions to 1959 contained chapters extolling men such as David Livingstone and Cecil Rhodes in Africa, Lawrence of Arabia and even Ghandi. In one chapter it describes an old Matabele woman meeting Rhodes who she says is a great chief who will bring peace, justice and plenty to the Matabele. Rhodes is more generally known as an imperialist who looted South Africa's diamond mines and oversaw the founding of Rhodesia, believing that the Anglo-Saxon race was the finest in the world, and 'the more of the world we inhabit the better it is for the human race' (MacFarlane 2007: 438). Rudyard Kipling and his co-author produced a *History of England* in 1911, which even then was criticised for its racial overtones. Despite this Kipling's writing has been influential through the decades, living through films and musicals such as *The Jungle Book* and *The Lion King*, but he specialised in propaganda for Empire, his poem 'Take up the White Man's Burden' exemplifying the labour of running an Empire (Kipling 1940). In January 2017 the then British Foreign Secretary Boris Johnson, could, on a visit to Burma (now Myanmar) colonised by the British 1824 until 1948, attempt to recite the poem 'The Road to Mandalay', while in front of a statue of the Buddha at a sacred Buddhist site.[4] The embarrassed British ambassador managed to stop him before the lines 'Bloomin idol made of mud, wot they call the Great Gawd Budd' (Booth 2017).

University influence

In 1905 a young lecturer at Oxford University told his class that instead of Greek that morning they were to study a most important historical event 'the victory of a non-white people over a white people' (Zimmern 1926: 2), This was the defeat of Russia by the Japanese in the Russia-Japan war. But, in general, university influence on imperial racial superiority could not countenance such a situation and the white race continued to be presented as superior. Most of the school textbooks and influential literature in the late 19th and early 20th century were produced by men who had studied at Oxford or Cambridge, as had their publishers. Universities colluded in the celebration of Empire and preferential colonial trade. Professor Herbertson in the second edition of *Commercial Geography* noted above gave more detailed trade statistics on the imports and exports from 'British Possessions', exports from British South Africa being mainly gold bullion, diamonds and in 1911 £2,253 worth of ostrich feathers, presumably to decorate Edwardian ladies' hats (Herbertson and Cossar 1916).

A Rhodes Chair of Imperial History was set up in 1919 to celebrate a man who in modern terms had looted South Africa and Rhodesia. In Oxford, Rhodes House is still named after him. In 2017 Oxford students attempted to have his statue removed from outside Oriel College, but the statue remains in place, as does his portrait in the Department for International Trade in London. Groups of scholars in Oxford and in Cape Town, South Africa, set up movements for 'Rhodes Must Fall', although in their book *Rhodes Must Fall: The Struggle to Tear Out the Racist Heart of Empire* (Chantiluke, Kwoba and Nkopo 2018) noted that this was not simply about pulling down a symbol of British imperialism. It was removing a monument glorifying a colonial conqueror but also about confronting the toxic inheritance of the past and the pernicious influence of colonialism in education to the present day. Professor Halford Mackinder, one of the founders of the London School of Economics (LSE) set up a School of Geography in Oxford in 1899 and developed a series of Empire lectures for teachers in the 1920s. The Empire Marketing Board endowed a Professorial Chair at LSE in Imperial Economic Relations in 1926, which was intended to promote protectionist trade and that Empire Christmas Pudding.

Literature for youth

From the 1880s the expansion of popular publishing and the creation of wider readerships came at the same time as the development of mass education and improved literacy. A publishing market which made millions until well after the Second World War was the juvenile literature market – children's' magazines, story books and comics. Much of this literature took the form of an adventure tradition full of militarism and patriotism where 'violence and high spirits became legitimised as part of the moral force of a superior race' (MacKenzie 1984: 199). The adventure literature was mainly designed for boys and many of the fictional tales were set in public schools, which provided another way by which imperial values could be spread. Roberts (1971) wrote of the way he and his friends in back-street Salford became avid for the fictional world of the public school, especially Grey Friars, the public school invented by Frank Richards, which was the setting for stories in the popular magazines *Magnet, Gem* and *The Boys' Own Paper*. Rudyard Kipling's book *Stalky and Co* (1899) extolled the high spirits, patriotic pride and intrepid bravery of the public school boys destined to be leaders of Empire, and this book was the basis for a TV series filmed in the 1980s.

An influential magazine produced from the 1880s to 1933 was *Union Jack*, whose editor G.A. Henty had fought in colonial wars. He employed well-known writers for the magazine, including Conan Doyle (of Sherlock Holmes fame) Jules Verne and Robert Stevenson. Henty's schoolboy heroes exhibited both class snobbery and racism, and their superior morality was associated with their superior education and Nordic complexions. Many of the stories were openly anti-Black and anti-Semitic, Black people being presented as unfit to govern themselves and the energy and self-reliance of Northern Europeans contrasted with the lethargy and ignorance of 'the natives'. Imperial arrogance became an acceptable value. The Tarzan stories, written by Chicago-born Edgar Rice Burroughs, offered an example of this view of the world, the stories being presented on film, later television and in magazines and comic strips. Tarzan's aristocratic breeding (he is really Lord Greystoke) enabled him to be an educated gentleman in the jungle, continually fighting treacherous savage natives. His breeding apparently allowed him to kill Black people with deliberate cruelty (Burroughs 1919). Tarzan was called back to the jungle in a film released in 2016, although one review of this film described it as a myth wrestling with history in the mud. But the imperial adventure stories, in which intellect was not prized – physical power and fighting were more important – ensured that 'the world became a vast adventure playground in which Anglo-Saxon superiority can be repeatedly demonstrate vis-à-vis all other races, most of who are depicted as treacherous and evil' (MacKenzie 1984: 204). Stories stressed the romance of Empire, which went along with the starched uniforms and plumed hats of British Officers and officials. The Seeley Service Library included such titles as *The Romance of Savage Life*, and in these stories the bravery of heroic white individuals was a constant theme, with naval adventure stories in particular stressing role of the brave navy.

> England is a gallant little nation, whose power and conquests are obviously the reward of merit, since all opponents are bigger and uglier

than she is. ... The British tar is superhuman in his bravery, endurance and discipline ... the officers are wonderfully good at inspiring their men and able to carry out audacious manoeuvres under the noses of lumbering befuddled foreigners. (Bratton 1986:83)

There are parallels here with the Navy's views of the Falklands campaign in 1982. To be white and British provided the moral and ethical base for judging foreigners and races who were always found wanting. While many of these publications went out of print by the 1920s other publications came to replace them, particularly the comics *Rover* (1922), *Skipper* (1933) and *Hotspur* (1933), and later the *Dandy* and *Beano*, which in the 1950s had a circulation of around 2 million. Girls were not well catered for, their major magazine being *Sunny Stories*, mainly written by children's author Enid Blyton until the 1940s. Her story in the first issue in January 1937 introduced 'The Tricky G******g', and g*******s featured in further stories. The popular writer Angela Brazil, in her stories of girls' boarding schools, wrote a tale of 'A Patriotic School-girl' in 1918, and Katherine Hughes has documented the 'Dorm feasts and red-hot pashes' that figured in many of her novels (Hughes 2015). But in imperial literature girls and women usually were reduced to admiring men or in need of rescue.

Summary

This chapter has indicated the way in which the development of state education, its values and teachings, were inextricably tied up with the ideologies of imperialism and the values of nationalism, militarism and racial arrogance which filtered down from public schools to secondary and elementary schools to both the middle classes and the 'slum' boys, and which still form the base for many 21st-century views of other nations, races and 'foreigners'. It underpinned beliefs that somehow an 'Empire 2.0' would be created after Brexit (Olusoga 2017). The intensity of ethnocentric beliefs in the glories of Empire, and white racial superiority, uncritically reflected in textbooks, university writings, youth literature, films and later television, were reinforced by teaching which did little to combat unthinking acceptance of a value-laden imperial curriculum. Imperial nationalism created a unity across social classes and gave all classes a sense of owning the world. Earl Attlee, retired Labour prime minister, a major in the First World War, deputy prime minister in the Second and creator of the Welfare State, gave the Chichele lectures at Oxford in 1960. For his first lecture he chose 'Empire and Commonwealth'. In common with Robert's 'slum' boys, he described the excitements of youthful imperialism and 'the great map with large portions coloured red, (which) was an intoxicating vision for a small boy ... we believed in our great imperial vision' (Attlee 1960: 5). Political opposition to decolonisation persisted until well after the Second World War, as did opposition to educating all children beyond 15. A school-leaving age of 16 was not implemented until 1973, but visions of imperial greatness persisted in the curriculum into the 21st century. Countries colonised internally by the English over the centuries, Ireland, Wales and Scotland also had mixed relationships with their imperial masters, as discussed in the next chapter, when those landladies' signs of 'No Dogs, Blacks or Irish' for rental property began to appear.

2

Internal colonialism and its effects

> I am haunted by the human chimpanzees I saw along hundreds of miles of that horrible country ... if they were black one would not feel it so much, but their skins, except where tanned by exposure, are as white as ours.
>
> Charles Kingsley on Ireland, quoted in Curtis 1968: 84

This chapter is not in any way a definitive history but is included because there is much ignorance about the creation of a 'Great Britain' and the internal wars, conflicts and atrocities that took place as it was all notionally united.[1] Some understanding of the past and present is important as after the general election in 2017 the Conservatives were only kept in government and able to pursue leaving the European Union (EU), with the support of ten votes from the Democratic Unionist Party (DUP) of Northern Ireland. There is a general ignorance in England about Irish history and affairs. After an episode in the television production on the life of *Queen Victoria* (ITV 1 October 2017) when she exhibited concern about the Irish famine in 1845, there was widespread sharing on social media from people who knew nothing about the death of over a million and the emigration of 2 million from the island. It also notes that the 19th century often vicious denigration of the people in these internal colonies, was similar to that accorded to the overseas colonised and also extended to the English working classes. English elites especially regarded the Welsh and Irish and the 'natives' overseas with the same arrogant contempt they accorded to the English working classes. But there were also similar fears of uprisings and challenges to authority. As Kiernan wrote, 'Discontented natives in the colonies and labour agitators in the mills were the same serpent in alternative disguises. Much of the talk of barbarism and darkness of the outer world, which it was Europe's mission to rout, was a transmuted fear of the masses at home' (Kiernan 1969: 316).

Significant events

1169	Norman invasion of Ireland.
1177	Henry II made his son John Lackland Lord of Ireland.

1282	Edward I invades and conquered Wales.
1536	Henry VIII called himself King of Ireland.
1536	England annexed Wales. English law, language and church imposed.
1614	An Irish parliament in Dublin with a Catholic majority.
1641–53	Oliver Cromwell conquered Ireland for 'British Commonwealth'.
1690	Battle of the Boyne. Protestant William of Orange defeats deposed King James II.
1707	Act of Union with Scotland.
1745/6	Jacobite rebellion in Scotland. Defeat at Culloden.
1801	Irish Parliament dissolved and Act of Union with the United Kingdom.
1845–9	Irish potato famine. Population reduced from 8 to 4 million.
1914	Home Rule (Ireland) Act passed and then suspended.
1916	Easter Rising. Partition created 22 Free counties and 6 Union ones.
1921–22	Anglo-Irish Treaty. Irish Free State becomes a Dominion of the Commonwealth.
1921–72	Northern Ireland becomes a Protestant province within the UK.
1968/9	Civil disturbances and 'The Troubles' in Northern Ireland. British troops brought in.
1971	Ian Paisley sets up Democratic Unionist Party (DUP).
1972	(January) Bloody Sunday.
1998	Good Friday Agreement in Belfast (opposed by DUP).
1999	Devolution of governing powers to Scotland, Wales and Northern Ireland.
2016	In the referendum a majority in Northern Ireland vote to remain in the EU. (The Irish Republic is part of the EU.) DUP Leader Arlene Forster makes an informal agreement with Conservatives.
2017	In the UK general election DUP wins 10 seats and agree to support Theresa May's minority Conservative government.
2018	Brexit negotiations debate the issue of the border between Ireland and Northern Ireland interminably. A white paper (HM Government 2018) was criticised by Eurosceptic MPs. Government went into its summer recess with no agreement on trade over the border.
2023	(October) After five more years of arguing Rishi Sunak, the fourth prime minister after Brexit, put forward the 'Windsor Framework'. This was a legal agreement between the EU and UK which adjusted the terms of trade with Britian, accepting that Northern Ireland remained in the EU single market but giving the Norther Ireland Assembly powers over changes to EU trade regulations with a Scrutiny Committee set up.

What the Romans did for us

Most children still learn about the Roman conquest of Britain and Julius Caesar's invasion. Then after AD 43 they learn the country became a Roman province known as Britannia. Less well known is Caractacus, a

Welsh chief, who fought against the Romans, or the history of the Celts, whose lives, cultures and languages in Wales, Ireland and Scotland, were eventually taken over as the countries were internally colonised by the English. A major difference between these conquests and the oppression which followed was that, as Charles Kingsley, Cambridge University historian and author of the famous children's book *The Water Babies* (1863) helpfully pointed out, the Celtic people were white. Despite this the ethnic racism and the denigration of the cultures and languages meted out, especially to the Welsh and Irish, was similar to the treatment of colonised Black people. Kingsley was another fervent believer in the superiority of the white English race. Primary school children still learn that after the Romans, what is now called England was made up of immigrant Saxons, Angles, Jutes, Vikings and Danes all fighting each other, until Cnut (Canute) who is remembered for sitting in the sea ordering the waves back, married a Norman French woman.

Then we remember '1066 and all that', when William the Conqueror defeated Harold and from then on all the kings and queens were of French, Dutch or German descent. The Normans invaded and colonised Ireland in 1169, and Henry II handed the country over to his son. Edward I, now called an English King, invaded Wales in 1282 and there has been an English Prince of Wales ever since. A GCSE textbook in 2016 claims that the Normans were 'foreign invaders taking over a proud country' (Clarke 2016: 22). This is a myth or invention as no one can know how 'proud' the majority of peasant inhabitants were, and Saxon lords would presumably have been keener to keep their own wealth and property than feeling proud. At least the Normans documented who owned the country's wealth in 1086 in their Doomsday Book.

In 1536 Henry VIII, in between getting rid of his second wife and marrying a third, titled himself King of Ireland and married his sister Margaret to the Scottish king. Scotland, with its warring clans, was always a harder country to colonise. It was not until 1707 that there was an Act of Union between England and Scotland, and in 1715 the English Parliament tried to ban the Scottish kilt, on the grounds that it was indecent when men bent down! The mass-produced kilt with its varied tartans was actually created by an English Quaker from Lancashire (Ranger 1983). As noted in the introduction, a major reason for early colonisation was a search for food, especially to feed urban populations and expanding armies and navies. This also applied to Wales and Ireland, where from the 1500s their grain and cattle fed the English (Tilly 1976). It was only in the later 1700s that the myth of a 'Great Britain' began to emerge, as the German Hanoverian Kings took over and the early Empire was emerging. A poem by a Scottish poet was set to music by Thomas Arne in 1740. This was 'Rule Britannia' which is one of the many patriotic songs still sung especially at the end of the Last Night of the Proms broadcast world-wide from London. The poet, James Thompson, was given a pension for patriotism by the then Prince of Wales (German-speaking Frederick Ludwig of Bavaria who only arrived in England in 1728). No other country calls itself 'Great'. The nearest any other European state gets to giving itself a superior label is the Grand Duchy of Luxemburg.

Internal colonialism and its effects

The Celtic peoples of Ireland and the Scottish Highlands were originally close politically and economically. Ranger has claimed that the Highlanders of Scotland were 'simply the overflow from Ireland' (Ranger 1983: 15), and arguments as to which were the original invaders continued until the 1700s. Scotland soon claimed that it had the original Celtic culture, and rivalries have continued to be played out in literature and especially in football. If a supporter of Celtic you are likely to be Catholic and/or Republican. A Rangers fan is likely to be Protestant and Unionist. Although the Scots made a bid for independence from England in 1745, the Jacobins were defeated at the battle of Culloden and it was not until 2014 that Scottish nationalism was resurrected in a referendum for independence which was also defeated. A majority in Scotland did, however, vote in the 2016 Referendum to remain in the European Union.

The fierce fighting of the Scots was noted by the English government of Prime Minister Pitt the Elder, who encouraged the creation of Highland regiments to fight in imperial wars. Ironically, a major effect of the colonising of the three countries was to supply armies to fight in the wars to take over the overseas colonies of the British Empire. Highland and Irish regiments fought to claim and retain imperial land in India and South Africa, and Irish-American soldiers fought on both sides of the American Civil War in 1861–65. Historians of internal colonisation have documented the expansion of an English state as it attempted to anglicise the countries. There was a 'political incorporation affecting the course of developments in the Celtic fringe by contributing to its economic, cultural and political dependence on England' (Hechter 1975: 80; Brendon 2007). As England benefited from this dependence, it is not surprising that hostilities and antagonisms between the three countries and the English persist to the present day. The Scots probably made the best of their colonisation, after James VI of Scotland became James I in 1603 calling himself King of Great Britain, France and Ireland. Scotland had its own parliament and legal system, was largely Protestant and developed a profitable banking and investment system.

After the Act of Union between Scotland and England in 1707, local elites were co-opted to run the country, a colonial policy successfully applied to the Empire as 'indirect rule', although one positive effect in

Scotland was that local elites were prepared to help develop a national education system which served all communities. After devolution of powers to the Scottish Parliament in 1999, the country had control of its whole education system, setting up a Department for Education and Life-long Learning. By 2014 Scotland was noted by the Institute for Fiscal Studies as the most highly educated country in Europe, although it had private schools based on the English public schools which served both Scottish and some English elite members. King Charles was educated at Gordonstone, Prime Minister Tony Blair at Fettes while former Education Secretary Michael Gove had to content himself with being a day pupil at Robert Gordon school. In a blog in 2013, a former pupil at the Scottish public school Glenalmond described the way the activities in his school, typical of the British public school system, functioned to build 'the class solidarity of the British elite'. All the sport, uncomfortable beds and Spartan diet were originally designed to produce generations to run an Empire now vanished. In his view, it later functioned to produce a culture that exuded confidence, created old boys' networks and sneered at the working and middle classes. 'The middle classes are taught to believe they will succeed through hard work and gumption. The upper classes know this is nonsense' (Ramsey 2013: 8).

The Welsh had a tougher time than the Scots under their colonisation. Even before the Act of Union with England in 1536, Welsh people were forbidden to buy much land, could not officially carry arms, fortify their houses, hold assemblies, become judges, and any Englishman marrying a Welsh wife was deemed to be Welsh. Any Celtic traditions were outlawed and after Union the Church of England was the official religion, although many non-conformist groups continued to hold services in Welsh. The Welsh language came in for particular denigration. A Commission in 1846 reported to the English Parliament that 'Because of their language the mass of the Welsh people are inferior to the English in every branch of practical knowledge and skill' (Coupland 1954: 186). Both external and internal colonisation meant that local languages were denigrated, and 'It is not surprising that the Commissioners should have swept aside the ancient language of Wales as ruthlessly as MacCaulay ... had swept aside the ancient languages of India' (Coupland 1954: 190). Arguments over the use of the Welsh language in politics and education continue to the present day (Cosslett 2017). The policy of indirect rule was successful in Wales as Welsh local gentry acquired land and influence at the expense of a rural and urban working class, but the dependence of the Welsh economy on England had similar effects to that of overseas colonised countries, its production and labour being subject to English demands. Wales acquired its own Welsh Assembly after devolution in 1999, with full control of its own education system.

A further effect of internal colonisation, more apparent initially in Wales and England than in the other two countries, was hostility and racism directed against Black settlers.[2] Fryer has documented in some detail the divisive role of racism, especially in Cardiff, where white workers were in economic competition for diminishing work with men from colonies who had served in the armed forces in the First World War or served on merchant ships. In 1919, South Wales 'experienced one of the most vicious outbreaks of racial violence that has yet occurred in Britain' (Fryer 1984: 303). The violence began with the familiar colonial charge that Black men were consorting with white women. Settlers from West Africa, Somalia and Arab countries were attacked by white mobs. A former colonial governor, Sir Ralph Williams, wrote in *The Times* (14 June 1919) 'that sexual relations between white women and coloured men revolt our very nature' and called for repatriation. *The Times*, to its credit pointed out that 'black girls in the colonies were subject to the "lust" of white seducers' and a measured response was printed from Felix Hercules, one of the leaders of a national liberation movement in the West Indian colonies, that if Black men were to be repatriated on sexual grounds, then so should white men in the colonies, and a result would be 'a downfall of the British Empire' (*The Times* 19 June 1919).

Fighting colonialism in Ireland

Ireland, where 'the denigration of Irish culture has a longer and more distinguished history than the Welsh culture' and where after colonisation in 1169 the English fought continually to 'subdue this barbarous country' (Hechter 1975: 76), can now be regarded as place where internal colonialism has been contested and 'to some extent overcome. Myers (2015) discussing the post-war histories of Irish and Afro-Caribbean people in England noted the ways in which the histories of subjugated states and peoples have always been marginalised or misrepresented in the national history story. Former Education Secretary Michael Gove, for example, told the Conservative Party Conference in October 2010 the 'children are growing up ignorant of one of the most inspiring stories I know – the history of the United Kingdom' (Myers 2015: 4). But that would be his version of the national story and certainly did not include the miseries inflicted on the Irish.

Northern Ireland, has been a problem for the Westminster Parliament since 1922. The most recent being the 2017 general election after which the ten votes of the DUP allowed the Conservative government to remain in power. After the vote to leave the European Union in 2016, the question of the border between the Irish Republic and Northern Ireland, still in the UK, but with a majority voting to remain the EU, remained contentious. As journalist Polly Toynbee pointed out, the Irish border question was a roadblock to the fantasies of Brexit supporters in the government 'reviving the centuries-old deep-dyed contempt for the Irish' who dismissed the question 'with an imperial fly-whisk, as a minor irritant' (Toynbee 2017).

In the very large literature on Irish history (Connolly 2007; Myers 2015; Bourke and MacBride 2016) historians generally agree that the Norman invasion of 1169 was followed by around 800 years of English rule, with resulting violent conflicts, centred round land and religion surviving to the present day. Henry VIII attempted to make the country Protestant, importing English and Scottish Protestant settlers and introducing a plantation policy similar to that in overseas colonies. Catholic landowners were displaced and Oliver Cromwell and his army, victorious in 1649, ensured that religious differences became the dominant cleavage in the society, the Anglo-Irish Protestants becoming the ruling class. The Battle of the Boyne in 1690, where Protestant King William of Orange defeated deposed Catholic King James II ensured Protestant ascendancy in Northern Ireland for generations, and an Orange Order still celebrates the battle on 12 July, usually causing retaliation from Catholics. Thereafter the English attempted to Anglicise the country through language and education, especially holding the Irish language in contempt. An Act of Union with what was described as a United Kingdom in 1801 dissolved the Irish Parliament. Absentee landlords caused much misery among the Irish poor, culminating in the famine of 1845–46, when the potato crop failed and a million starved, while 2 million emigrated. Despite famine conditions the English continued to import food from the island (Woodham-Smith 1962) and the resulting poverty and anger helped to create the Irish Nationalist movement. The English Prime Minister Sir Robert Peel, drew his ideas of a police force from the Royal Irish Constabulary, established in 1822 to keep control of Irish dissidents.

It was during the famine that the Cambridge academic the Reverend Charles Kingsley, visited Ireland after a visit to Jamaica. He later became a Chaplain to Queen Victoria and tutor to the Prince of Wales. He made his dislike of Black people, the Irish and Jews plain in his writings, although as noted previously, he felt that the Irish 'human chimpanzees' were at least, not Black. In his well-known children's book *The Water-Babies* (1863), he managed to include a dishonest Irish woman as a character. A further example of Victorian contempt for the Irish came from Sir Charles Trevelyan, who helped administer famine relief in Ireland but wrote that 'death by starvation' was a discipline for unruly behaviour, He later served on the board of the Charity Organisation Society in England, working to control 'defective populations' (Tomlinson 1982: 43).

Prime Minister Gladstone was sympathetic to the idea of Home Rule for Ireland, and eventually in 1914 a Home Rule Act was passed, but almost immediately suspended. Nationalists fought in an Easter Rising in 1916 which was brutally suppressed, but independence for most of Ireland arrived in 1922, when an Irish Free State of 22 Catholic counties became a separate nation and a dominion of the Commonwealth. By 2017 the Taoiseach (Prime Minister) of Ireland was Leo Varadkar, who had an Indian father and Irish mother. The remaining six counties became a Northern Ireland Protestant province within the UK, sending MPs to Westminster but with an Ulster Unionist party in government from 1921 to 1972. By 1969 discrimination against Catholics led to conflict which lasted over 30 years and became known as 'The Troubles', and in 1971 the DUP developed from a Protestant Unionist party, led by the Reverend Ian Paisley, who was totally opposed to any power sharing with Catholics, whom he referred to as breeding like rabbits. Enoch Powell, having stirred up anti-immigrant feeling in England, and opposed entry into the European Economic Community, became a Unionist MP in 1974 and devoted himself to defending the province as part of the British nation, as the 'soil of the province is British soil' (Cooke 2012: 254).

Ending the Troubles?

The para-military groups linked to Nationalist Republican parties and the military groups linked to Unionist parties, fought each other over the years with over 3,000 civilians killed, The Westminster government sent in British troops who, after an incident on 'Bloody Sunday' in January 1972 when 13 unarmed people were killed by the army, exacerbated the conflicts. The British government took over the province with Direct Rule until 1998 when a Good Friday Agreement (The Belfast Agreement), brokered by the British government under Prime Minister Tony Blair, notionally put an end to open conflict and eventually a handing in of weapons. Blair and his children hold both British and Irish passports as his mother was Irish.

The DUP was opposed to the Belfast Agreement, which they regarded as an 'imperfect peace'. In October 2016 the DUP MPs, led by Arlene Foster, attended a champagne party at the Conservative Party conference and agreed to support the Conservatives in the Westminster government after any elections. After the June 2017 general election they were the largest party of the 18 Northern Irish parliamentary places with ten seats. The Republican Party Sinn Fein took seven seats but does not attend the Westminster Parliament. In subsequent votes the DUP did indeed vote with the Conservative and Unionist party, and kept the government in power. The Republic of Ireland, under its Prime Minister Leo Varadkar, and also Northern Ireland seemed more open to the arrival of migrants both globally and from the EU, and around 17 per cent of the population of Northern Ireland are migrants, including many from Romania. However, cultural racism knows no borders, as when, in an international football match against Switzerland, in November 2017, the Northern Ireland team lost by a penalty awarded by the Romanian referee. This led to racist comments on Twitter insulting Romanians in general.

By the middle of 2018, two years after the vote to leave the EU, the question of a border between Northern Ireland and the Irish Republic still dominated discussions on Brexit in both the Westminster parliament and the EU negotiators in Brussels. The progress was followed in a series of papers written by the Institute for Peace, Security and Justice at Queens University Belfast (Haward and Komarova 2018). In July 2018 Prime Minister May produced a green paper (HM Government 2018a) which included plans for a 'soft' border between the two countries. The proposals were welcomed in Ireland by Declan Breathnacht, Ireland's Spokesperson on North–South Bodies and Cross Border Co-operation (Breathnacht 2018). In England the Paper was criticised by members from all parties and several ministers resigned from her government, including Foreign Secretary Johnson. A Customs and Trades Bill was passed in the Westminster Parliament on 18 July by just three votes, after four amendments by 'hardline Tory Brexiteers' were accepted (Sabbagh and Stewart 2018). Moves to challenge the leadership of Prime Minister May were deferred until after the summer recess, and the question of the Irish border after Brexit rumbled on for the next four years until in October 2023 Rishi Sunak's government produced what became known as the 'Windsor Framework', which was an acceptable trade agreement all round.

Class and the white colonised

English elites in the 19th and 20th centuries treated the overseas and the internally colonised, and the English working classes with the same arrogance and contempt. There were similar fears of insurrection and uprisings among the 'natives' abroad and the lower classes at home. In 1819 at the Peterloo Massacre in Manchester, when English workers holding a peaceful meeting over workers' voting rights were attacked by the military, leaving 16 dead and over 600 injured, Irish workers had joined the meeting. This was not something the authorities could tolerate and one way of dealing with this was to exacerbate divisions between the English working class and any of the internally colonised. This worked well, especially with the Irish. In the 19th century Irish labour was used to dig canals and build railways. But incursions into the textile industry, especially when the Irish were brought in to break strikes, was not tolerated as described by Elizabeth Gaskell in her novel *North and South* (Gaskell 1855). Karl Marx studied the working class in Ireland carefully, noting that Ireland sent its surplus labour to the English labour market, which forced wages down. As a result:

> Every industrial and commercial centre in England now possess a working class divided into two hostile camps, English proletarians and

> Irish proletarians. The ordinary English worker hates the Irish worker as a competitor who lowers his standard of life ... the Irishman sees in the English worker at once the accomplice and stupid tool of the English domination of Ireland. (Marx 1870: 220)

Winder documented anti-Irish riots in the 19th and early 20th century and the stigmatising of Irish migrants, particularly if Catholic. In 1923 the General Assembly of the Church of Scotland approved a report on *The Menace of the Irish Race to Our Scottish Nationality*, which documented fears that the Protestant Church would be swamped by an alien population (Winder 2004: 203). It is noteworthy that the references to 'aliens' and 'swamping' re-occur in speeches and reports from eminent figures over the decades when referring to Black, Asian, Jewish or Irish people. Creating divisions through emotive and negative language has long been a tool of political and military ruling classes. One especially emotive area was that of the notices in landladies' windows requesting 'No Blacks, no Dogs, no Irish' and how widespread these actually were. In 2015 there were letters in *The Guardian* newspaper describing the signs as old myths of the 1960s, while others claimed they saw such signs. Summing it up, O'Dowd wrote that 'The era of no Blacks, dogs or Irish is over but should never be forgotten' (O'Dowd 2013). A photograph of one such sign is held in the Irish Studies Centre at London Metropolitan University.

But further divisions between social and racial and migrant groups, especially the Irish and Welsh, continued to be provided by eugenic theories supporting claims that the lower classes, colonised and migrant groups have lower cognitive abilities than other groups (Tomlinson 2017). For well over a hundred years there was been a plethora of writing and research on ability, intelligence, mental measurement and eugenic and their educational implications. Usually dating from Francis Galton, second cousin to Charles Darwin who worked to provide a 'scientific' base for selective breeding to improve the genetic inheritance of the human race (Galton 1869), there have been attempts to suggest that lower classes and racial groups had supposedly less educable minds. It was no accident that early industrialising countries needed to rationalise the unequal treatment of urban slum and migrant populations by popularising notions of inherited differences between these groups, a situation which has continued into the 21st century (Astbury and Plomin (2014). A book published by University of London Professor Hans Eysenk in 1971 was notable for conflating lower class, Black (Negro in some of the book) and the Irish, as likely to have lower IQs, although he blamed historical injustices for this:

> If, as the data suggests, the Negroes show some genetic influence on their low IQs, this may very well be due to the crimes committed

against their ancestors, just as the Irish show a similar low IQ on account of the oppression they suffered for so long at the hands of the English. (Eysenck 1971: 142)

Eysenck also worried that racial quotas in university admissions might disadvantage whites and recommended that a small upper segment of Blacks could 'share the pursuit of happiness with their fellow whites' (Eysenck 1971: 149) but only if they escaped the ghetto. He actually recommended the 'abolition of the lumpenproletariat as a whole – both black and white' (Eysenck 1971: 150), which was astonishing coming from a man who had escaped from Nazi Germany before the Holocaust.

Summary

This chapter has briefly described how both before and during the creation of a British Empire and its overseas colonisation, Scotland, Wales and Ireland were internally colonised by the English, with similar economic consequences and rationalisations. Most adults did not learn much through schooling about the Empire or the English internal colonisation of Scotland, Wales and Ireland and were confused over the interminable discussions of trade deals and backstops as goods moved over the Irish sea. The three countries had different views about the continued link with a European Union and while the DUP of Northern Ireland held a balance of power in the Westminster Parliament they were able to hold discussions up until Theresa May's government ended. It was Rishi Sunak's government which finally made the breakthrough on trade agreement with his Windsor Framework.

The chapter noted that, despite myths about a proud British heritage all the rulers (kings and queens) for over 1,000 years in what became Britain, have been of European descent. It particularly indicated similarities in the contemptuous and arrogant views that the colonisers held about both the internally and externally colonised, and their lower classes. These were reinforced by 19th-century eugenic views, which have persisted into the 21st century The next chapter links the slow ending of Empire and the independence of former colonies with post-war education policies and the unequal treatment of migrant and minority children in all four countries, although schools and higher education institutions in England were particularly bad at incorporating minority and lower class children fairly.

3

Ending Empire: education for ignorance, 1945–60s

> Despite a restructuring of education in post-war Britain there were initially few challenges to its underlying colonial-imperial value base which supported beliefs in the superiority of white people and white social institutions.
>
> Tomlinson 1990: 44

In Andrea Levy's novel *Gilbert*, a Jamaican man, arriving to join the wartime RAF in what he had assumed to be the 'Mother Country' meets an American officer from a segregated USA who cannot understand that Black men can mix with white troops in England. The insulting language he uses, used later by the husband of an English friend, makes Gilbert say, 'You know what your trouble is, man? Your white skin. You think it makes you better than me. You want to know what your white skin makes you? It makes you white. That's all, no better, no worse than me' (Levy 2004: 525). This message is incomprehensible to the English man, whose education and war time service as a lower-rank soldier in India had convinced him of the superiority of white over all 'coloureds' and foreigners. In the real world an English officer serving in India who passionately supported the British Empire, Enoch Powell, later an MP, had already written a paper in 1946 opposing any Indian migration to Britain. But the British Nationality Act in 1948 gave all imperial subjects the right of free entry into Britain, although distinguishing between citizens of independent (white) Commonwealth countries and those in colonies and dependent territories.[1] The Act was possibly, as Winder suggested, to demonstrate that the British Empire was still a vibrant entity (Winder 2004: 332).

The fictional Gilbert had arrived back in England in 1948, on a real captured Nazi troopship which had been refitted and called *The Empire Windrush*. Some 490 men and women came from the Caribbean on this ship, skilled workers of whom over half already had jobs agreed in England. A British government that had overseen the post-war immigration of 200,000 Polish and other European displaced persons was so alarmed at the potential arrival of a few hundred 'coloured' workers that the Foreign Office was instructed that 'no effort be made to help these people, otherwise it might encourage a further influx', and they were initially housed in an old air-raid shelter in Clapham in South London. There was some opposition to the Polish migration from union leaders, and also from the communist party, worrying about the threat to jobs (Smith 2015) but none from the government. This contrasted with the hostile political and public reactions to postcolonial immigrants, their descendants and subsequent migrants, which can be traced to imperial beliefs in nationalism, racism, exclusion and a culture of Empire that was 'built into the very fabric of their (white) lives' (Mackenzie 2015: 197).

This chapter links the ignorance of empire firmly to the failure to challenge the colonial value system, as noted above by the author. It links this ignorance, as people arrived from former colonial countries, many skilled but taking over unskilled jobs the indigenous population did not want, to developments in education. While under the post-war Labour government a welfare state was coming into existence, education policy was largely based on a social democratic consensus that governments should regulate and resource education to achieve redistributive justice and some kind of equality. But this equality did not encompass the children of migrants, who from the outset were regarded as problems to be treated differently, dispersed, or incorporated unequally into a system which itself remained unequal. The relationship between the British class system and the class structure of Empire had embodied a permanent status barrier between citizens in the 'mother country' and those in the Empire. Whatever class conflicts went on in Britain, all social classes were, to some extent, united in hostility to the arrival of former colonial subjects and their children. Reaction ranged from attempts to remove the arrivals, or limit their entry, to some liberal and business welcome for their labour. There were mixed reactions from socialists and trade unions fighting for working class justice but confused when this class incorporated an unwelcome colonial 'underclass'.

The chapter documents the dissolution of Empire, as former colonies gained their independence during the 1950s and 1960s, some by planned handover of power, some by bloody conflict and the ignorance of the way in which a 300-year-old Empire disintegrated in some 20 years. The nearest many children came to learning about Empire and decolonisation was when they or their relatives did their compulsory military service (ended in 1962) in former colonies. Even a Professor of Modern History and Empire admitted that 'When I was at school and university in the 1950s and 1960s I was taught nothing at all about the British Empire' (Porter 2015: 397). He did not need to be actually taught, as the presence of Empire was there in all schooling. Former Prime Minister Gordon Brown wrote in his memoirs that in the 1950s and 1960s 'people could be forgiven for believing the British Empire was going to last forever' (Brown 2017: 33). Despite attempts to differentiate or remove new arrivals from former colonies, they were British subjects with rights to remain. This was in contrast to the German notion of 'guest worker' (*Gastarbeiter*) where migrants were initially regarded as work units and not expected to settle or bring their families.

Significant events

1944	Education Act. Secondary education for all to 15. Selective system of grammar, technical and secondary modern schools. General Certificate of Education O and A levels established in 1951.
1945	Labour government elected. Clement Attlee prime minister.
1945	United Nations organisation set up.
1947	India/Pakistan gain independence.
1948	British Nationality Act. Burma, Ceylon, gain independence.
1948	Israel to be an independent 'homeland'. Right of Palestinians promised.
1948	United Nations Universal Declaration of Human Rights.
1951	Conservatives elected.
1956	Suez canal invasion and British troops withdrawal.
1957	Ghana and Malaya (1963 Malaysia) gain independence.
1958	Race riots in Nottingham and Notting Hill.
1959	Independence for Somaliland (former British Protectorate).
1960	Independence for Nigeria and Cyprus.
1960–61	Proposed immigration restrictions lead to more immigration from the Asian sub-continent. Birmingham sets up the first Department for Teaching English as a Second Language. The Birmingham Immigration Control Association and Southall Residents Association set up to oppose immigration of 'non-whites'.
1961	Independence for Tanganyika (now Tanzania) and Sierra Leone. Enoch Powell makes a speech on English Nationhood and a vanishing Empire.
1962	Conservative Immigration Control Act. Minister of Health Enoch Powell encourages migration of health workers from the Caribbean.
1963	Kenya becomes independent. Singapore (colonised in 1819) gains independence. Short courses for teaching English as a second language set up. White parents in Southall protest against immigrant children in 'their' schools. Minister Edward Boyle rejects ideas of segregated education. Newsom report on *Half Our Future Secondary Modern Pupils).* Robbins Report on university expansion.
1964	Labour government elected (October). Harold Wilson PM. Voucher system restricts immigration. A Campaigns Against Racial Discrimination set up and an immigrants Advisory Council suggests dispersing immigrant children.
1964	Malta, Malawi and Zambia become independent.
1965	Circular 7/65, DES suggests no school to have more than 30% immigrant children. Eleven LEAs adopt dispersal by bussing. A North London West Indian Association expresses worry about children referred to ESN schools.
1965	First Race Relations Act. Race Relations Board and a National Committee for Commonwealth Immigration set up.

1965	Circular 10/65 requests all schools to reorganise on comprehensive principles. Sierra Leone and Gambia gain independence.
1966	Labour re-elected and a new MP declares 'we have buried the race issue'. Roy Jenkins envisions a society based on cultural diversity, mutual tolerance and equal opportunity. Botswana, Lesotho, Barbados and Guyana gain independence.
1966	Local Government Act to provide rate support grant for school staff in 'high-immigrant' areas. 10% Census personal data for England & Wales (Unpublished). Shows 'coloured population' as 924,000.
1967	Plowden Report on *Children and Their Primary Schools* includes a chapter on immigrant children. Independence for Aden (South Yemen).
1968	Commonwealth Immigration Act: Those 'patrials' with a father or grandfather born in the UK have priority. Second Race Relations Act passed but discrimination in education not mentioned.
1968	Enoch Powell makes 'rivers of blood' speech in Birmingham.
1969	Black Paper attacks comprehensive schooling and child-centred education. Mauritius, Swaziland and Nauru gain independence.
1970	Second report on public schools. Labour fails to integrate public schools into the state school system.
1970	Conservative government elected.

If the education system either failed to include information about Empire or did so in a distorted form; there was also little attempt to explain the process of decolonisation or why migrants from former colonial countries were entering Britain during the 1950s and 1960s. There was no change in a value system that supported the superiority of 'white' institutions. Political suggestions that unwanted migrants could 'go home' have formed a permanent background to debate on nation identity and who belongs in a nation-state in a globalised world. A Liberal member of the House of Lords, Gladwyn Jebb, declared that 'the process of de-colonisation has left us without any positive and generally accepted notion of our position in the world' (Jebb 1961). 'Us' did not include the former members of colonies who now lived in Britain. The white British continued to mainly define themselves by who was not regarded as British. There was also, as suggested in Chapter 1, a desperate need to maintain a fiction of a benign withdrawal from colonies. Cobain (2016) has recorded the ways in which hidden caches of documents recording brutalities and injustices during colonial rule, were destroyed by burning or, in some cases, taken out in crates and dropped into the sea, with the precaution that they would not be washed up by tides.

In 1945 a post-war Labour government was elected, to the discomfort of Winston Churchill and the Conservative Party. A war-torn Britain did not want to return to pre-war inequalities, and the new Prime Minister Attlee promised a new contract between the state and citizens. He had one woman in his Cabinet, Ellen Wilkinson, who was made Education Minister. Attlee, a product of Haileybury public school and Oxford, believed that the Empire was a force for good, and self-government with a rule of law would prevail in former colonies, although he was uneasy about the militarism and racial superiority that went along with it all. He was present at a Paris Peace Conference in July 1946 which attempted to settle border issues in Europe and its colonies, and agree to minority rights. The USA was at that time supreme in world affairs; a cold war was developing between it and an expanding USSR and there was agreement in the British government that 'the British Empire was unsustainable in its current form' (Bew 2016: 412). Attlee hoped that the newly created United Nations organisation might be an example for a British Commonwealth that was supposedly a United Nations in miniature. Despite war-time conflicts with India (which included arresting and jailing Ghandi), he agreed to a date for Indian/Pakistani independence on 14 August 1947. This proved a costly and horrific undertaking and debates still linger as to who was to blame. Attlee was not unduly worried by labour immigration, despite a group of his MPs sending a letter claiming that:

> This country may become an open reception centre for immigrants not selected in respect of health, education, training, character, customs and above all whether assimilation is at all possible ... and while the British people are blessed by the absence of a racial problem ... an influx of coloured people here is likely to impair the harmony, strength and cohesion in our public life. (Watson 1996; 157)

The letter suggested immigration control would be 'universally approved by our people', and uncontrolled migration would impair cohesion in public life – a claim that would resurface over the years. In the long term it would appear that politicians of all parties, then as later, gave no leadership to welcoming new potential citizens despite the need for their labour. Meanwhile, over the decade around 2 million people emigrated from the UK especially to 'white' Commonwealth countries.

The Conservative Party was elected in 1951 with Churchill again as prime minister. Churchill continued his opposition to decolonisation and immigration and in 1955 proposed that a slogan for another election in 1955 should be 'Keep Britain White'. Following Churchill's retirement, Anthony Eden led Britain into what was regarded as a fiasco over attempts to retain the Suez Canal in Egypt after General Nasser had nationalised it. The affair was widely regarded as signalling the end of much of British military power 'east of Suez' and decolonisation continued apace. In 1959 the British protectorate of Somaliland was declared independent. As an illustration that colonial countries were used as sources of food, this country in the north of the Horn of Africa was initially used to supply camel, goat and sheep meat to the British colony of Aden, taken by the British in 1839, and gaining independence in 1967 as part of South Yemen. UK governments have continued into the 21st century to supply arms to Saudi Arabia to use in a civil war in their former colony against the Houthi, a rebel group supported by Iran.

By the end the 1960s over 30 major colonies had achieved independence, welcomed by Harold Macmillan, then Conservative leader who in 1964 spoke in South Africa about the 'Winds of Change' blowing through the continent. By 1960, 17 new African States had joined the United Nations. The Colonial Office, founded in 1768, merged with a Commonwealth Office in 1966 and in 1968 became the Foreign and Commonwealth Office. Between 1945 and 1965 the number of people under British colonial rule reduced from 700 million to 5 million. Those at school during this period were unlikely to have heard all this mentioned, and although universities took in some students who would later go back to rule in their decolonised countries, the increase in overseas students was yet to begin.

Of the several bloody conflicts preceding independence, which were usually reported in the British press along the lines of 'ungrateful natives fighting our troops', Malaysia, Ceylon (Sri Lanka) Rhodesia and the Central African Federation and Kenya were major examples. African opposition to colonial rule in Kenya centred round the expropriation of land by white settlers and militant action by Africans. A state of emergency during the Mau Mau insurgency led to many atrocities. Cobain's view was that the truth about 1950s Kenya is still unknown (Cobain 2016:107), but only recently the British government paid reparations to elderly Kenyan men tortured during the war. By the end of the 1950s some land was released to Africans but the state of emergency was still in place. Brendon wrote that while club members at the Meru Club in Nairobi were worried about admitting Black men to the club as they might dance with the officials' (white) wives, 11 men were beaten to death in Hola camp by British troops (Brendon 2007: 563).

A more peaceful but arrogant example of de-colonisation which also involved relationships was illustrated in the British Protectorate of Bechuanaland (Botswana in 1966). The story was documented by Williams (2011) and a film, *A United Kingdom*, was released in 2016. The heir to the Kingship of the major nation in the Protectorate, Seretse Khama, while studying law in London, married a white woman. There was a need to placate apartheid South Africa, as the country supplied uranium and other minerals which were urgently needed. The Labour Colonial Secretary who circulated the Cabinet with a memo advising banishment for Seretse was Patrick Gordon-Walker. Ironically when a Labour government was finally returned to power in 1964 Gordon-Walker lost his West Midlands Smethwick seat to a Conservative who had campaigned on the slogan 'If you want a n****r neighbour, vote Labour'. Sir and Lady Seretse Kharma and their descendants went on to rule in Botswana.

A further example of the assumption that imperial governments could move their colonial people around as they pleased came in the later 1960s when the people in the Chagos Archipelago in the Indian Ocean were forced to leave their islands. The islands had been taken from the French in 1814 and used as a slave trading post. In 1967 the British government bought most of the plantations which deprived the Islanders of their income and at the request of the USA forced them to leave. The largest military base in the world was then constructed by the American military on Diego Garcia. The island was supposedly returned to Mauritius in 2024, with the Americans retaining their base, but there are still debates over possession.

Political hypocrisies

In England, anti-immigrant antagonism towards post-war colonial immigrants found support in all social classes and surfaced in all subsequent elections. Later hostility to European migration was added, which was evident in the vote to leave the European Union (EU). While racism against Black and Asian migration was developing, anti-Irish and anti-Semitic racism continued, although in 1948 there were only some 400,000 Jews and 600,000 Irish in England (Kynaston 2007: 270). All political parties colluded in the hypocrisy of recognising that labour migration was needed while passing immigration control measures. There were outbreaks of violence against immigrants throughout the 1950s and 1960s, and two bills attempting to outlaw discrimination in the 1950s failed. It appeared that liberal beliefs in equality before the law were sustained when white youths were jailed for attacking Caribbean migrants in Nottingham and Notting Hill in 1958, but this did not last.

Ideological self-images of a tolerant Britain came under strain in the 1960s as more migrants arrived, including those invited to work in transport and hospitals, and after a period of intense hostility to immigration the Conservative government passed an Act in 1962 which limited Commonwealth immigration by the introduction of vouchers. This was initially opposed by Labour leader Hugh Gaitskell, but the Act led to a 'beat the ban' surge in migration from families from the Indian sub-continent just before it was passed. After Gaitskill's early death at the age of 57 in 1963, the new Labour Prime Minister Harold Wilson endorsed the voucher system in 1965 and went on to introduce a 1968 Immigration Act. This was designed mainly to limit the entry of Kenyan Asians by distinguishing between 'patrials' with a father or grandfather born in the UK and others. The Act led E.J.B. Rose and his Associates in a study of 'race relations' in England, to assert that: 'A Rubicon was crossed in the spring of 1968. This was when the British government decided, on grounds of expediency rather than principle, that it could no longer accept responsibility for certain of its citizens because of the colour of their skin' (Rose et al 1969: 11).²

The Labour government attempted to retain a liberal stance on race and migration with Acts in 1965 and 1968 notionally outlawing discrimination (education was not mentioned until 1976) and set up a Race Relations Board and a National Committee for Commonwealth Immigration, but all political parties were nervous about 'coloured immigration'. MP Richard Crossman wrote in his diary that 'Since the 1964 general election it is clear that immigration can be a potential vote-loser for the Labour party if we are seen to allow a flood of immigrants to come in and blight the areas of our inner cities'(Crossman 1979). A rhetoric of floods, blights and blaming immigrants for inner city decline had taken hold early. In the relatively affluent city of Birmingham with a million people and some 50,000 Caribbean and Asian workers, there were objections to immigrants doing the unskilled work local people did not want and complaints about their housing in multi-occupied lodgings. Rex and Moore (1967) documented the actual poor housing and work conditions of migrants in a book which was reviewed by Enoch Powell. His review was mainly a polemic against 'coloured immigration' and suggestions of repatriation. He appeared to have forgotten that as minister of health in 1962 he had encouraged migration from the Caribbean for hospital workers. In 2018 some of the nurses recruited by Powell reminisced in a BBC TV programme about their reception. A common experience was of patients telling them to 'keep your black hands off me'.

In the 1960s England was searching for a new post-imperial identity, As American Secretary of State Dean Acheson famously put it, 'Britain has lost an Empire but has not yet found a role.' Powell's outright nationalism provided this and his speeches continued to articulate a romantic view of the Empire and promised a 'lyrical, indeed sublime way forward for a bemused and resentful people conscious of having lost their place in history' (Roberts 2012: 128). But romanticism was not extended to the former colonised. In speeches in the West Midland in 1968 and 1969, he deplored the immigration of those he described as 'coloured, Negro and piccaninies' and used the well-known 'rivers of blood' allusion to the writings of the Latin poet Virgil. He claimed without evidence that the white working class could not obtain houses, hospital beds or school places and that employers favoured migrant workers, and 'the sense of being a persecuted minority is growing among ordinary English people' (Powell 1968). All these assertions were to resurface over the years up to and beyond the Brexit vote (Tomlinson 2018).

The main issue in the 1960s was whether immigrant minorities could be incorporated into a working class which had only partially achieved legal, political and social citizen rights (Marshall 1951). Assimilation and absorption of migrants dominated political debate; a government white paper in 1965 demanded 'control of the entry of immigrants so that it does not outrun Britain's capacity to absorb them' (Home Office 1965: 2). Roy Jenkins, while home secretary in 1966, claimed that there could be an integration of minorities which was 'not a flattening process of uniformity, but cultural diversity coupled with equal opportunity in an atmosphere of mutual tolerance'. But evidence of white tolerance of Black immigrants or their British-born children was hard to detect.

Although Powell was sacked from the Conservative Cabinet for his anti-immigrant speeches, they were followed by dock workers and market traders in London marching in his defence and claiming support for a white nation-state. In fact, these supposedly spontaneous marches were, according to a memo sent to Harold Wilson by the security services, organised by extreme right-wing groups, including remaining members of Oswald Mosley's fascist party (Norton-Taylor and Milne 1999). Writer Sarfraz Manzoor recalled the effect Powell's speeches had on him as a boy of Pakistani origin for whom 'Repatriation was the most terrifying word for those who feared it might happen if Powell and his supporters ever gained power' (Manzoor 2008). It was by no means only racist working-class people who supported these views. By 1969, some 327 out of 413 Conservative Associations, mainly in middle-class areas with few minorities, had voted to stop all 'coloured immigration'. Race policies in the later 1960s were influenced by the civil rights movement and fear of city riots as in the USA, and a language of assimilation was superseded by a government language of cultural pluralism and equal opportunity, while at the same time further immigration control legislation was passed. Subsequent debates have centred round whether assimilation had been a long-term government policy, but even the most obtuse policy makers would have been aware that minorities in nation-states generally do keep their own languages, religions and customs, providing they do not conflict with the law.

Education policies

The post-Second World War education system was intended to be central to a welfare state which would distribute resources more fairly and encourage economic growth. Growth demanded all kinds of labour to reconstruct the country.[3] A labour shortage was partly due to women who had worked during the war, leaving work to become 'housewives', a group always assumed to be white. Kynaston (2007) noted that the middle classes felt a greater sense of deprivation in the austerity years into the 1950s and a sense of losing privileges, especially servants and golf. But education policies were to continue to favour the middle and upper classes. Before the 1944 Education Act some 88 per cent of pupils had left school by 14, only 10 per cent passed public examinations and 5 per cent went into higher education. The Act introduced secondary education for all to 15, with children separated at age 11 on the basis of 'age, aptitude and ability' into grammar, secondary modern and technical schools, the latter remaining undeveloped. It soon became apparent that the Act benefited middle class children with some 80 per cent of mainly working class children going into modern schools and the middle classes dominating grammar schools with some concessions to the 'bright' working class child. The practice of streaming in primary schools worked as a form of social selection and middle class and the aspirational lower middle classes did their best as they has always done, to ensure that their children were more successful in competitive examinations for the best state schools.

The Labour government actually increased inequality, preventing secondary modern pupils from entering for public examinations and openly stated that these schools were 'for children whose future employment will not demand any measure of technical skills or knowledge' (Ministry of Education 1946: 13). It was not until 1963 and the introduction of the Certificate of Secondary Education (CSE) that secondary modern schools were allowed a public examination. Simon noted that 'even under Labour governments elected with a massive majority the mediation of class relations was still a major function of the education system' (Simon 1991: 115). But the post-war government was concerned to hurry as many young people as possible through schools into jobs at age 15 into a workforce needed for economic reconstruction.

The rich and influential, including most members of the government, continued to send their children to private schools, especially those in the prestigious Headmasters' Conference (HMC). Although the public schools were initially concerned that a Labour government might interfere with their status, this did not happen, and they continued to inculcate beliefs in their superiority over the working classes, colonials and immigrants, as the testimony of numbers of ex-public school boys can testify (Gaythorne-Hardy 1977; Green and Kynaston 2019). A report in 1944 had considered the integration of these schools into the state system, but this was quietly forgotten. Both Prime Minister Attlee and future Labour leader Hugh Gaitskell, educated at public schools, had little interest in the issue and Tony Benn recorded in his diary in October 1953 that 'Gaitskell still wants an elite learning Latin verse' (Benn 1974: 172.). Future public-school educated ministers perhaps showed that Latin verse was not the best preparation for government, and the Brexit negotiations after 2016 demonstrated that it was mainly men educated at public schools, notably Boris Johnson and Jacob Rees-Mogg, schooled at Eton, who failed to support Theresa May in her negotiations.

The idea that children could be separated on the basis of testing for assumed intelligence or ability was soon challenged by research but enduring eugenic beliefs and assumptions that social and racial groups could be differentiated as more or less intelligent, cast a long and pernicious shadow into the 21st century. Even the report by Liberal Lady Plowden in 1967 referred to the difficulty of deciding whether an immigrant child 'lacks intelligence, or is suffering from culture shock or an inability to communicate' (Plowden Report 1967: 70). Two reports in 1963 on the education of 13–16-year-olds (Newsom Report 1963) and higher education (Robbins Report 1963) rejected deterministic theories of intelligence, and the Newsom Report recommended raising the school leaving age to 16. By the 1960s, governments around the world were recognising the need for expanded education systems, and a broad consensus emerged that non-selective comprehensive schooling be established with the middle classes realising that working class children might enter grammar schools in larger numbers and displace their children. Even before Labour won the election in 1964, some 90 out of 163 local authorities had submitted plans to become non-selective and comprehensive, although this was only requested, not required, in a 1965 circular (DES 1965). This allowed some 15 local authorities to retain selective schools.

Optimistic beliefs that a democratic society should educate all its young people to high levels rather than just selected elites, was always under attack from a right wing dedicated to preserving a traditional hierarchical society. Both during the 1960s and afterwards the decade was presented as a period of liberalism when traditions were destroyed and education standards lowered. A series of Black Papers published by right-wing academics and policy groups between 1969 and 1977 resurrected deterministic theories of intelligence and presented in lurid and inaccurate detail the lowering of standards and the feckless behaviour by the working classes which hindered their school achievements. The national media demonised some urban schools as 'blackboard jungles' a term redolent with the supposed primitive behaviour of 'natives' depicted in 19th- and 20th-century imperial literature. While Black Papers blamed the poor for their failings, more liberal policies advocated compensatory education along the lines of the Headstart Programmes in the USA. In Britain, remedial education for children falling behind was intended to alleviate what were described as cycles of deprivation and cultures of poverty (Rutter and Madge 1976). There was little discussion, then as now, of economic conditions that create poverty

Education for ignorance

Ignorance about colonial immigrants and where they came from was widespread and the education system was not about to enlighten children. A survey of 2,000 people in 1948 reported that 67 per cent of people thought those living in the Colonies had a lower standard of living than in Britain, 62 per cent thought they were mainly 'coloured' but only 49 per cent could name one colony (Kynaston 2007: 272). While the report noted that housewives, the unskilled and those over 60 were least well-informed, even managerial groups were not well informed, especially on knowing the difference between a colony, a dominion and a protectorate. A history textbook published by an association of assistant masters in secondary schools, thought that this was something to be clarified for grammar school boys. By the time the post-war period was reached, it was suggested that there should be some teaching to the boys about developments in the Empire and 'possibly a lesson or two on the peculiar problems of India and its recent crisis', presumably the partition and massacres (IAAM 1950: 49). Press reporting at the time blamed sectarian violence on 'gangs of Muslims attacking Hindus' with no mention of the hasty departure of the British or Britian's responsibilities. A white paper in 1943 suggested that history, geography and modern languages should be taught to give all pupils more interest in 'the responsibilities of citizenship in this country, the Empire and the world' but that it remained only an aspiration. The national narrative of imperial superiority, based on ignorance of what was actually happening, clashed with the reality that supremacies were vanishing (Cannadine, Keating and Sheldon 2011: 141). Into the 1970s school curricula continued to be based on understanding from Social Darwinist and eugenic beliefs in different 'races' with the white race superior. Stembridge's three-volume *New World Geographies* recorded in Volume one, that 'mankind is divided into three races' (Stembridge 1951: 1). This textbook was still used in the 1970s when Prime Minister Theresa May and her Foreign Secretary Boris Johnson were at school. Colonial historians in other countries with disappearing empires have also recorded that 'Geography text books remind us of the most simplistic and over-determined classification system of them all, that of skin colour' (Fremeaux and Maas 2015: 386).

In Britain, teachers from former colonies, even when fully qualified, found difficulty in finding work. One, Eustace Braithwaite with a physics degree from Cambridge, eventually found a job teaching science in a London school and, as apparently the only Black teacher in London, suffered abuse. He eventually wrote a book about his experiences, which was made into the successful film *To Sir, With Love*. There was little evidence that primary or secondary modern school pupils were learning anything other than the pre-war imperial stories, supplemented by comics and films. Films by this time were mainly focusing on the defeat of Germany and the Nazis had taken over as despicable enemies. Parents, brought up on an imperial curriculum, were not in a position to enlighten their children. Although the Festival of Britain, organised in 1951 under the Labour government to promote British trade with a post-imperial world, was a great success with the public, Churchill regarded it as socialist propaganda and ordered the site demolished when he came to power. Business was more enlightened and many schools continued to receive a book called *The British Trades Alphabet*, which gave information about companies and their trade around the world and offered competitions and prizes. Cadbury's Chocolate was especially remembered for free samples of chocolate (British Trades Alphabet 1955).

Education policy makers in the 1950s and 1960s were more concerned with developing new school and local authority structures and a rising birth rate to worry about changing views and attitudes concerning the Empire and its aftermath. A teacher shortage post-war led to ex-servicemen being offered a nine-month training programme and sent into schools. Many of these (mainly men) had similar experiences of 'the natives' overseas as had the character in Levy's novel, and they had no experience of treating Black or other minorities as equals. Public schools often took graduates with no teacher training and continued with their own traditional curriculum. Civil servants who drafted Education Acts and guidance, were, like their political masters in all parties, mainly educated at public schools. The experiences of one National Service recruit, educated at a public school and given a National Service commission, and who subsequently became a teacher, illustrated the incomprehension of some young men sent out to colonies to oversee independence. He had been brought up on patriotic tales and was surprised to find 'British good-will' was not reciprocated in former colonies (Hawkes in Shindler 2012: 229). But at least he was more understanding than the officers encountered by another National Service recruit sent out to Singapore before Malaya fought for independence. He recorded that:

> We had eight Malays on our fire crew and we were told they were not our equals. Officers told us we must be firm but fair with them but they were not our equal. I thought that some of the officers, if they had not been to public school, wouldn't have made lance corporal in charge of the toilets. (Perry in Shindler 2012: 33)

By the 1960s it was clear that teachers in both private and state schools had little idea of their importance in helping along what was a developing multiracial and multicultural society. This was not surprising, given that most had been educated in the ethnocentric curriculum with the pink maps on classroom walls and a curriculum which combined elements of nationalism and racial arrogance with beliefs in superior moral and Christian benevolence towards imperial subjects. In the literature on the education of immigrant children in the 1960s, assimilationist approaches were dominant. Jenny Williams, studying schools in Birmingham wrote that 'teachers see their role as putting over a set of values (Christian), a code of behaviour (middle class) and a set of aspirations in which white collar jobs have higher prestige than manual' (Williams in Tomlinson 1982: 98). One head teacher, responding to a survey in the 1960s, replied that 'I do not consider it the responsibility of an English state school to cater for the culture and customs of a foreign nature' (Townsend and Brittan 1973:13). Historians of Empire, whether champions or critics, appear to agree that the spread of modern ideas and institutions, democracy, the rule of law, secularism, rationalism, technology, capitalism and human rights, along with football shirts, came from western nations (Porter 2015). The idea that these noble ideas were spread peacefully to former colonies lingered on, without any mention of force or guns. Beliefs that colonial populations were inferior in their culture and lifestyles were expressed openly.

Education and minorities

Britain was not alone in its contradictory responses to migration and the incorporation of migrants and their children. Post-war migration had led to world-wide debates, especially in Western countries, about the merits of assimilation versus pluralistic co-existence. Assimilation required that a nation-state should have one majority culture with minorities abandoning their own cultures and languages to become effective citizens. This view initially was espoused by both liberals and traditionalists, and education was to bring this about. The second report from the Commonwealth Immigrants Advisory Council asserted that 'a national system cannot be expected to perpetuate the values of immigrant groups' (CIAC 1964). Assimilationist ideologies were soon challenged as civil rights protest movements emerged during the 1960s. Within these movements racial discrimination had emerged as a major factor to be challenged. In Britain a first generation of settlers had incentives to move towards some kind of absorption into a society promising social and economic equality, but they soon realised that hostile assumptions about race and culture prevented equal educational and employment opportunities for them and their children. Black and Asian movements against injustice quickly developed. A West Indian Standing Conference which brought together various groups was established after the Notting Hill riots. The Indian Workers' Association, with a history from the 1930s continued to defend workers' rights in and out of trade union movements, a Campaign against Racial Discrimination was set up in 1964 following a visit to Britain by Martin Luther King and a North London West Indian Parents' Association was active in voicing concerns over the education of Black children. There was initially no central policy or planning to meet the incorporation of immigrant children, The DES defended this on the grounds that 'Neither the scale of future immigration or the patterns of settlement could be seen until the early 1960s' (DES 1971: 14). This was nonsense as it was clear that settlement was where labour was needed in inner cities. But these were places where schools serving the working classes were already neglected and ill-resourced. Government papers continued to refer to undesirable concentrations of Commonwealth immigrants which should be broken up and a Birmingham Association of Schoolmasters lamented that racial enclaves were here to stay.

White parents in Southall complained about the numbers of immigrant children in 'their' schools and it was suggested that no school had more than 30 per cent of minority children. The 1964 Commonwealth Immigrants Advisory Council recommended dispersal of children on the grounds that they affected the progress of other children and hindered their assimilation into 'normal' school life. Dispersal by bussing became official policy, although only 11 local authorities adopted this and the policy was ruled illegal in 1975, and there was never any suggestion that white children be bussed. Despite confusion over numbers of immigrant children, one specific policy was from the Home Office, not the Education Department, to distribute money via Section 11 of a Local Government Grant, to areas where immigrants from the Commonwealth had languages and customs different from their local communities. The then respected school inspectors (HMI) focused on teaching English to immigrants and brought together specialist language teachers. Policies aimed at all deprived communities included Educational Priority Areas, and an Urban Aid programme, set up by the Labour government in 1968 partly as a response to Enoch Powell's inflammatory speeches (Tomlinson 2008).[4]

Blaming minority children

As policy makers and schools could not admit to, or were not aware of, their own ignorance of colonialism and subsequent migration, they were not in a position to consider changes that were needed to educate all children in a society where literally the Empire had come home. So the default position was to blame migrant children and their parents for deficiencies. Black, Asian and other minority children had barely arrived before psychologists and educational researchers began to conduct psychometric tests to measure 'intelligence' and ability, and used tests of attainment standardised on white populations to declare the children were of low ability or under-achieving. The issue of the over-placement of Black children in what were then schools for the 'educationally subnormal' (ESN-a category not abolished until 1981), caused much anxiety for Caribbean parents and in 1969 the North West London West Indian Association complained to the Race Relations Board that it was racial discrimination (Tomlinson 1981). Bernard Coard published his classic paper *How the West Indian Child Is Made ESN in the British School* system in 1971 (Coard 1971).

Parents from Caribbean countries, where there had been no general secondary education until 1953, had assumed that even if they took low-paid work, their children would have educational and job opportunities, and were shocked and angry at the levels of discrimination they and their children faced. Even well-qualified parents found their qualifications did not lead to equal treatment by schools – a situation continuing over 40 years later (Rollock et al 2015). Supplementary schools became popular with parents, both to supplement poor school teaching and to give a fairer historical account of colonialism and Caribbean and African development. Any course labelled Black Studies was regarded as a dangerous activity, and in 1972 the Chief Education Officer in Birmingham visited a school where a Black Studies course was incorporated into a Community Studies course and closed it down (Rex and Tomlinson 1979: 186). But by 1981 the DES were lamenting that 'minority parents appear to be losing confidence in what schools are teaching their children' (DES 1981: 41).

Official explanations for any lower educational performance of minority children over the years ran along the lines of lack of English, interference from Caribbean dialects, migration shock, family disorganisation, male dominance, male absence, female dominance, cultural difference, child-minding, low self-esteem, identity problems and low socio-economic status. School difficulties, low teacher expectations, stereotyping of children and the experience of racial hostility were also explanations, but overall assumptions remained that Black and Irish children had a lower intellectual capacity for learning. Jensen (1969) in an article in the *Harvard Educational Review* concluded that compensatory education for Black children was misplaced due to their inferior intelligence, and, as noted in Chapter 2, his former student, Hans Eysenck, later a London University professor, demonstrated a peculiar historical view when he concluded in his 1971 book that 'Negroes and the Irish' had lower mental capacities due to crimes committed against their ancestors (Eysenck 1971: 142).

Positive practice

There was, however, a growing awareness in urban schools that blaming immigrant children for their deficiencies was not good enough and teachers had been left to solve to the problems of educating for a multiracial society, in which all people would live together harmoniously. The first collection of essays by practising teachers in the 1960s was *The Multiracial School* (1971) edited by McNeal and Rogers, Julia McNeal being the daughter of former Labour leader Hugh Gaitskell. This collection showed that some teachers were taking seriously the need for resources and a changed curriculum for all children, and they were aware that white children needed an education to 'combat the indifference and hostility that exists between different national and racial groups' (McNeal and Rogers 1971: 15). They were also aware of the children grouped themselves along ethnic lines, a recurring issue not just in the majority but also in the minority groups. Teachers' willingness to deal with these issues depended on their training, and as teachers came through their own schooling with an acceptance of the Empire and an ignorance of its consequences, training was desperately needed. It was not until 1969 that there was recognition that 'all teachers should be equipped to prepare children for life in a multicultural society' (Select Committee on Race Relations and Immigration 1969: para 214). But the cultural values filtering down through all social classes still encouraged beliefs in the economic social and racial superiority of white Europeans. As Gilbert in Andrea Levy's novel found, even after finding a job, his white work mates were still asking 'When are you going back to the jungle … when are you going back where you belong?' (Levy 2004: 317).

Summary

This chapter has linked the dissolution of Empire in the 1950s and 1960s as former colonies gained their independence, with education policies in England. It suggests that imperial beliefs and images were still engrained in public understandings and educational structures, policy makers and schools were not able to, or interested in, changing this. The arrival of former colonial immigrants was met with hostility and incomprehension and education did little to enlighten people about the reasons for migration or combat the nationalistic sentiments spread by prominent politicians. There was considerable hypocrisy from politicians of all parties over migration. Post-war education was based on a social-democratic consensus that governments should regulate and resource the whole system fairly and improve schooling for all children. Although to a certain extent this happened, the middle classes continued to benefit most. It did not happen for the children of migrants, who from the outset were regarded as 'problems' to be dispersed, or treated unequally in poorly resourced urban schools. Positive treatment eventually came from HMI and money for teaching English, and from some teachers who realised that there was a need for what in a later report became an 'Education for All' (DES 1985). Political antagonisms ensured that educational ignorance about Empire and migration continued.

4

Post-imperial anxieties and conflicts, 1970–90

We all thought the empire was a marvellous thing. It was a force for good throughout the world. When Britain chose to give her empire away we were rather saddened – the colonial people had all the blessing of colonial rule and look how casually they dismissed them.
National Service cadet officer quoted in Shindler 2012: 92

If we went on as we are, by the end of the century there would be four million people of the New Commonwealth or Pakistan here. Now that is an awful lot and I think it means people are rather afraid this country might be swamped by people with a different culture.
Margaret Thatcher interview on Granada Television,
30 January 1978

An Empire mindset never really died. For some, colonial rule was a blessing given up by ungrateful people, and for many, including a prime minister, the arrival of former colonials subjects into the colonising country was to be regretted. By 1978, Margaret Thatcher claimed that just 1.5 million Black and Asian people, a third actually born in Britain, might 'swamp' the other 55 million. National servicemen who had served overseas were, as Colin Schindler has noted, among many who regretted the ending of the British Empire. From the 1970s, all political parties were in agreement that immigration from those former colonies euphemistically termed New Commonwealth countries, should be limited. Whereas in the 19th and earlier 20th centuries, politicians, adventurers, academics and others were openly racist over colonial conquests of supposedly inferior peoples, by the mid-century an ideology of conservative imperialism had developed to try to smooth moral dilemmas. '*Civis Brittanicus sum*' (I am a British citizen) and accompanying legal rights was a claim all people in the Empire could make, but it assumed colonial people would stay put in their countries. Conservative imperialism, liberal ideologies concerned with human rights and socialist notions of the brotherhood of all workers disappeared with the invited arrival of colonial workers and their families. By the 1970s, notions that might earlier have been dismissed as morally unacceptable became the unspoken assumptions of all political parties.

This chapter documents the continuation of an anti-immigrant ideology and its linkage with the idea of an exclusive British identity, and the developing reactions of a younger generation becoming more race-conscious. By the 1980s, conflicts surrounding the acceptance of Black and other minorities into what was becoming a multiracial and multicultural society and their equal participation as citizens became the major contested issue. The old British Empire had been transformed into a Commonwealth of former colonies, dependencies and British overseas territories.[1] This was not a process without conflict, as the issue of Grenada, independent in 1974, and the Falkland Islands, acquired in 1833 and still an overseas territory, indicated. Closer links with Europe were becoming a reality, with a referendum in 1975 cementing entry into a European Economic Community, and Prime Minister Thatcher signing up to the Single European Act in 1986. In 2018, when papers were released after 30 years, her 1988 speech in Bruges, Belgium, suggested that she was in favour of developing a single market and 'Our destiny is in Europe, part of the Community' (Thatcher 1993). What was described as globalisation and a global economy was developing, which was causing further migrations of people and their labour world-wide. In Britain, questions of identity became crucial, with much antagonism to minorities based on whether differences of colour, culture and religion were at odds with notions of a British national identity. In the 1980s a radical restructuring of public welfare provision began to take shape with the introduction of market forces into education, health and other social services, and an extended market in housing, which resulted in more inequalities and disadvantages for working class and minority groups. A working class openly at war with government, was subject to a defeat when the miners' strike of 1984–85 ended in capitulation. A racism based on culture and religion as well as colour encouraged Powellite views of an exclusive national identity and provided more rationalisation for xenophobia and hostility towards minorities.

Education policies were moving towards non-selective schooling and some curriculum change, accompanied by what was to become a familiar charge that educational standards were too low and failed to produce a literate and skilled workforce. A need to play down any special arrangements for immigrant (Black and Asian) children to placate a hostile white population underpinned policies, and minority children were subsumed under the label of disadvantage. 'Immigrant children share with indigenous children the disadvantages associated with an impoverished environment' (DES 1974: 2). Despite more Race Relations legislation the terminology of race or racism was avoided in education policy documents. In 1984 a paper produced by the Council for National Academic Awards (CNAA) on including multicultural understanding in teacher training courses, had any references to anti-racism deleted by DES officials (Tomlinson 2008: 86). Despite all this, the 1980s was actually a period of some educational advance for minorities, and there was more focus on the needs of a society by then being described as multicultural or multi-ethnic. The Swann Report (DES 1985a) was regarded as 'the boldest, most comprehensive statement on multicultural education so far produced in Britain' (Williams 1988: 6), with the resulting right-wing backlash from nationalists seeking to preserve imperial notions of a national identity free from the contamination of 'alien cultures'.

Significant events

1970	Conservative government elected. Circular 7/70 cancels expectations that secondary schools need to become comprehensive.
1971	Immigration Act limits right of abode to patrials with a father or grandfather born in the UK. Others to obtain work permits and register with the police. Home Office sets up a Race Relations Research Unit.
1971	McNeal and Rogers publish *The Multiracial School*. Hans Eysenck publishes *Race, Education and Intelligence*, suggesting Black and Irish people have lower IQs than other groups. DES produces two surveys on *The Education of Immigrants*.
1972	Expulsion of Ugandan Asians by Idi Amin. 27,000 arrive and many go to Leicester despite the city council claiming that 'Leicester is full'. DES discontinues collection of statistics on immigrant pupils.
1973	School leaving age raised to 16. Select Committee on Race Relations and Immigration publishes a report on education, making 24 recommendations. Trevor MacDonald becomes ITV's first Black news reader. (He retired in 2005 and was given knighthood.)
1973	War in the Asian sub-continent. Pakistan secedes from the Commonwealth. Bangladesh becomes a separate country. Recession as price of oil increased, collapse of youth labour market.
1974	Labour forms a minority government. Roy Jenkins announces an amnesty for illegal immigrants. Abolition of direct grant schools. DES publishes *Educational Disadvantage and the Needs of Immigrants* (DES 1974). A Centre for Disadvantage was set up in Manchester but closed in 1980.
1974	Grenada, claimed by the British in 1763, gets independence.
1975	(February) Nationwide vote to join the European Economic Community (EEC). 17,300.000 voted to join, 8,400,000 were against.
1975	Home Office report on *Racial Discrimination* and Bullock report on *A Language for Life* published. Sex Discrimination Act passed. Mrs Thatcher becomes Conservative Party leader.
1976	Gurdip Singh Chaggar murdered at a Southall bus stop. Police say it is not a racial crime. Shadow home Secretary William Whitelaw says 'The British Empire has paid its debts' and calls for inner city programmes to defuse racial tension. Third Race Relations Act and Commission for Racial Equality (CRE) set up. James Callaghan makes Ruskin College speech.

Education and Race

1977	Select Committee on Race Relations and Immigration reports on *The West Indian Community* and claims 'we are a multiracial, multicultural country' (Cox and Boyson 1977). Black Papers (Cox and Dyson) attack comprehensive education and 'Marxist infiltration' in education.
1977	In by-elections in Stechford and Ladywood in Birmingham the National Front come third with Liberals fourth.
1978	Warnock committee reports on *Special Educational Needs* (DES 1978) with no mention of Caribbean parents' anxiety about their children. Viv Anderson becomes the first Black footballer to play for England.
1979	Conservatives win the general election. Mrs Thatcher first woman prime minister.
1979	Rampton Committee set up to enquire into the education of children from minority groups. During confrontations with the National Front in Southall, Blair Peach, a teacher, is killed.
1980	Education Act. *A Framework for the School Curriculum* (DES).
1980	Rhodesia becomes independent Zimbabwe.
1981	Race riots in Brixton, Toxteth and other cities. Home Office reports on *Racial Disadvantage* also Rampton Report on *West Indian Children in Our Schools*. Special Education Act abolishes 'categories of handicap'.
1982	Falklands (Malvinas) War (April), against Argentina.
1982	Scarman Report on the Brixton disorders. Schools Council for the Curriculum abolished. Lower Achieving Pupils (LAPP) for bottom 40% of pupils Twenty LEAs have multicultural education policies. New guidelines for Section 11 funding. Some 40 Black supplementary school in operation.
1983	Conservatives re-elected. The USA invades British Caribbean island of Grenada.
1984	Honeyford affair in Bradford. Council for the Accreditation of Teacher Education set up (CATE).
1985	Lord Swann's Committee reports on *Education for All* (DES 1985a). Archbishop of Canterbury's report *Faith in the City* called a Marxist document. Riots in Toxteth and Handsworth. National Anti-racist Movement in Education set up. DES publishes a white paper on *Better Schools* (DES 1985b) stressing all pupils should understand the traditions and values of British society. Oliver Letwin advises Margaret Thatcher that race riots were caused by individual bad character and attitudes.
1986	Parliament ratifies the Single European Act which sets up a single market and allows free movement of labour. DES offers Education Support Grants for multicultural projects in white schools (120 funded by 1988). 'O' levels replaced by GCSEs. Corporal punishment outlawed in state schools. Ahmed Ullah stabbed to death in Burnage School, Manchester.
1987	Conservatives win a third general election (four Black MPs elected). DES creates a post for inner-city education and education for a multicultural society. White parents in Dewsbury set up a school in a pub for their children. A *Campaign for Real Education* set up to support British culture and the Christian religion. Black History Month introduced in schools.
1988	CRE publishes *Learning in Terror*. St George's Medical School admit their selection procedures discriminate against ethnic minorities and women. Immigration Act removes right for New Commonwealth citizens to bring in marriage partners. Section 28 of a Local Government Act forbids the 'promotion' of homosexuality in education.

1988   Education Reform Act. National Curriculum. Key Stage Assessments. Parental right to 'choose' school continued. Schools able to opt out of Local Education Authority control and be 'grant maintained'. Inner London Education Authority abolished. National Curriculum Council (NCC) set up.

1989   Schools in Birmingham with largely Muslim intakes vote to become grant maintained. Copies of Salman Rushdie's book *The Satanic Verses* burned in Bradford. Secretary of State for Education requests the NCC to take account of the multicultural nature of society and sets up a working group. Their subsequent report being censored. Labour Party produces *Multicultural Education: Labour's Policy For Schools*.

1990   Education Secretary rules that a parent in Cleveland has a right to remove her child from a multiracial school as parental 'choice' takes precedence over Race Relations legislation. Norman Tebbit MP argues that Asian loyalty to Britain can be judged by whether they cheer for the English cricket team.

Politics and ideologies, 1970s

By the 1970s there was a general consensus among politicians, their advisers, the public and academics of various theoretical persuasions, that 'race' was a problem and a likely cause for conflict and violence. Rex and Tomlinson, undertook an empirical study and concluded that by the 1970s 'crucial decisions had already been taken, and the status of black and brown men (sic) in Britain, had already been declared different from and inferior to, that of the native-born British citizen' (Rex and Tomlinson 1979: 47). Researchers at the Birmingham Centre for Contemporary Cultural Studies, under the direction of Stuart Hall, further concluded that a 'siege mentality shaped the 70s', and political class struggles incorporated a racism which linked a Black presence, illegal migration, young unemployed people and white people who identified with 'alien cultures' as enemies (Centre for Contemporary Cultural Studies 1982: 27–29; Hall 1978).[2] Sir Alfred Sherman, a former Communist Party member turned right wing, and a political advisor to Mrs Thatcher, declared that 'The imposition of mass immigration from backward alien cultures is just one symptom of this self destructive urge reflected in the assault on patriotism, the family ... the Christian religion, in public lives and schools ... and all that is English and wholesome' (Sherman 1979).

Although in 1970 Conservative Prime Minister Edward Heath told his local party that 'There is no reason why cultural diversity should not be combined with loyalty to this country' (Heath 1970), both local and national parties were asserting ideas of patriotism and a national homogeneity that excluded minorities. There was much opposition to the arrival in 1972 of some 27,000 Asians with British passports, mainly educated people with entrepreneurial skills, expelled by Idi Amin from Uganda. Despite hostility, many settled in Leicester and rejuvenated business there. There was similar hostility to the arrival of Asians expelled from Malawi and Vietnamese boat people taken in as refugees, both the results of British and French imperialism. The Conservative Monday Club in Parliament campaigned for repatriation of Caribbean and Asian people, and took exception to what they called a 'race industry'. This comprised the various Commissions and groups supporting the legislation against discrimination, especially the 1976 Race Relations Act, which included education for the first time and created a Commission for Racial Equality (CRE). In 1976, in a speech in Leicester, Shadow Home Secretary William Whitelaw, referring to immigration, announced that 'the British Empire has paid its debts' (Whitelaw 1976), by allowing the entry of the former colonised into Britain.

The 1971 Immigration Act had gone some way to satisfying the anti-immigrant lobby, by distinguishing between 'patrials' and non-patrials', and subsequent Acts controlled the entry of wives and children. Although former imperial subjects, from rural and urban backgrounds, had settled where their labour was needed and white flight, and discriminatory housing policies had ensured spatial segregation, minorities, especially with different languages, religions and cultural traditions were openly regarded as a threat to a British national identity. Trade unions were not much help, despite industrial disputes being led by Asian workers.[3] One trade union leader, William Carron, referred to people not born in the country who 'dip their fingers' into the National Health Service and other benefits to which they had not contributed (Rex 1973). This was as untrue then as it continued to be over the years, as migrant workers' tax contributions have always been more than any benefits claimed.

Enoch Powell's role was important as he had moved from being an advocate of imperialism to being an arch advocate of a nationalism that excluded New Commonwealth immigrants. His concern with immigration control could be linked to a concern with his own political advancement (Foot 1969), but other political parties were also playing to popular antagonisms. Through the 1970s the neo-Nazi National Front, developing out of fascist anti-Semitic movements in the 1930s, made electoral gains particularly in the West Midlands.[4] Although Powell had been demoted from the Conservative Shadow Cabinet by Heath when he made his anti-immigrant speeches, he turned his attention to opposing the 1972 European Communities Bill, bringing Britain into the European Economic Community (EEC), a forerunner of the European Union (EU). He gave a speech in Lyon telling the French that 'the British people are profoundly opposed to the Community' (Powell 1971), although most of the Conservative Party were in favour, and most of the Labour Party opposed the move. It was Prime Minister Harold Wilson who held a referendum in 1975 whereby a majority of the British People voted to stay in the EEC. Powell went to Northern Ireland where he became an Ulster Unionist MP in 1974–87. His major ambition there was to keep the province as part of the 'British Nation'.

A major political issue in the 1970s was the reaction of a younger second generation of immigrant descent, mainly schooled in Britain who were aware of their own disadvantages in obtaining equal rights to education and jobs. With increasing youth unemployment, despite the variety of youth training schemes developing, Caribbean and Asian groups faced discrimination (Troyna and Smith 1982). Between 1973 and 1979, unemployment of Black youth increased at twice the rate as that for white youth. Influenced by the civil rights movement in the USA, the Pan-African National Congress and the anti-apartheid African National Congress, many young Caribbeans asserted a militant Black identity, and relations with the police deteriorated, with 'SUS' laws (questioning on suspicion of crimes) and a tabloid media asserting fears of Black crime. The police were reluctant to bring a prosecution when a white teacher, Blair Peach, died from injuries in 1979 sustained during a march opposing a National Front rally in Southall. By the 1980s, what the media described as race riots and the government termed racial disturbances took place in Bristol, Brixton, Southall, Toxteth and Birmingham. The Home Affairs Select Committee noted a deteriorating state of race relations and the 'grim realities' of young people and their parents whose expectations of life in Britain had not turned out well (Home Affairs Committee 1981: vii). More eloquently, poet and writer David Simon wrote that for Black people 'the 1980s was a decade of blood and tears' (Simon in Richardson 2005: 68).

Politics and ideologies, 1980s

By the 1980s the old British Empire had been transformed into a Commonwealth of former colonies and protectorates, still leaving the government responsible for a few overseas territories, including several which were havens for tax avoidance by rich individuals and multinational companies. Rhodesia, having been subject to white rule for longer than most colonies, became Zimbabwe in 1980. Prime Minister Thatcher, in power from 1979 to 1990, made much of the nationalist sentiment created during the Falklands War, declaring at a victory parade, 'The war had dissolved secret fears that Britain was no longer the nation that had built an Empire and ruled a quarter of the world' (Brendon 2007: 635). She wrote tetchily about how uncooperative the Commonwealth heads of government were, especially when they wanted her to support sanctions against the apartheid regime in South Africa. During a Special Conference of Commonwealth Heads of governments in London in 1986, she noted that 'Kenneth Kaunda (Zambian President) was in a thoroughly self-righteous and uncooperative frame of mind when I dropped in to see him' (Thatcher 1993: 521). She also found it 'intensely irritating' when Kaunda told her that Africa was not her area. She made a visit to Kenya in 1988, but it confirmed her worst fears of the 'backwardness' of African countries. She wrote 'At the government guest house Denis (husband) tried to run a bath but found there was no water and it had to be brought up in dustbins from the cellar' (Thatcher 1993: 524). Despite her apparent support she was no fan of the EEC and wrote much in her memoirs of her dealings with EEC politicians, most of whom she appeared to despise. But she did believe closer trading links were necessary and in signing up to the single market in 1986, wrote that 'We must have a European Single Market with the minimum of regulations – a Europe of Enterprise' (Thatcher 1993: 745).

A global economy was developing which encouraged the movement and migration of people, bringing about both cultural convergences and more hostile resistance to migrants. Challenges to the old Empire continued. In 1982, Argentina occupied the Falkland Islands off their coast in the South Atlantic and which they had always claimed were their Malvinas Islands. Argentinean people had been moved off the island when the British moved in. A war resulted, in which, as noted in Chapter 1, David Tinker, a naval officer, wrote to his father that his fellow shipmates regarded the Argentineans as only 'w**s' and assumed they could easily be defeated. His father was Hugh Tinker, a Professor of Politics, who had spent his career writing against imperialism. It was a supreme irony that David was killed, aged 26, by a French Exocet missile supplied to the Argentineans (Tinker 1982). An editorial in the *Sunday Telegraph* managed to link the war with a denigration of citizens in the UK, asserting that 'If the Falkland Islanders were British citizens with black or brown skins, spoke with strange accents or worshipped strange Gods, it is doubtful whether the Royal Navy would fighting for their liberation' (Worsthorne 1982). A further challenge to Britain was when, in 1983, the USA invaded Grenada, a former British colony in the Caribbean, without informing the British government. Bernard Coard, whose book on the miseducation of Caribbean children galvanised several generations of practitioners and activists (Richardson 2005) had returned to the island as deputy prime minister.[5]

Whose identity?

During the 1980s there was a grudging acceptance of the reality that colonial immigrants and their children were 'here to stay' and conflicts surrounded the acceptance of Black, Asian and other minority people into a multiracial and multicultural society. Their equal participation as citizens became a major contested issue. Questions of national identity continued to be raised and antagonism to minorities centred on whether differences of colour, culture and religion were permanently at odds with a British identity. Young people responded with open conflict. In 1980 there was rioting in the St Paul's' area in Bristol. The local National Union of Teachers reported that

Black frustration over discrimination in schooling and employment, and police harassment, were the cause (Avon NUT 1980). By June 1980, some 40 minority organisations had established a National Council for Black Organisations and criticised policing of minority people. In January 1981 a fire broke out in a house in New Cross, London, in which 13 young Black people died. After police had discounted a racial motive, 15,000 people marched from New Cross to Westminster demanding an end to racial murders. In response, the police launched 'Operation swamp' to check on Black people in Brixton, where rioting broke out in April 1981, followed by riots in Toxteth, Liverpool, Manchester, Birmingham, Coventry, Leeds and other towns. Home Secretary Whitelaw appointed Lord Scarman to hold an inquiry into all this, and his report blamed negative police practices, poor education and youth services, and discrimination in employment and housing (Scarman 1982).

Papers released 30 years later showed that Oliver Letwin, then a young adviser to Margaret Thatcher, later an MP and a chief adviser to David Cameron, wrote that as 'lower class unemployed white people had been living for years in appalling slums without a breakdown in order', riots and criminality by Black people were the result of 'bad moral attitudes' and if given money they would use it for Rastafarian arts and crafts and a disco and drug trade (Travis 2015: 3). Letwin, educated at Eton and Cambridge University, in 2003 became well known for declaring that he would rather go out and beg on the streets than allow his children to go to local comprehensive schools. He retired from Parliament in 2019. But urban rioting in the 1980s forced the government to give more attention to racial disadvantages. Michael Heseltine was appointed as Minister for Merseyside to co-ordinate ameliorative policies with an urban programme and Youth Training schemes. In 1983 a Conservative election poster featured a young Black man, with the slogan 'Labour says he's Black. Tories say he's British'. After the Conservatives were elected again there were riots in Handsworth, Birmingham and Tottenham, London, and in other areas in 1985.

Paul Gilroy pointed out that the idea of national belonging used military and patriotic metaphors of war to describe minorities after conflicts. Some descriptions included the enemy within, unarmed invasion, alien encampments and New Commonwealth occupation, which were all used to describe the Black and minority presence in cities. He wrote that by the 1980s there was a 'racial nationalist portrait of Blacks as fundamentally alien' (Gilroy 1987: 153). But while the majority society was attempting to define itself by who was 'not British', business leaders working in a global economy noticed that discrimination was bad for business. Free-market supporters and a racist nationalism were in competition, although they had in common 19th-century beliefs that the state should not interfere or regulate markets or worry about inequalities in wealth or low wages. The governments during the 1980s encouraged privatisation and markets in the public as well as the private sphere with consequent inequalities and insecurities, including in education. In 1988 an Action for Cities programme was initiated to make inner city areas more attractive to business, but over the following decade around one and a half million jobs were lost in inner cities.

By the 1980s religion had been added to race as a source of white hostility, as Muslim communities began to request funding for Muslim schools on a par with the existing religious schools – Anglican, Catholic and Jewish. Salman Rushdie's book *The Satanic Verses*, regarded as insulting Islam, was burned in Bradford in January 1989 and a death threat (Fatwa) issued from Iran against Rushdie. As Winder pointed out, the notion of tolerance was now debatable. The idea of a 'benign elite graciously tolerating the outlandish habits of its inferiors' was now challenged (Winder 2004: 415).

Norman Tebbit's cricket test, by which he claimed that loyalty to the country was judged on whether people cheered for the English team, was put to the test when Caribbean and Asian cricketers played in the English team. Although Labour lost the 1987 election, four Black MPs were elected – one being Diane Abbott who by 2018 was the longest-serving Black (and female) member of Parliament. And an Asian Councillor, Ajeeb, became the first Muslim lord mayor in the city of Bradford. Labour ended the decade by producing a paper which claimed that 'Britain is manifestly a multicultural society with a plurality of cultures. We believe that any education system ... must ensure that all children develop an understanding of and sensitivity too, this plurality of cultures and traditions' (Labour Party 1989: 2) something which, as Shakespeare might have said 'Is a thing a thing devoutly to be wished'!

Education policies, 1970s

The 1944 Education Act emerged out of a consensus between a Coalition government, the churches and the education system at all levels. Secondary education was compulsory to 15, although children were to be separated on the basis of 'age, ability and aptitude'. However, as Simon later noted 'Even under a Labour Government elected (in 1945) with a massive majority, the mediation of class relations was still seen as a major function of education' (Simon 1991: 115). In the 1970s Labour encouraged comprehensive schooling, improved education for children with special needs, and although they failed to address divisions created by a private school sector, education seemed ready to break with the past. What happened was a determination to hold onto a past of selection and division. After the Conservatives were elected in 1979, Mrs Thatcher became education secretary and her first act was to cancel free school milk – those little bottles of milk at break time which had seemed as permanent as Empire. Her next act was to announce that local authorities need not develop comprehensive schools. The ideological battles over education in these decades have been documented by, among others, Benn and Chitty (1996), Lawton (2005) and Tomlinson (2005). The 1970s brought a retrenchment of egalitarian and innovative policies. Global economic events put schooling under stress, as the effects of a rise in oil prices led to a recession and resulting youth unemployment. This was partly solved by raising the school leaving age to 16 in 1973 and setting up a series of Youth Training Schemes run by a Manpower Services Commission.

Ironically, Labour Prime Minister James Callaghan made speech at Ruskin College Oxford in 1976 claiming that what he called – and subsequent ministers have delighted in quoting – the 'education establishment', was not adequately preparing children for the world of work, and he called for a great debate on education. The speech and resulting publicity pleased Conservatives and those opposed to comprehensive schooling, demoralised teachers, and was regarded as an own goal by Labour. Despite accusations of lowered standards, Shirley Williams, Labour Education Secretary, produced a 1977 green paper *Education in Schools* (DES 1977), which made clear that more children were now in schools for longer and improvements in education were continuing. This did not prevent education becoming a permanent scapegoat for a troubled economy with consistent attacks on schools, teachers and later on colleges and universities. Reactionary views of education were encapsulated in a series of *Black Papers* mainly produced in the later 1970s (Lawton 2005: 85).

Education policies, 1980s

The focus of education policy during the 1980s was on free markets and privatisation. The ideology underpinning reforms was that of a 19th-century liberal individualism in which consumers of education (children, young people and their parents) embraced the laws of markets and the values of self-interest and family profit. Mrs Thatcher had attended a direct grant grammar school, direct funding from the DES having been abolished by Labour in 1975, and she was determined to bring this back, which she did through grant-maintained schools 'free' from local authority control. There was also money to encourage assisted places for supposedly brighter pupils to attend private schools, a scheme which benefited middle class children more than minority children (Whitty et al 1998).

Most of her ministers had been privately educated, especially at Eton. Her vision incorporated an appeal to moral authoritarianism and a nostalgic imperialism in which individuals were to have a hierarchical understanding of their class, gender and racial position. As she wrote, 'I never felt uneasy about praising Victorian values ... because they summed up what we are now discovering – they distinguished between the deserving and the undeserving poor' (Thatcher 1993: 627). By the 1980s, she may have softened her stance on the very Victorian practice of beating children, as corporal punishment was outlawed in state schools in 1987 but not in private schools until the 1990s. In 1961 she had voted in favour of birching young people. Education from the 1980s was to be a commodity with parents notionally free to choose schools, which was in effect an invitation for the middle classes to compete to take over the best state schools. The curriculum was also to be centrally controlled and local education authorities (LEAs) eventually disappeared. The 'left dominated' Inner London Education Authority, was the first to go (Thatcher 1983: 590). The idea for a Black History Month, originating in the USA, was taken up in 1987 by a Ghanaian teacher, Akyaaba Addai-Sebo, who coordinated projects for the Greater London Council. This was a particular irritation to Mrs Thatcher.

Ten Education Acts were passed between 1979 and 1988, and eventually every area of education was subject to reforming zeal. The relationship between central and local government, funding, school structures and governance, curriculum, assessment, pedagogy, teacher autonomy and training, inspection, early years and post-16 training, relations with parents, vocational and higher education, were all subject to scrutiny, criticism and legislation. Although many more comprehensive secondary schools came into operation during the 1980s, by 1990 some 90 per cent of children attending these schools, there was continued pressure to retain forms of selection and ration education. It was a decade when the realisation by government that all children and young people were capable of being educated was a cause for anxiety. As one civil servant told a researcher, 'We are beginning to create aspirations we cannot match. In some ways this points to the success of education in contrast to the public mythology that has been created … we have to select, to ration educational opportunities, people must be educated once more to know their place' (Ranson 1984: 241). This sentiment appeared to be implicit in most subsequent education policies, especially with persistent Conservative support for selective grammar schools.

Having led the Conservative Party to a third election win, Mrs Thatcher claimed that raising the quality of education was a major aim of her government. Teachers and local education authorities, especially those attempting to come to terms with a multiracial society, were the enemy apparently opposing this. Even the Church was regarded as an enemy. A report by a committee led by the Archbishop of Canterbury criticising conditions in inner cities was condemned as Marxist-inspired (*Faith in the City* 1985). She told the Party Conference in October 1987 that the chances of 'youngsters getting a decent education … was often snatched from them by hard-left education authorities and extremist teachers … children who need to be able to count and multiply are learning anti-racist mathematics – whatever that may be' (Thatcher reported in Hughill 1987). For good measure, children were not being taught to respect traditional moral values and were apparently being taught that they have an inalienable right to be gay! A section in a 1988 Local Government Act put a stop to local authorities supposedly promoting homosexuality, a measure only repealed in 2003. The Education Reform Act of 1988, introduced by Education Secretary Kenneth Baker, contained 238 sections, 13 schedules and gave the Secretary of State 451 new powers. The Reform Act was intended to increase the influence of the central state on education and reduce local powers and teacher influence. A major feature of the Act was the introduction of a subject-centred national curriculum assessed at four Key Stages, KS 4 being the GCSE (formerly the 'O' level). School admissions changed, and through local management schools were to receive their own budgets. Control of education in London passed to 12 boroughs. Mrs Thatcher was not happy with the National Curriculum proposals and the subject working groups Baker had set up. Teachers and task groups on assessment had to become the opposition, and she was particularly concerned with the English and history proposals. Indeed, when the history working group produced a suggested curriculum in 1989 'I was appalled ... there was insufficient weight given to British history ... not enough emphasis on history as chronological study' (Thatcher 1993: 596). Right-wing beliefs, fears of left-wing influence and of any developing multicultural schooling, dominated this 1988 reform. As a Cambridge professor recorded, 'the 1988 Act should have looked forward with confidence to a better multicultural, multilingual and multifaith Britain entering a new relationship with itself and the rest of the world ... but it did not' (Hargreaves 1993: viii).

Miseducating minorities

It was not surprising that the education of the children of post-colonial migrations to Britain should be a problem for educators. Policy makers, civil servants and teachers at all levels, had themselves been educated through an imperial curriculum and had no training and little understanding of how to incorporate the children into a system which was itself unequal and hierarchical. There was eventually more pressure on government to produce policies and funding for what the House of Commons Select Committee in a report on *Education* described as immigrant children with an ethnic background. The report made 24 recommendations for improved education, criticised the DES for not being well informed of what was being done locally or nationally and 'was frequently struck by the haphazard was a crucial part of human race relations has been dealt with' (Select Committee 1973: 55). With imperial hindsight, it now appears inevitable that the denigration, slurs and stereotyping of Black and minority people over the past 200 or so years, would continue. Poet Benjamin Zephaniah summed up nicely the attempt by his head teacher to fit him into the stereotype of Black sportsman, insisting he should be good at cricket and boxing. Eventually 'trying not to look Afro-Caribbean', he replied 'I am very good at formation flying, Sir' (Zephaniah 2005: 157). A major poet and musician, Benjamin died in 2023.

Although the National Union of Teachers took the view that 'The curriculum should have a wide international outlook and the future must lie in an education directed at the needs of a multiracial society and not the specific question of educating children from immigrant families' (Tomlinson 2008: 53), the DES preferred to lump all minority children, whether immigrant or not, into a category of 'disadvantage' – a euphemism for 'poor' which has endured over the years. Thus the Department asserted that minority children shared with the indigenous children in urban areas 'the educational disadvantages associated with an impoverished environment' (DES 1974: 2), and the Home Office concurred. Basically, Black and minority people should not complain, as poor whites shared their neglected urban environment of poor housing, schools and health services (Home Office 1978). USA scholar Kirp noted that governments used the language of disadvantage, deprivation or non-English speaking and preferred almost any label to a racial one (Kirp 1979). And as noted, whites took flight from these areas if they could.

It was astonishing that a committee set up in 1973 to look into *Special Educational Needs* (DES 1978) ignored the over-representation of Black and other minority children in special schooling of all kinds, and the anxiety Black parents had demonstrated over the years about this issue. A study carried out during the 1970s on the way Black and working class children were regarded as candidates for the then schools for the educationally subnormal (ESN) recorded much ignorance among the professionals – head teachers, psychologists, social workers and medical officers – about minority children, and much racism, covert or overt was evident. Some of their comments were noted in the book *Educational Subnormality: A Study in Decision-Making* (Tomlinson 1981), and some were not included in the book as the personnel were still in work. Thirty head teachers were interviewed and tended to operate within a framework of stereotypes about Black children. There was an assumption that the children would be slow learners, create disciplinary problems and come from disorganised or violent homes. Some comments were:

> They [West Indian children] are bound to be slower, It's their personalities, they lack concentration.
>
> They are slower than Asian children – not as bright.
>
> The temperament of the West Indian child is more volatile, disruptive, easily stirred.
>
> They are violent – a lot of none of you whites are going to tell me what to do.

One female head of a girls school commented that 'Enoch Powell is right. He has an avid love of his country as many people have, There are enough immigrants and there is going to be trouble' (Tomlinson 1981: 145–7). In notes not published at the time, this head also considered that 'some of the girls are not fit to clean Enoch Powell's shoes'.

The educational attainments of minority children and young people continued to be a focus for anxieties, especially for Caribbean parents. A Black–white gap in achievements turned into a 40-year farce, with researchers initially using tests standardised on white children in a climate of assumptions of the inferior 'intelligence' of Black children (Eysenck 1971; Herrnstein and Murray 1994). This was reinforced by comparisons between Black and other minority achievements, Chinese and Indian pupils eventually becoming 'model minorities' as their school achievements improved. Caribbean and Pakistani (Muslim) pupils usually lagged behind, with explanations focusing on families and culture. As Gillborn and his colleagues eventually pointed out, the goalposts were consistently moved to redefine achievement, which had the effect of restoring historic levels of race inequity (Gillborn et al 2017).

A major issue in the 1970s was the use of Creoles and dialect speech by Caribbean children, which many teachers regarded a sloppy and lazy, despite the Bullock Report (Bullock 1975) pointing out that Jamaican and French Creoles had their own linguistic grammars and structures. The Rampton Committee inquiring into 'West Indian' achievement, set up by the Labour government before the 1979 election, and almost closed down by Mrs Thatcher, also repudiated language issues as causing underachievement (DES 1981). In the 1980s, young Black people were developing the speech as part of a cultural identity, linked to the Rastafarian movement and Reggae music, which together with the 1980s riots, created more fear and hostility from police and public.

Multicultural policy

A combination of riots and reports persuaded the government that education for an ethnically diverse society was important if only to combat public order, and the Rampton Committee was allowed to continue its work, chaired now by liberal Lord Swann. Their 807-page report, complete with evidence and consultation, constituted a high point in positive recommendations for all pupils living in a multiracial, multicultural society and briefly commented on the education of Chinese, Vietnamese, Ukrainian, Cypriot, Italian and Travellers' children as well as the children of established Black and Asian communities. The Report did feel it necessary to include a chapter on research into IQ testing and 'intelligence' as a sop to the persistent assertions of a lower Black IQ (DES 1985a). During the 1980s a number of local education authorities began to produce multicultural education policy documents. Bradford LEA, with a large Asian population, published a memorandum suggesting ways of improving education for all young people and countering racial hostility and discrimination. The head teacher of one local school did not share these aspirations and wrote an article in the *Times Educational Supplement* suggesting that 'The responsibility for the adaptions and adjustments involved in settling in a new country lies entirely with those who have come to settle' (Honeyford 1982). After a further article complaining about multicultural bigots and the hysterical political temperament of the Indian sub-continent, a campaign was launched against him and he took early retirement. Bradford and the Honeyford affair led to an open polarisation of views on the education of minorities in a system designed for white children. In Dewsbury in 1987, a group of white parents insisted that their children should not be taught in a school with Asian children and opened a school above a pub, and in Cleveland a parent won a case for her daughter to be transferred to a predominantly white school as she was 'learning Pakistani' (Tomlinson 2008). In 1989 copies of Salman Rushdie's book *The Satanic Verses* were burned in Bradford by clerics who considered that the book insulted Islam. Rushdie had to go into hiding after a Fatwa (death threat) was issued against him by Iran. He survived to write much more, although a serious attempt was made to kill him in 2022 by a young Lebanese man who admitted he had not read the book. A similar book-burning incident had occurred in 1960 when a Catholic priest in Ireland had publicly burned copies of a novel by an Irish woman writer. The incident went unremarked by politicians, with much of the media castigating the writer for criticising Irish life (O'Brien 1960).

Manufacturing ignorance

The 1970s and 1980s set the stage for the manufacturing of ignorance about the nature of a post-imperial society. On the whole, the white population were aghast that former colonial people from the Empire had now come to live, work and remain in Britain. Demands from minorities, most now confirmed as British citizens, that they be accorded equal rights, accompanied by angry conflicts, were taken as proof that 'these people' should never have been allowed into the country. Immigrant settlement, as noted, was mainly in urban areas where there was work, but housing and schooling was poor. A white working class were united with other social classes against Black and other minorities. Successive governments understood that racial discrimination and hostility was a source of potential conflict, but it was always understood that overt action in support of minorities or offering leadership in a post-imperial world, was not something any government could do if it wished to be elected. But governments also understood that the nature of British society was changing in a global context, and joint ventures with Commonwealth countries were making it uneconomic to hold hostile attitudes towards former colonial settlers.

The antagonisms towards attempts by teachers, local education authorities, Her Majesty's Inspectorate (HMI), Black parents and organisations attempting to develop education for a multiracial, multicultural society suggested an educational nationalism which was not just a white backlash against ideas of democratic pluralism and equality (Tomlinson 1990). It supported a myth that Black and other minorities in Britain had full opportunities to assimilate into a British way of life. Educational nationalism denied that there are barriers placed in the way of minorities achieving in education and employment, other than obstacles they created for themselves. It also depended on a mythologized British heritage, culture and values, assumed to be shared by all white individuals regardless of class or gender. Roger Scruton, who had made numerous contributions over the decades to political and educational nationalism, especially when he edited the Conservative journal *Salisbury Review*, wrote that 'a child brought up in the British way of doing things is encouraged to question and criticise … a child brought up in such a culture does not need "alternatives" which so many educationalists wish to foist on him [sic]' (Scruton 1986: 132). Scruton was knighted in 2016 and died in 2020, with Boris Johnson, who had previously criticised Scruton for his anti-Islamic views, claiming that 'we have lost the greatest modern Conservative thinker'. Education Minister Keith Joseph, in a retirement speech, acknowledged that Britain was now an ethnically mixed society but reiterated the view that 'a tradition of tolerance was one of Britain's most precious virtues and British history and cultural traditions are, or will become, part of the common heritage of all who live in this country' (Joseph 1986: 6).

The problem with this was, as has been noted, imperialism largely took the form of military conquest, taking over of land and labour, slavery and denial of human rights, and migrants from colonial countries had always been subject to discrimination and a conspicuous lack of tolerance. The working groups preparing the content of subjects for the new national curriculum from 1988 were all subject to central government scrutiny and omissions. The mathematics working group report, overseen by the DES included the comment that:

> It is sometimes suggested that the multicultural complexion of society demands a 'multi-cultural' approach to mathematics with children being introduced to different number systems, foreign currencies and non-European measuring and counting devices. But this would confuse children and we have therefore not included any multi-cultural aspects in our attainment targets. (Bishop 1993: 34)

Even that classical mathematician and engineer Archimedes was given short shrift.

It was not surprising that research into white children's views of minorities in the 1970s and 1980s mainly showed racism, stereotyping and rejection, Many schools in all-white areas thought that notions of a multicultural society did not apply to them. In the 1980s researchers for Lord Swann's report interviewed children in white schools. A typical comment was, 'There are too many Pakys and foreigners in our country' (DES 1985a: 253). At one school the researcher was told by older pupils that 'We've got to talk to you about n*****s and w**s and things' (DES 1985a: 292). Teachers found it difficult to come to terms with the racial antagonisms and cultural ignorance displayed by pupils. There was evidence of longstanding white parental antipathy to their children being educated alongside minority children. Parents in their turn had been through an imperial education. Various organisations opposing any multicultural, anti-racist or multifaith educational efforts were set up, supporting an 'English and Christian' curriculum. A *Campaign for Real Education* had some political support and the *Parental Alliance for Choice in Education* was supported by the Dewsbury parents, who also supported the demands of Muslim parents for separate state-funded Muslim schools as this would separate Muslim children from the rest (Naylor 1988). In 1986 a disturbed white boy stabbed fellow pupil Ahmed Ullah in the playground of a Manchester school. As the school had an anti-racist policy, sensational media coverage followed the murder giving the impression that the policy was to blame (MacDonald 1989). LEAs and schools with multicultural anti-racist policies were presented by right-wing politicians and media as 'looney left'.

Curriculum possibilities

After James Callaghan's intervention in the education world in his Ruskin College speech in 1976, bureaucratic control of the curriculum was strengthened, with more questioning of the acceptability of curriculum content. A Green Paper produced by Education Secretary Shirley Williams in 1977 noted that: 'Ours is now a multiracial and multicultural country and one in which traditional social patterns are breaking down ... The curriculum appropriate to our imperial past cannot meet the requirements of modern Britain' (DES 1977:10).

Although no national policies followed this claim, a large literature advocating and suggesting varieties of multicultural education followed, and an equally large literature critiquing suggestions. Claims that Black pupils were diverted into a different curriculum rather than the formal subject centred one were hard to demonstrate. They were just taught badly by teachers who had no training in how to teach all children. Black Studies,

World Studies, Peace Studies and changes in subject areas were all attacked, although Supplementary Schools did their best to supplement teaching and learning outside formal schooling. The report by Lord Swann's committee suggesting that a plural democratic society might require a re-thinking of national identity, was regarded by the Conservative MPs in the Monday Club as a 'profoundly dangerous document aimed at re-shaping British society' (Pearce 1986: 136).

But by the later 1980s there was some agreement that the curriculum in all schools, not just those with minority children, needed changing. Teachers began to write about their practices and publishers and writers of textbooks began to think more carefully about the incorporation of multicultural and global information in all curriculum subjects. Kenneth Baker as education secretary, encouraged Education Support grants for 'Educational needs in a Multicultural society' and 23 projects in 'white' areas from North Tyneside to the Scilly Isles, were set up between 1985 and 1988. Good intentions did not last long. Baker approved the setting up of a Multicultural Task Group in 1989, to produce 'Guidelines on Multicultural Education in the National Curriculum'. The Group, comprising HMI, headteachers, advisors and professors (six members from minorities) duly did this, but their report was never published. The most that was conceded was one page in a National Curriculum Council Newsletter (Tomlinson 1993). By the end of the decade an editorial in the *Times Educational Supplement* noted that 'Unspoken anxieties about ethnic differences underlie several bits of educational policy ... there seems to be a definite though unformulated attempt to starve multicultural education of resources and let it wither on the vine' (TES 1990).

Summary

This chapter has covered post-colonial politics and ideologies, and education developments over two decades to 1990. Nostalgia for a lost Empire was accompanied by continued hostility to the former imperial subjects who were invited to bring their labour into the country. While a British Empire had been transformed into a Commonwealth of former colonies, closer links with Europe were developing, with Parliament agreeing to a single market in which trade barriers and tariffs would be agreed among EU countries. The welfare state was being dismantled, privatisation and markets in public services encouraged, and New Commonwealth citizens excluded from a narrowing concept of a national identity. At the same time, what would now become a continuing debate over immigration in the coming decades the need for labour was developing. Politicians of all parties continued to believe that policies directed at migrants and their children was bad for their electoral chances, and the children were lumped together with that intractable group 'the disadvantaged'. Race riots galvanized government into some action, and there was a slow realisation the country really was multiracial and multicultural. Suggested curriculum and other changes in the education system were met with much hostility, especially on the grounds that British cultural traditions and sense of identity were being attacked or contaminated. Into the 1990s, things did not get much better.

Appendix

Independence was acquired by the following British colonies and protectorates in the 1970s and 1980s:

1970 Fiji, Tonga. Western Samoa
1974 Grenada (invaded by USA 1983)
1975 Papua New Guinea
1976 Seychelles
1978 Solomon Islands. Tuvalu (Ellice Islands) Dominica.
1979 St Lucia, St Vincent and Grenadines. Kiribati
1980 Rhodesia (Zimbabwe). Vanuatu (new Hebrides)
1983 Brunei
1997 Hong Kong

5

Inequalities and education markets, 1990–97

The historian and author Max Hastings for once got it wrong when he claimed that not much of lasting significance happened in the seven years John Major was prime minister (Hastings 2007). A great deal happened during the years of Major's premiership. He took over as prime minister in November 1990 after excusing himself with toothache in hospital while his colleagues removed Margaret Thatcher from her post. Despite being regarded as a 'grey man' of politics with cartoonists depicting him as wearing his underpants outside his trousers, global conflicts, financial mistakes, the European Union (EU), immigration and asylum seeking, race and religious issues, all marked his time in office. Another view of the period was that 'sleaze built up slowly through the 1990s' (Tiratsoo 1997: 208), and Major became a prisoner of a strident and undisciplined Eurosceptic right. What was to be a most contentious policy, the signing up before the 1992 general election to the Maastricht Treaty which created a European Union, did not figure much in this election, which Major won against all expectations. He inherited from Thatcher support for a single market to replace the old rules of a Common Market where separate countries had their own trade rules, and this boosted trade, employment and investment over the decade. But in signing the Treaty he argued for an 'opt out' from a single euro currency and a Social Chapter which included workers' rights. He also pushed the Thatcher privatisation of public utilities even further, especially selling off the railways to private companies, and replaced an unpopular 'poll tax' with a Council Tax on households.

The education policies of his years in office helped to dismantle the influence of local authorities on education, created education markets, school privatisation, and set the stage for a break up of a state education system. A further crucial event during the period was the murder in 1993 of 18 year old Black student Stephen Lawrence by five white youths. This led to the 25-year search for justice against police and judicial racism led by his mother, now Baroness Doreen Lawrence. Doreen, initially meting 'arrogance and contempt' from the authorities (Lawrence 2007: ix) eventually saw two out of the five men responsible for killing her son gaoled and another named many years later. This chapter documents the issues and tensions arising from the signing of the Maastricht Treaty on European union in 1992. It also notes the surge in the number of asylum seekers and refugees escaping wars and conflicts, often from countries once colonised by Britain. There was a surge in popular racism directed at Islam, and the murder of Stephen Lawrence became a catalyst for understanding the way in which post-imperial racism permeated the whole society. While education policies were turning education into a competitive market, with 'naming and shaming' of schools, and government taking control of curriculum and assessment, there was a concerted effort to dismiss any multicultural dimensions and any attempts to educate all young people in the art of living together.

Policy preview

While Major was acquiescent if not enthusiastic over the EU, he did find determined opposition from those who became known as Eurosceptics. Prominent among these was a young *Daily Telegraph* journalist, Boris Johnson. He produced ludicrous stories about European regulations demanding straight bananas and cucumbers, and other anti-European newspapers and their owners and editors were also keen to produce myths and lies about the Union (Smith 2017). In dealing with the parliamentary Eurosceptics, Major did what Prime Minister Theresa May was to do some 26 years later – he appointed them to his government, although he had in an interview described them as 'bastards' (Castle 1993).[1] James Goldsmith, a rich businessman and father of former MP Zac Goldsmith, set up and funded the Referendum Party in 1994, which gained 2.6 per cent votes in the 1997 general election. Eventually this Party merged with UKIP. By 1996 the Eurosceptics were demanding a referendum on staying in the EU and were still around and agitating for a referendum in the Cameron government from 2010.

During the period the arrival of workers from EU countries, asylum seekers and refugees from global conflicts – notably from the collapsed Yugoslavia after 1992 – raised more tensions about immigration. Economic migrants from former East European communist countries arrived after the collapse of the Berlin Wall in 1989. Issues of race, culture, religion, spatial segregation and discrimination were downplayed, although after the first Gulf War in 1990 popular racism began to be directed against Islam as a world religion. There was, as Stuart Hall noted, more understanding among the public that the tea and sugar in their 'cuppa' came from post-imperial India and the Caribbean (Hall 1991), but this probably owed more to developing global communication and advertising than to education in schools. While world migrations, cultural convergences and the effects of wars became more obvious, policy makers continued along familiar lines of regarding minorities as problems and politicians continued to deride multicultural education as a left-wing activity. Although between 1988 and 1996 one or more Education Acts were passed each year and the Secretary of State for

Education was handed some 1,000 new powers, a new National Curriculum was more a vehicle for testing and assessment than any new content to help understanding of a post-imperial world. John Major, who left grammar school with 'O' levels, left office in 1997 after his election manifesto had promised a 'grammar school in every town', a policy still urged by the Conservatives nearly 30 years later.

Significant events

1990	Saddam Hussein attacks Kuwait in first Gulf war (November). John Major takes over from Margaret Thatcher. Poll tax becomes a Council Tax.
1990	Nine EU countries signed the Schengen Accord allowing free movement of people and attempts to create more equitable immigration policies.
1990	Education Secretary turns down a request for a private Muslim school in Brent to become state-funded. Over 500 children in Tower Hamlets have no school place. Court absolves the local authority of blame.
1991	Census in Britain includes a question on ethnicity for the first time
1991–99	Break up of former Yugoslavia. Ethnic conflicts result in some 2–4 million refugees in European countries. Serbs, Kosovans, Albanians and others seek asylum in Britain. Civil war in Somaliland, a former British protectorate, granted independence in 1991, brings Somali refugees.
1991	Culloden Primary School in Tower Hamlets attacked in the tabloid press for giving too much attention to second language speakers.
1991	(September) Rioting by white youths in Newcastle and North Shields. Economic deprivation and policing blamed. Also riots in Oxford on the Blackburn Leys Estate.
1992	Conservatives win the general election. John Smith takes over from Neil Kinnock as Labour Leader. Major signs the Maastricht Treaty but with an opt-out from the Social Chapter and the euro currency. 'Black Wednesday' 16 September. Sterling currency left the European Exchange Rate (ERM). Conservative economic policy in crisis.
1992	White paper *Choice and Diversity* and an Education (Schools) Act which creates an Office for Standards in Education (Ofsted). DES becomes the DfE. Higher Education Act allows polytechnics to become universities. Further education colleges to be independent of local authorities.
1992	National Union of Teachers (NUT) publishes anti-racist guidelines for schools. At the October Conservative Conference Major says teachers should teach children how to read and 'not waste their time on the politics of gender, race and class'. An inquiry by the Commission for Racial Equality noted that the assignment of minority pupils to lower ability sets and bands is unlawful.
1993	Asylum and Immigration Act. More controls on asylum seekers.
1993	(April) Stephen Lawrence murdered in Lewisham by white youths. No arrests and government refuses an inquiry. First Chair of NCC confirms that it was made clear to him by ministers that any multicultural anti-racist education was a 'no-go' area. Mrs Thatcher's memoirs make clear her distaste for multicultural education and changes in the history syllabus.

1994	John Smith dies. Replaced in July by Tony Blair as Labour Leader. Teacher Training Agency created. No special training for teaching in a multiethnic society. New syllabus for religious education approved. Herrnstein and Murray publish *The Bell Curve* claiming people in a Black underclass have lower IQs.
1995	Hackney Downs School becomes the only school closed down by an Education Association which includes Michael Barber. (In 2017 Barber was appointed Head of an Office for Students with the power to close universities.)
1995	Riots in Bradford between young Asians and whites. Major resigns as Conservative leader and is re-appointed. Volcanic eruption on Island of Montserrat, acquired by Britain in 1632, brings half its population to Britain.
1996	Two Education Acts repealed and consolidated much previous legislation. A clause reiterates that religious education should reflect Christian traditions. A further Act controlling immigration passed.
1997	Fourth PSI Report notes differences in education and vocational qualifications and life chances between ethnic groups (Modood et al 1997).
1997	General election. Major promises a 'grammar school in every town' and leaves office asserting that 'education policies must be colour blind, they must just tackle disadvantage'. New Labour elected. Tony Blair becomes prime minister.

The politics of wars and immigration

Wars and migration in the early 1990s had crucial consequences for issues of race and religion in Britain over the next decades. A month before Major took office in November 1990, Saddam Hussein, President of Iraq, invaded Kuwait. Iraq had become a British Mandate in 1920. Although becoming notionally independent in 1933, it had, for most of the 1980s, fought a war with Iran over territory and religion, which had killed over half a million young men. A British arms firm, Matrix Churchill, had during this period, exported weapons claiming they were 'machine tools' to the Iraq military. In January 1991 a coalition, led by the USA and Britain, attacked Iraqi troops and forced a withdrawal from Kuwait. This war was supported by both Conservative and Labour politicians. Hussein continued in power until the second Iraq war in 2003, the consequences of this conflict still terribly apparent in the Middle East and also in Britain today.

During the first Gulf war, Hussein attempted to represent the war as a *Jihad* (holy war) against the West and some Muslims in Britain felt that their communities and religion was under attack again after the Honeyford and Salman Rushdie affairs. In East London, especially centred round the East London Mosque, young Muslims were joining radical Islamic groups.[2] Mutual fears surrounding the presence of Muslims in European countries had escalated over the years, and as Rex (1996) noted, 'Islam as a focus for racist hostilities was at least as important as colour' (Rex 1996: 8). The label 'Islamophobia' to describe this situation had been popularised in other

European countries (Karakasoglu and Luchtenberg 2002), although it had been present since Queen Victoria's reign, when her friendship with the Muslim Indian 'The Munchie' was derided by her court.

The 1991 British Census was the first to include an ethnic question and 94 per cent of the population described themselves as white British or white Irish, with 5.9 per cent claiming to belong to one of the ethnic groups specified.[3] In 1994, a fourth survey by the Policy Studies Institute demonstrated that a 'Black–white divide' which had provided a political label up to the 1980s, was now more complex (Modood et al 1997). Modood noted that the differences between minorities had become as important and significant to the life chances of minorities as the similarities. The more open identification of a Muslim identity created a situation where popular racism began to be directed at Islam as a world religion. In Britain as in France and other countries, Muslim women's dress became a permanent focus for hostility. In 1990 a school in Altrincham, Cheshire, banned two Muslim girls from wearing the hijab (headscarf) in school. Young Black people, demonised as an 'enemy within' during the 1980s, were overtaken by a spiralling demonization of Muslims.

Political attention in the early 1990s focused on immigration from various quarters. Post-1989, when the Berlin Wall came down, economic migrants from former communist countries began to arrive in Britain. In 1992, the Maastricht Treaty created a European Union out of a European Economic Community, with 15 member countries at that time. The Treaty, intended to 'promote economic and social progress which is balanced and sustainable, in particular the creation of an area without internal frontiers' (Maastricht 1992 section B-3) guaranteed an internal single marker with an elimination of customs duties and the free movement of goods, persons, services and capital. Movement of people was initially not excessive. European Roma, who had long suffered rejection and persecution, was one group who arrived in Britain, and Home Secretary Kenneth Clarke recorded in his memoirs that 'We managed to keep things reasonably under control and immigration was not in my time the crisis ridden and poisonous subject of public debate it became in later years' (Clarke 2016: 285). He had earlier recorded that he objected to 'nostalgic nationalistic protectionism in which people indulged ... the British economy benefits from the fact we are open and welcoming to inward (and outward) investment' (Clarke 2016: 176). By September 1992, benefits to the economy disappeared when the sterling currency was ejected from the European Exchange Rate Mechanism (ERM), interest rates increased and mortgage holders were threatened with repossession of their houses (Geddes 2013).

It was war and conflict around the world, often proxy wars actually fought between the 'Great Powers', that brought asylum seekers[4] from civil wars which included people from the first Iraq war and groups from Somaliland,

Southern Sudan, Sierra Leone and Zimbabwe (all former British territories), Kurds of Turkish origin, Somalis from the former Italian colony, and during the Balkan wars, people from Bosnia, Kosova and Albania. The pre-EU member states, excluding Britain, had signed the Schengen Agreement in 1990, allowing passport-free movement between countries but with increased border policing and a database on criminals, asylum seekers and visitors. All countries were anxious to limit the numbers of people from outside Europe, and in England an Asylum and Immigration Act in 1993 and a further Act in 1996 restricted numbers of immigrants from outside the EU, and brought in 'fast-track' detention and removal of those refused asylum. The Major government also had to deal with the consequences of the Northern Irish Troubles, as the Irish Republican (IRA) took its war to mainland Britain.

There was considerable debate over the possibility of citizens from the colony of Hong Kong, due to be returned to China in 1997, coming into the UK and the government ensured that only a limited number arrived. In the event, many went to Vancouver in Canada and helped create a booming economy there. Similar negative treatment was handed out to the British overseas citizens of Montserrat, a Caribbean island which suffered a volcanic eruption in 1995 and people had to leave. Half of the population came to Britain where they were treated as homeless and offered little help. A study of the experiences of the children arriving in London schools found teachers denigrating their language and some asking the children 'where is Montserrat?' (Shotte 2002).

The politics of sleaze

While all governments have their share of corrupt and questionable activities, the Major government was either unlucky or more questionable in that over the seven years a number of senior politicians, were found to have indulged in financial and/or sexual peccadilloes. In 1995 journalists on the *Independent* newspaper collected enough stories about parliamentarians to compile a 'Sleaze List' (Independent 1995). This included MP David Mellor, Secretary of State in the Department of National Heritage who resigned in 1992 after tabloid revelations of an extra marital affair which involved toe-sucking. In 1994 Tim Yeo, minister in the Department for the Environment, resigned having fathered a child out of wedlock. More important were the financial scandals – journalists from *The Sunday Times* having asked MPs to submit questions in Parliament in return for money. The 'cash for questions' became a lasting scandal especially when MPs Neil Hamilton, a Trade and Industry minister, and MP Tim Smith took £2,000 each to ask questions on behalf of Mohamed Al-Fayed, the owner of Harrods. Hamilton later became a local councillor in Wales and after his death Al-Fayed was found to have been a sexual predator. More scandal ensued when MP Jonathan Aitkin, former Chief Secretary to the Treasury, sued *The Guardian* newspaper over allegations that he had taken money from Saudi businessmen for a stay at the Ritz in Paris and had procured prostitutes for them in England. He was found guilty of perjury and imprisoned, later studying theology and being ordained. It was also perhaps unfortunate that an inquiry into selling what were described as machine tools to Saddam Hussein in the 1980s was published in 1996 (Scott Inquiry 1996). The inquiry showed that government departments and ministers had been lying about the sales.

The lies published in tabloid newspapers about EU regulations over the period could also be classed as sleaze. Smith (2017) documented some of the Euro-myths put forward which included the EU banning corgi dogs, prawn cocktail crisps and mushy peas, and requiring standard-sized condoms, Christmas trees, curved bananas, cucumbers, and even banning saucy postcards and double-decker buses. Some of this nonsense, as noted, was published by Boris Johnson, later to be British foreign secretary until resigning in July 2018. It was unfortunate that at the Conservative Party Conference in October 1993 Major had made a speech which urged the country to go 'back to basics' and learn more honest self-discipline, respect the rule of law and take responsibility for one's own actions rather than relying on the state, and he set up the Nolan Committee to report on standards in public life. His own reputation was later called into question when former MP Edwina Currie revealed in her diaries (Currie 2002) that in the 1980s she had enjoyed a four-year extra-marital affair with him. When the activities of former MPs who were leaving government and joining companies they had helped privatise became public, it was not surprising that historian Tiratsoo described the period as characterised by 'Sleaze which damaged the Tories to their core' (Tiratsoo 1997: 209) and helped a Labour victory in 1997.

Education did not escape questionable activity on the part of those in charge. John Haggitt Charles Patten, education secretary from 1992 to 1994, a former lecturer in Geography at the University of Oxford, who had taught Geography to future Prime Minister Theresa May, was in charge of implementing major Education Acts. He described Tim Brighouse, chief education officer in Oxfordshire and then Birmingham as a 'nutter' and 'a madman walking the streets frightening the children' (Pyke 1994). Brighouse sued him and won £25,000 in damages, which he gave to schools, and went on to improve London's schools in a 'London Challenge'. Patten went on to enter the House of Lords and to write a book *Things to Come: the Tories in the Twenty-first Century* (Patten 1995). The book did not sell well. Chris Woodhead, appointed as chief inspector of schools in 1993, was also shown to have a dubious past – a questionable relationship with a young pupil at a school where he had previously taught (Bright 1999). The early 1990s was certainly a period which illustrated the hypocrisy of politicians criticising schools and teachers for 'lowered standards' and 'failing pupils' when those in government acted so irresponsibly.

Class and deprivation

When John Major signed the Maastricht Treaty in 1992, French politician Jacques Delors accused him of making Britain a 'paradise for foreign investors', a charge to which Thatcherites could happily plead guilty (Judt 2010a: 543), with everything from bus companies to electricity supplies having been sold to competing private companies, and citizens now being consumers and 'stakeholders'. But 'as a society Britain suffered a meltdown, with catastrophic long-term consequences … for Thatcher, class warfare, suitably updated, was the very stuff of politics' (Judt 2020a: 543). Class war, of a kind unknown since the 1930s and harking back to Victorian views of the dangerous poor, certainly reappeared in the 1990s. Inequality and poverty took on new dimensions after a decade when bankers and investors enjoyed increased wealth, but many working class people were 'Caught in permanent poverty. Private affluence was accompanied by public squalor' (Judt 2010b: 544).

The default position was as usual, to blame the victims. American Charles Murray, fresh from bemoaning the rise of an underclass in the USA, wrote in 1990 about *The Emerging British Underclass* (Murray 1990). According to Murray, the ways to identify an underclass were mainly by babies born to single mothers, criminals and drop outs from the labour force, with poor people especially defined by their 'deplorable behaviour' in not taking jobs. He likened the spread of an underclass to a contagious disease (Murray 1990: 68). He continued to be an important influence on conservative policies, writing again in *The Sunday Times* in 1994 that well-educated people will become New Victorians, returning to traditional morality, while a New Rabble of a low-skilled working class, especially those single parents, would continue to be a drain on society (Murray 1994). Murray was presumably not well informed about the sleaze in the political class documented above at this time.

Murray's views on an American underclass, apparently mainly Black single parents, was elaborated further in his book with Richard Herrnstein, which purported to demonstrate the lower intelligence of Black Americans, who are likely to create social problems, especially crime (Herrnstein and Murray 1994). David Willetts, a Director of the Centre for Policy Studies set up by Prime Minister Thatcher, supported Murray's notion of genetic determinism in producing a lower class during a Policy Studies seminar in 1990 (James 1990). Willetts, an MP from 1992 to 2015 when he moved to the House of Lords, became a crucial figure in higher education. He was appointed Minister of State for Universities and Science in David Cameron's

Coalition government from 2010 to 2014, introducing the rise in tuition fees from £3,225 to £9,000 in 2010, and later selling student loans to a debt collecting agency, removing £160 million from the public debt at that time. He also managed to infuriate women, by suggesting that social mobility for men had stalled because of the increased entry of educated women into the workforce.

Although in August 1991 Michael Heseltine, environment secretary, had set up a bidding process for urban aid grants for deprived areas, the following month it was the white socially and economically deprived who came to political and public attention as an 'underclass' made its presence felt. In September there were riots on white housing estates in Newcastle on Tyne (Meadow Well), North Shields (Rye Lane) and in Oxford on the Blackbird Leys Estate, and also in many other towns and cities that were less well recorded nationally. As many riots began with young men stealing cars and inviting police retaliation, the then Education Secretary Kenneth Clarke came up with a novel explanation – he blamed the Society of Motor Manufacturers for enabling easy car thefts (MacIntyre 1991). What was needed were more car alarms and more police! Murray returned to his theme of family collapse and community disintegration in 1994, returning to Newcastle's Meadow Well and those single mothers, and he forecast the scenario of *New Victorians and the New Rabble* (Murray 1994).

What was actually happening was a widening gap between rich and poor families. The Thatcher government had encouraged income inequality and reduced Social Security as a supposed incentive to work, despite much work disappearing. On the European Community definition, the proportion of people in poverty in Britain rose from 8 per cent in 1979 to 19 per cent in 1993. Low-income families were concentrated in certain geographical areas, especially council estates and inner cities, while other urban and suburban areas became more prosperous. A report by the still respected old HMI concluded that 'Schools in disadvantaged areas do not have the capacity for sustainable renewal, beyond the school gates are underlying social issues of poverty, unemployment, poor health, and inadequate housing' (Ofsted 1993: 45).

At least in the media discussions following white riots there were no suggestions that however feckless the underclass might be, they were not intellectually deficient; they were merely undeveloped due to poor education. This was in contrast to the rise of a 'New IQism' (Mirza 1998), which again covertly connected Black children's ability with lower intelligence, which affected teacher perceptions. In 1995 race was a feature in riots between white, Indian and Pakistani young men in Bradford. Asian community leaders blamed problems of unemployment, poor housing and low school expectations as alienating a younger generation and noted that Asian young people were not prepared to put up with the racism their parents had suffered (Donegan 1995). Future 'riots' as Britain became more multiracial and multicultural, were a mix of white versus minorities, minority groups fighting each other and minority groups plus whites fighting racist groups. All this was linked to poverty, deprivation, alienation and racial injustice. Even as a Black and Asian middle class developed, and professional people from overseas were fast-tracked into the country, the default position remained that 'for people of colour, race is in everything we do, Because the universal experience is white' (Shukla 2016: 6).

Race and harassment

One consequence of European policies on immigration was a resurgence of fascist neo-Nazi parties especially in Germany, Austria, Holland and France. In Britain the British National Front, now the British National Party (BNP) continued its recruitment of young white racists, and racial violence and attacks on minorities and immigrants continued. Much of the press, especially some of the papers owned by Rupert Murdoch, kept up a stream of denigration of asylum seekers as 'bogus welfare scroungers', 'stealing British jobs' and 'swamping' Britain all over again, and the BNP exploited fears of both legal and illegal immigration. The number of refugee children had always been difficult to establish but by 1997 there were estimates of around 40,000, living mainly in London, with schools receiving no extra assistance for them. Political interest in racial harassment and violence was minimal during the early 1990s, although evidence mounted as to its extent. The Runnymede Trust, established to study issues of racial justice and equality, published a report in 1993 on *Racist Attacks and Harassment: The Epidemic of the 1990s* (Runnymede 1993).

The views of white parents had never been well researched, but evidence had mounted that white parental antagonism to those regarded as racially of culturally different. Kelly and Cohen researching *Racism in Schools* (1988) had produced a list of a hundred derogatory insults aimed at minority children and suggested that white parents followed politicians in ignoring or condoning racist behaviour. In June 1992 the House of Commons held its first debate on racial equality for six years, led by the then Shadow Home Affairs Secretary Roy Hattersley. The government response was that 'we have forceful policies to tackle racial discrimination and disadvantage' (Hansard 1992: column 149). In September a Black Chelsea football player was attacked with an iron bar by a white youth and the Chair of the Commission for Racial Equality asked for new legislation on racial violence, but it was refused. Then in April 1993, the 18-year-old Black 'A' level student Stephen Lawrence was attacked and killed at a bus stop in Lewisham by five white youths. The eventual inquiry into his murder became a defining moment in the history of race and racism in the country.

His mother, Doreen Lawrence, described the shocking way she and her family were treated by the police. Even in the hospital she was treated badly and initially denied seeing her son's body. It was not until, at a press conference arranged several days later, she heard that five white youths had approached Stephen and his friend Dwayne Brooks shouting 'What, what n****r' before Stephen was stabbed (Lawrence 2007: 73). The Major government refused an inquiry into the murder, and it was left to Doreen and Neville Lawrence to pursue a private prosecution. It was not until 1997 that the Labour government agreed to an inquiry and a report was finally published in 1999 (Macpherson 1999). In 2012, almost 18 years after the murder, two of the youths were convicted of killing Stephen, and it was 20 years before it was confirmed that one of the police actions was to spy on the Lawrence family. The Macpherson report introduced the notion of institutional racism, another way of describing the underpinning of police and other public institutions with beliefs in the inferiority of Black and minority people. Nothing much had changed since the 19th century. The concept was much derided, then and later, the favoured explanation continuing that it is just a few 'bad apples' or hostile individuals who are racist, rather than whole social structures. In 1994 pupils at a school in East London were moved to other schools as racial harassment increased after the election of a BNP councillor in the area, and police reported a rise of 33 per cent in racial violence in London. Racial hostility and harassment was not confined to cities, a study in rural Norfolk interviewing minority residents, which included Black, mixed race, Asian, Japanese, Cypriot, Irish, travellers and Jewish groups, found that all had experienced some form of racism and harassment (Derbyshire 1994).

Education policy

The Major government was characterised by what seemed to be a frenzy of education legislation but was actually part of a long-term strategy to change the whole education system from a national system democratically run, to a semi-privatised centrally controlled system. There were four education secretaries during the seven years: John Macgregor took over from Kenneth Baker from 1989 to 1990 but was thought to be too nice to teachers. Kenneth Clarke took over until mid-1992, later boasting in his memoirs that he introduced the league tables showing winners and losers in school testing. But he regretted that when he decided that polytechnics should become universities, some of them opened what he considered were second rate arts faculties, to gain a greater veneer of respectability. John Patten, despite the Brighouse incident reported previously, was appointed to implement the policies set out in the white paper *Choice and Diversity* (DfE 1992). He wrote in the Introduction to the white paper that 'Good schools that attract most pupils will get more money. Poor schools that cannot attract pupils must improve standards or wither and perish' (Patten, in DFE 1992: Introduction). He was rapidly moved on and Gillian Shepherd was in post 1994–97, making an example of those 'failing schools'.

Aims of legislation included strengthening a market ideology to be achieved by parental 'choice' of school, government control of the curriculum and assessment, further eroding of the powers and responsibilities of local government, teachers and their trainers, and demands for accountability from individuals and institutions. This applied to universities, increasing in number by 1992 when a Further and Higher Education Act allowed polytechnics to become universities and further education (FE) colleges became independent of local authorities. FE colleges had long been a destination for Black and minority students to gain vocational and academic qualifications, but Clarke decided the colleges were 'fairly unimportant', and 'did not matter to their local councils' (Clarke 2016: 277). Universities were to be funded by a Higher Education Funding Council (HEFC) and a group of vice-chancellors of research-dominated universities, calling themselves the Russell Group after the hotel they met in, claimed to be the top universities.

Teachers and their training were a particular target for the Major government, with teachers gradually stripped of their professional status and becoming more a technical workforce delivering a National Curriculum. Much publicity was given to beliefs that university education departments and remaining higher education (HE) colleges were hot-beds of left-wing theory, multicultural education and 'progressive' child-centred methods. A Teacher Training Agency (TTA) was created by the 1994 Act. Schools were to be inspected by the new Office for Standards in Education (Ofsted). There were widespread objections to the TTA, including those from the National Union of Teachers. The Union's then Assistant Education Secretary, Michael Barber, wrote that the TTA would lack independence and would be subject to political interference (NUT 1993), although his views changed when he became a government adviser.[5] Ofsted, superseding the old HMI who had conducted independent inspections of schools and gave schools and government helpful advice, now employed private teams of inspectors. The first chief inspector, appointed by the government and retained by Labour after 1997, was Chris Woodhead, noted previously as having a somewhat unusual private life but whose willingness to criticise schools and teachers proved useful to succeeding governments and initiated a climate of pointless fear in schools that persisted into the 21st century. When Woodhead was accused of amending an Ofsted report on reading, carried out in three boroughs, deleting sections referring to poverty and bilingualism, a chair of one of the boroughs observed that 'Mr Woodhead is as much use in the battle for higher standards, as a chocolate teapot' (MacCleod 1996: 2). Mr Woodhead was also credited with referring to anyone with a professional interest in education as 'The Blob', a phrase used later by Michael Gove when education secretary.

Following the 1988 Education Act, open enrolment and local management of schools whereby funds followed pupils, was the mechanism that made some schools richer and some poorer. It also led to a diversion of funds into marketing and public relations, and encouraged parents to become vigilantes and complainers rather than partners. A long Education Act in 1993 made further attempts to make schools grant maintained (GM), including the notion that failing schools could be made to 'go GM' just as in later years under-performing schools were to be forced into becoming 'academies'.

The operation of market choice of school was quickly shown to be a crude method of social selection. This escalated over the years as house prices near 'good' schools shot up. Grant-maintained schools funded directly from the Education Department, replicated the direct grant grammar schools which Labour had abolished. Even the Conservative Education Association worried that 'if schools do opt for GM status an even larger part of the £14.5 billion spent annually on schools will be spent by bodies that are not democratically accountable' (CEA 1992: 2). This was a foretaste of the large amount to be spent in the future by undemocratic academy trusts which came to control large numbers of schools and their funding. The publication of league tables comparing schools' test results became an annual media event and a political weapon for subsequent claims that effective and poor schools could be easily identified. American scholar Michael Apple later commented that 'While race talk may be absent in the discourse of markets, it remains an absent presence that I believe is fully implicated in the goals and concerns surrounding support for the marketisation of education' (Apple 1999: 12).

Failing schools

By the 1990s a new educational phenomenon appeared in Britain. This was the 'failing school' – a demonised institution whose teachers and governors were deemed to be responsible for the underperformance of the pupils.[6] They were also blamed for failing local communities and, that permanent category of citizen, 'the disadvantaged'. Press coverage of failing schools was negative and insulting, as journalists competed to discover the 'worst school in Britain' (Brace 1994). The notion of failure was not new but had previously been mainly associated with individual pupil failure. In England and Wales from 1945 the secondary education system was premised on the assumption that 80 per cent of pupils at age 11 would fail to demonstrate potential for academic learning. The expansion of comprehensive schools, expanded access to examination courses from the 1960s, changed attitudes to girls education and improved teaching, had allowed larger numbers of pupils to pass public examinations, and the 1940s figures were reversed.

By the 1990s over 80 per cent of young people were achieving passes in academic courses, numbers gaining vocational qualifications increased and by 1993 around 33 per cent of 18–19-year-olds were attending university – some at the 'new' universities. A public consciousness was developing that recognised the importance of qualifications and a decline in the deference that 'education is not for the likes of us'.

This success was of little interest to politicians or the media, and persistent propaganda claiming low standards and incompetent teachers was used to establish an increasing hierarchy of schools and centralised control of education. Margaret Thatcher, always supporting selection at secondary level, expressed 'deep personal dissatisfaction with schooling', and continued to blame teachers who were 'less competent and more ideological than their predecessors' (Thatcher 1993: 598). Local education authorities (LEAs)', especially if Labour-controlled, were also blamed for low standards, with migration, second language speaking and families that did not value education also coming under attack. Less attention was paid to lack of resources, crumbling buildings, under-paid teachers and the spread of poverty and unemployment. Neither was there much interest in the situation which had developed in Tower Hamlets in London where by 1990 some 500 Bangladeshi children were without a school place, the local authority, short of money to build more schools, blaming parents who would not travel out of the area for fear of racial attacks. The local law centre took the case to a judicial review and Lord Justice Wolf gave the curious judgement that the duty of an LEA to provide school places was 'not absolute' (Tomlinson 1992: 444).

But pillorying individual schools became a policy, with initially around 200 secondary schools targeted as failing and in need of 'special measures'. Unsurprisingly, these schools were in predominantly urban areas attended by minority children, second language speakers and those with special educational needs. Culloden Primary School in Tower Hamlets was criticised in the tabloid media for giving too much attention to second language learners and to children with special needs. While national education systems had become a key focus for the incorporation of racial and ethnic minorities into the economy and civil society the educational policies of the early 1990s contributed to disadvantages by race and class. Minority students had to bear additional market burdens, as they were likely to be regarded as undesirable, attend 'failing schools' and those with reduced budgets. A classic example of the failing schools policy was Hackney Downs School in Hackney, which became a by-word for a failing school. In 1986 this former grammar school turned comprehensive in 1974, had boys achieving public examination passes on a par with similar London schools but by the 1980s was taking in large numbers of minority and migrant pupils and those expelled from other schools. The intake included pupils with backgrounds from African, Caribbean, Indian, Pakistani, Bangladeshi, Kurdish, Turkish and other groups. In the 1990s there had been four head teachers in six years, and buildings were in severe disrepair. The chair of the Hackney Education Council from 1988 1990 was Michael Barber, who was not initially critical of the school. Arguments between the local authority, the chief education officer (Gus John – one of the first Black CEOs of an education authority to be appointed), parents, governors and the DES ensued over the next five years, as to whether the schools should be closed (see Barber 1995, 1996; Tomlinson 1995, 2005; O'Connor et al 1999).

The failing schools legislation allowed for the setting up of an 'Education Association' to inspect schools and take over their running if necessary. In July 1995, when Hackney Council had decided to keep the school open and a week after the Secretary of State Gillian Shepherd had decided not to intervene in Hackney Downs School, she changed her mind and appointed the one and only Education Association to go into the school. Despite parents taking the closure decision to court in a judicial review, the school was closed with precipitate haste, and the boys transferred to a neighbouring school, where the examination performance in the following year was no better than at Hackney Downs.

Eventually the school was demolished and a new school, Mossbourne, endowed by shipping businessman Sir Clive Bourne and costing some £35 million of tax-payers' money, was erected on the site with Michael Wilshaw, a future head of Ofsted, as head teacher. With a selected intake, the school would later be accused of taking few pupils with special needs, but claiming 'traditional' teaching, the school initially had good examination results and became a favourite for visits from Tony Blair when he became prime minister. Michael Barber, later to head Blair's Standards and Effectiveness Unit, claimed in an interview in 2011 that 'The stand we took on Hackney Downs became a foundation of New Labour's education policy' (Wilby 2011). The Labour government under Blair continued the policy of naming and shaming schools, which, as 'choice' policies developed, ensured that these failing schools were largely attended by pupils from poor, minority, refugee, special needs and second language backgrounds. It eventually became clear that it was easier to blame schools than to restructure education or plan the economy to ensure all young people had an educated future.

Whose National Curriculum?

With wars, migration, an EU, privatising public utilities and those extra-curricular activities, it was not surprising that the Major government had little time to examine in detail the content of the school curriculum or debate existential questions such as what kinds of knowledge would young people need as the 21st century approached. The main interest was in developing tests which would demonstrate winners and losers in the educational market, The National Curriculum, pride of Baker's 1988 Education Reform Act, developed over several years, and much of the work was left to civil servants and advisors, who had themselves largely been educated at private schools which were exempt from a national curriculum.[7] There was certainly no enthusiasm for examining Britain's place in relationship to her former Empire or her new European partners. Instead there was a growing and determined attack on any changes by the educational nationalists, the right-wing groups around Mrs Thatcher and John Major who demanded a return to what they termed a traditional curriculum. They labelled any of the 1980s activities that went under the name of multicultural, anti-racist education and global or world studies as subversive of British culture, likely to be associated with left-wing egalitarianism and leading to lowered standards (Palmer 1986).

Empire as a topic was an 'absent presence' and although royalty was still touring Commonwealth countries, the inclusion of former colonial subjects as citizens was still a matter for regret and the school curriculum was not about to provide the *Education For All* Lord Swann's committee had envisaged (DES 1985a). The committee was clear that national identity could not be understood without understanding British imperialism, colonial expansion and the way imperial ideologies entered the school curriculum. Despite the efforts made by educators from the 1970s to develop a curriculum more meaningful in a multicultural society and develop anti-racist strategies, those influencing a national curriculum were still clinging to notions of the cultural, linguistic and political superiority of the English nation and wished the curriculum to define the boundaries of a national identity and assert a 'traditional'(Victorian) culture and heritage. While a national curriculum with recognised standards in state schools was generally agreed by the later 1980s to be necessary, it was a relatively small group of politicians and lobbyists who determined that it should be an 'English' curriculum and certainly not international. Political attack on any content suggesting equal opportunities, anti-racist or multiculturalism was a feature during the creation of a national curriculum and these areas were banished from discussion.

Duncan Graham, appointed as the first chair of the National Curriculum Council (NCC) by Kenneth Baker in 1988 – who welcomed him with a malt whisky – wrote that it was made clear to him that references to multicultural education were a 'no-go' area and 'The right-wing of the Conservative Party was listening to lobbyists who were continually saying how terrible it was that none of the country's children – apart from their own – could read or write' (Graham 1993: 6). He noted that the educational traditionalists were the same people who talked of a return to Victorian values, and he pointed out two junior ministers who saw the NCC as dominated by professionals, educationalists and teachers who attempted to block much of the Council activities. He named one of these ministers as Michael Fallon, who 'believed the NCC was dangerously left-wing' (Graham 1993: 99). Fallon subsequently had a long career in Conservative governments, culminating in the post as defence secretary, before resigning in 2017 over 'inappropriate (sexual) conduct' (Castle 2107).

Secretary of State, Kenneth Baker, had determined on a broad, ten-subject National Curriculum, with working groups of teachers producing detailed suggestions on what each subject should contain with cross-curricular themes, a recipe, as Graham noted, for interference and argument. Geography, History and English were always the most contentious subjects. Geography, as noted previously, was up to the 1960s frankly imperialist and had moved slowly towards internationalism, but even in the 1980s taught material which was highly questionable. Dawn Gill, Head of Geography in a London school, and an intrepid anti-racist campaigner, pointed out, for example, that work sheets on a *Geography for Young School Leavers* project taught into the later 1980s contained a worksheet on Dallas USA, juxtaposing information that 'Dallas is a visual mess, its crime rate is a disgrace, and 19% of its population is Negro' (King and Reiss 1993: 94.) But the National Curriculum geography working group made a valiant attempt not to duck the issues and the final report of their group included a section on 'Geography for a Multicultural Society'. They were to be disappointed when the DES draft orders for national curriculum geography concluded that 'The Secretary of State recognizes that geography lessons will sometimes deal with conflicting points of view ... However he considers that the main emphasis. should be on teaching knowledge and understanding of geography rather than on people's attitudes and opinions' (DES 1991: intro).

History in the National Curriculum aroused fierce debates, especially over the History working group's wish to produce a curriculum for a multicultural society. Governments around the world, especially dictatorships, have often attempted to reinvent their national histories, recognising that what is taught as history is crucial to the creation of a national identity. Rob Phillips (1998) discussed in some detail the battle for control as to which historical stories should comprise the National Curriculum and the political interference that ensued. As he noted, the struggle for the 'big prize' of the nation's story led to thousands of articles, letters and editorials in the quality and tabloid press, and demonstrated the influence of those who wished to link history teaching to what they considered to be a patriotic nationalistic cultural identity. The final report of the National Curriculum History Working Group claimed that one of the purposes of school history was 'to contribute to pupil's knowledge and understanding of other countries and other cultures' (Booth 1993: 78), but this was not acceptable to the traditionalists. Kenneth Baker was sympathetic to right-wing views that school history paid to little attention to a British heritage and had become anti-patriotic (Graham 1993: 63). The final study units, and the statutory orders for history, came across as largely about white indigenous people. The group's chair, Commander Michael Saunders Watson, owner of Rockingham Castle in Nottingham, clashed with Margaret Thatcher over her views on history and also objected to Kenneth Clarke's proposal that history should end in 1945.

Graham's conclusion regarding history and geography interference by politicians raised serious questions about the role of ministers in the school curriculum and the dilemmas when politics clashes with educational views. The English Working Group suffered similar interference. This group, headed by Professor Brian Cox, included several members who were concerned about bilingualism and multicultural education. Cox wrote later 'Conservative politicians were over-confident they knew the right policies and to a large extent were contemptuous towards the professional teacher' (Cox 1991: 11). The negative influence of politicians was most clearly indicated by the open repudiation of the report of a Multicultural Task Group, set up by the NCC in response to a letter from the Secretary of State that the NCC was 'to take account of ethnic and cultural diversity and the importance of the curriculum in promoting equal opportunity for all pupils regardless of ethnic origin or gender' (Tomlinson 1993: 21).[8] The NCC had noted that multicultural education was a controversial area, and the Task Group were well aware that any debates prefaced by 'multi' or 'anti' were anathema to influential people with the ear of the government. The Group set about suggesting ways in which schools could incorporate multicultural issues into all subjects and the implications for local education authorities, school, teachers, governors and parents. The five-chapter report presented by the Task Group was never published. The only reference to it was in one page of an NCC newsletter which noted 'The NCC does not see multicultural education as a subject, but as a dimension which permeates the whole curriculum and the Council would draw on the work of the Multicultural Task Group to see that this would happen' (NCC 1991: 2) There was little subsequent evidence that permeation occurred.

Summary

This chapter has attempted to demonstrate that a great deal happened during the government headed by John Major, which had negative consequences for future dealings with the EU, with immigration issues, and with the education of all young people for a multiracial multicultural society, while the first Gulf war set the stage for future conflicts in the Middle East and retaliations that affected the British population. Politics was dominated by persistent euroscepticism and by the untruths and sleaze which came to be associated with some politicians. The period consolidated the education policies which enhanced market ideologies, competitive individualism and privatisation and which were to dominate the development and eventual possible break up of a state education system. It initiated a school inspection system which superseded a helpful and respected inspectorate, and introduced cruel and pointless policies of naming and shaming schools which did not do well in constantly updated tests and examinations. Markets and choice policies created new disadvantages for minority young people, as they were most likely to be attending urban schools regarded as 'undesirable' and likely to be labelled as failing. These policies were embraced by an incoming Labour government and its advisers. The period and preceding two years also saw the development of a determinedly 'national' curriculum, interfered with by the views of right- wing politicians and their advisers. It was not a curriculum for all children and young people, and certainly not one with which racial and ethnic minorities could identify. It did grave disservice to all young people who needed some truthful accounts of the past and present realities about living in a multiracial multicultural global world.

6

New Labour: wars, race and education, 1997–2005

After 18 years of Conservative rule, the British people were apparently ready for a new Prime Minister and a revamped Labour Party now known as New Labour. They got this on 1 May 1997 when public-school educated Anthony Charles Lynton Blair became prime minister age 43. Much was made of the notion that there was a 'new dawn' in politics. As his close adviser Alastair Campbell wrote in his diaries describing the Blair election win 'as we got to the Festival Hall. TB worked the crowd, then up to the lectern and a "new dawn" and they (the audience) cheered every word' (Campbell 2007: 187). A number of books were hastily written to celebrate this accomplishment and Campbell and Blair's own memoir (Blair 2010), gave their exhaustive account of the years after Blair took over as Labour leader after the untimely death of shadow leader John Smith in 1994. In his speech to the Labour Party conference in October 1997, he affirmed a commitment to social justice and to education as a means to a socially just society (Blair 1997a). Then in 1998 he referred to the equal worth of all individuals, claiming that 'The attack on racial discrimination, now commands general support, as does the value of a multicultural multiethnic society' (Blair 1998: 3) and in a later speech celebrated as his 21st-century message, asserted that 'nations that succeed will be tolerant, respectful of diversity, multi-racial, multicultural societies' (Blair 1999). So what went wrong? It might have gone wrong from the start of his government, as although he claimed beliefs in social and racial justice, by the end of his tenure he was blaming Black gangs and parents for racial violence, and supporting selective education policies for 'high flyers' (Gillborn 2007).

This chapter notes that the New Labour government initially embraced an ideology of a 'Third Way' joining capitalist market competition with social democracy and a reformed welfare state, with education as a means to help create a socially just society. It claimed education as a priority and continued the avalanche of market-driven education legislation and policy initiatives which had characterised 18 years of Conservative rule. But it did initially attempt to take on a number of social and racial grievances and inequities. This included setting up a Social Exclusion Unit in the Cabinet office, ordering an inquiry into the Stephen Lawrence murder, offering Muslim schools the same state funding as other voluntary-aided schools and creating an Ethnic Minorities Achievement grant. Race returned as a presence rather than an absent presence.

New Labour seemed eager to affirm Britain as embracing a national identity that valued cultural diversity and recognised the rights of minorities, although Blair had never expressed much support for this previously. By the second term in office from 2001 it was clear that the government had not grasped the scale of problems in creating a multicultural society, More conflicts in Northern English towns in 2001 ushered in another examination of what constituted a British 'national identity', and there was agonising over what constituted multiculturalism and how to create community cohesion. This was not helped by further immigration control acts, and a lukewarm view of the European Union (EU), with some dithering over whether to hold a referendum on joining a single euro currency. Echoes of Empire returned after terrorists attacks in New York on the World Trade Centre in September 2001 led to joint Allied invasions of Afghanistan in 2001 and former British territory Iraq in 2003. It was *Blair's Wars* (Kampfner 2003) that were to be the main legacy of his premiership, and at his handover as prime minister to Gordon Brown in 2007, notions of a progressive, inclusive Britain were giving way to xenophobia and disunity.

Significant events

1997	(May) New Labour wins the general election. European Year Against Racism. David Blunkett Education Secretary.
1997	Social Exclusion Unit set up. Brief to inquire into school exclusions and truancy with special reference to Black pupils. A Qualifications and Curriculum Authority set up. William Macpherson asked to chair an inquiry into the killing of Stephen Lawrence. Muslim faith schools to be offered state funding.
1998	Bernard Crick reports on Citizenship and the Teaching of Democracy in schools (two paragraphs on multicultural education). Education Action Zones (EAZs) set up to improve education in inner cities areas. Later part of an Excellence in Cities programme.
1998	Human Rights Act brings European Convention on Human Rights into UK Law. Crime and Disorder Act brings more penalties for racial crimes.
1998	School Standards and Framework Act. Ends grant-maintained schools but schools can become foundation, voluntary aided or community schools (the first two controlling their own admissions). Teaching and Higher Education Act.
1998	Enoch Powell dies. There are many obituaries and tributes to his patriotism.
1999	Final devolution of governing powers to a Scottish Parliament and a Welsh Assembly. The Belfast Agreement (Good Friday Agreement) devolved government to a Northern Irish Parliament, although the DUP voted against this Agreement.
1999	Excellence in Cities Programme. Includes gifted and talented programme. Sure Start Centres set up, focusing on disadvantaged children aged 0–3.

1999	Macpherson report on the murder of Stephen Lawrence suggests there is institutional racism in the police force. NUT passes a resolution against racism at its annual conference.
1999	Asylum and Immigration Act introduces vouchers instead of cash for asylum seekers, enforced dispersal and detention on arrival.
2000	Race Relations Amendment Act requires local authorities and schools to have race equality policies. Ofsted to inspect these policies, Teacher Training Agency produced guidelines online for teachers in place of taught courses on teaching for a multiethnic society. Chris Woodhead resigns as head of Ofsted.
2001	Census records 4.5 million (8%) of UK population identify as minority ethnic. with a younger age structure for those of Pakistani and Bangladeshi origin. David Blunkett becomes home secretary.
2001	(June) New Labour elected again with nine Black and Asian MPs. DfEE becomes the DfES. (July) Riots in Northern towns of Oldham, Bolton, Bradford and Burnley. Ted Cantle sent to visit and report. (9 September) Destruction of World Trade Towers in New York by men of Saudi Arabian origin. More hostility to Muslims as Blair joins the USA in war in Afghanistan.
2002	White paper presents new policies on nationality and citizenship, English language and citizenship tests. Proposal that children of asylum seekers should have separate schooling. Blunkett claims the children are 'swamping' some schools.
2002	Nationality and Immigration Asylum Act. More border controls and an increase in detention facilities and deportation orders. Citizenship courses to be mandatory in all schools. First Academy schools set up.
2003	(March) Invasion and war in Iraq.
2003	Victoria Climbié report by Lord Manning. White paper *Every Child Matters* (DoE/ Home Office).
2004	Higher Education Act allows for fees of up to £3,000 in universities and sets up Office for Fair Access (OFFA). Mike Tomlinson's report suggesting an overarching Diploma at 18 repudiated. David Blunkett resigns as home secretary.
2005	Trevor Phillips, head of CRE and designate head of a new Equalities and Human Rights Commission claims the UK is 'sleep walking into segregation'. (June) New Labour elected for a third Term. The Conservatives under Michael Howard run a losing campaign vilifying immigrants. Education Act increases school inspections and schools are 'causing concern' if they fail to achieve set targets for pupils. The term 'local education authority' abolished but continues to be used.
2005	(July) Four young Muslim men, educated in English schools, suicide bomb London underground trains and a bus. (August) 18-year-old Black student Anthony Walker axed to death in Liverpool. (October) Conflicts in Birmingham between Black and Asian young men.

Politics, ideologies and war

A month after New Labour's election, Prime Minister Blair spoke at a European Socialists Conference in Sweden, telling fellow socialists that 'our task is not to fight old battles but to show there is a third way, of marrying an open competitive economy with a just, decent and humane society'

(Blair 1997b). The Third Way, an ideology borrowed from Bill Clinton in the USA, was intended to marry market competition and deregulation of business with social democracy and a reformed welfare state. The European socialists were not convinced and continued to support social democracy and regulated capitalism. They were right to do so as what was going wrong in Britain since the 1980s was the growth in inequality of wages, wealth and life chances, and this was exacerbated under the Blair Years (see Wilkinson and Pickett 2009; Dorling 2010). Labour's historic ideological commitment to state intervention to achieve equality and social justice rapidly gave way to a continuation of neo-liberal policies from the right. This included privatisation, flexible labour markets and a competitive individualism with people supposedly lifting themselves out of poverty with the help of state authoritarian policies. While this worked for some families from overseas – 11 of the top 12 families in the 2017 *Sunday Times* Rich List were from India, Russia, Canada, Sweden and Italy – it did not do much to help the working classes and many minorities. Policies increasingly left the middle classes fearful for their children's futures. Inequality led to more blaming of immigrants and minorities as the cause of social problems.

But New Labour accepted that those living in countries internally colonised by England should be given a measure of independence, and powers were devolved to the Scottish Parliament, a Welsh Assembly and partial resolution of the conflicts in Northern Ireland through the Belfast Agreement in 1999. There was more open recognition that the country now incorporated large numbers of ethnic minority groups with different migration histories, economic positions and religions whose claims to be part of the society could not be ignored. The European Convention on Human Rights was incorporated in UK law in 1998, and as noted in Chapter 5, a defining moment in British race relations came after an inquiry into the murder of Stephen Lawrence was set up, and the report in 1999 brought the concept of institutionalised racism and problems in the police service to public attention (Macpherson 1999).

Home Secretary Jack Straw set up a Commission on the Future of Multi-Ethnic Britain in 1998 (Parekh 2000), but this proved to be a disaster with its report condemned by the media for attacking 'Britishness' and Straw and Blair hastily disassociated themselves from it. The report had actually suggested in one chapter that 'There has been no collective working through the imperial experience. The absence from the national curriculum of a rewritten history of Britain as an imperial force, involving dominance in Ireland as well as Africa, the Caribbean and Asia, is proving an unmitigated disaster' Parekh 2000: 25). It suggested better ways of supporting community diversity while fostering a shared national identity, a theme repeated in subsequent academic and political literature, but at the time even the *Times* newspaper criticised the findings of the Commission (the author was a member) asking 'who do these worthy idiots think they are' (Kaletsky 2000). In 1998 Enoch Powell had died and his obituaries praised his patriotism and support for an exclusive sovereign national identity. In a later book evaluating Powell's life and work Iain Duncan-Smith, a notable voice in the campaign to leave the EU, wrote praising Powell's opposition to the Maastricht treaty and his view that 'we have traded away Parliament's supremacy to others, whether to foreign institutions or the British judiciary' (Duncan-Smith 2012: xxii).[1]

While Blair had not demonstrated much interest in foreign policy, he was keen to demonstrate patriotism. One election poster for the 1997 election included a British bulldog but led to arguments as to whether the dog's testicles were too big on the poster. He subsequently led the country to war five times in six years, four of the wars in Muslim countries. He supported Bill Clinton and the USA bombing in Iraq in 1998,[2] sent troops to defend the government in Sierra Leone (a British colony until 1961), sent troops to Kosova in the Balkans, supported President Bush and the USA in invading Afghanistan after 2001 and Iraq in 2003 (Kampfner 2003) and, as noted, considered moving into Zimbabwe again in 2007. Blair's wars did not endear him to EU members or to Muslim and other Asian minorities in Britain, and wars in Afghanistan and Iraq subsequently encouraged some young people world-wide in terrorist activities.

Multicultural fears

Post-Second World War global migrations world-wide led to the development of a large literature on multiculturalism, recognising that there are now few or no monocultural societies in the world. In England, while the country was becoming more multicultural as more people from former imperial countries arrived and in due course became citizens, and others arrived as economic or refugee migrants, institutions were slow to catch up. Attempts in education to bring in multicultural and anti-racist perspectives in education continued to be met with hostility. But despite supporters being attacked as left-wing loonies, a political discourse had developed recognising the reality of multiculturalism, later incorporated into the language of 'diversity'. Despite New Labour's stated commitment to ending racial discrimination and creating a socially just society, any philosophies of the common good continued to be utopian in a society structured along class, gender, race and ethnic lines, with groups in competition for scarce resources. A shared identity seemed conspicuously lacking as the British National Party (BNP) continued to gain influence in high minority areas, gaining three council seats in Burnley in 2002 and 18 overall in England in 2003. Two weeks after the Parekh report (2000) was published, a young Asian prisoner was killed in his cell by a white youth who resented being in prison 'with someone whose race and origin he despised' (Kelso 2000).

Hostility to European migrants began to be documented in education. In 2004 a school in Stoke-on-Trent found that five newly arrived Czech Roma children dropped out. On questioning the other minority children in the school, they told staff that racism was so routine they did not really identify it and the BNP distributed leaflets in the town claiming that English was not the first language taught in the school (Wallace 2004: 8–10).

Despite New Labour's 2001 electoral commitment to a multicultural inclusive society, any policies or ideologies defining a multicultural society reverted back to simplistic assertions that minorities had failed to 'integrate', after riots in the Northern towns of Bradford, Bolton, Oldham, Burnley and others in July 2001. The destruction of the Twin Towers in New York in September 2001 by educated men originally from Saudi Arabia signalled a more general hostility to Muslims, any commitment to multiculturalism was weakened and there was pressure on minorities to embrace what were claimed to be the responsibilities of British citizenship. Meanwhile, British companies continued to buy oil from Saudi Arabia. A Ministerial Review team on Public Order and Community Cohesion led by Ted Cantle was sent up to visit Northern towns and also Southall in London and other cities. The team expressed surprise at the 'parallel lives' people lived and made recommendations about education which virtually repeated those made in the Education Support Grant (ESG) projects supported by Baker in the 1980s (see Tomlinson 1990). There were also reports on the disturbances from Lords Clarke, Ritchie and Ousley – the latter a former chair of the Commission for Racial Equality (CRE), and the final report drew the findings together (Ministerial Working Group 2001). In reality, despite talk of ethnic groups deciding to live parallel lives on the basis of ethnicity, the major factor was economic – where can you afford to live and where are the jobs. A later study in London demonstrated that people are more becoming more mixed in areas by ethnicity but less mixed by income (Dorling and Thomas 2016).

David Blunkett, home secretary in 2001 after his years in education, commissioned a white paper which outlined new politics for citizenship and nationality, requiring future citizens to learn English and pass a citizenship test despite funding for teaching English as an Additional Language (EAL) being cut. A Nationality, Citizenship and Asylum Act followed, which proposed separate schooling for asylum seekers children – a move hastily dropped. In April 2002 Blunkett had claimed in a radio broadcast that these children were 'swamping some British schools' (BBC News 2002). His remark was defended by the government and he never apologised. Policies of dispersal of asylum seeking and refugees meant that families were often housed in areas hostile to their presence and there was in increase in racist abuse and hostility, especially from young white people. Blunkett managed to conflate the presence of long established citizens with newer arrivals when he asserted that there were norms of acceptability and 'those who come into our home

… should accept these norms' (Tomlinson 2008: 135) and Oliver Letwin, then shadow home secretary, told the Conservative Party conference in 2003 that asylum seekers should be deported to a far-off processing island. This idea was put into practice with the 2023 scheme to send people to Rwanda. Blunkett had to resign his post in 2004 when it transpired that he had fast-tracked a visa for the foreign nanny of a former lover.

Centralising education

The New Labour government under Blair had three years to prepare for power, and three pages in his 40-page election manifesto promised smaller classes, demanded higher standards and setting in schools, and zero tolerance of under-performance. More funding was promised but compromised when the newly elected government announced it would stick to Tory spending and no raised taxes. Despite hyping a concentration of education, spending on education as a proportion of gross domestic product (GDP) actually declined, from 4–8 per cent in 1996 to 4.7 per cent in 1998. A raft of education policy initiatives and Acts followed between 1998 and 2005. Michael Barber, who had announced the closure of Hackney Downs School as 'failing' influenced future Labour policy, and he was made head of a Standards and Effectiveness Unit. Literacy and numeracy task forces were set up plus a plethora of other groups on Adult Learning, Special Needs, University for Industry and a New Deal advisory group and others. There was even a Red Tape working group to advise on ways of cutting bureaucracy. Barber went on in 2001 to head a Delivery Unit in the Cabinet Office, checking how targets set in education, health and other institutions were being met. Liberal leader Charles Kennedy worked out that the government had set up some 4,585 targets for schools, colleges and local education authorities (LEAs) to achieve. The targets could be broken down into 306,480,472 measures to be monitored (Kennedy 2000).

A major Education Act in 1998 abolished grant-maintained schools, but secondary schools could become Foundation, Aided or Community. The Conservative policy of specialist school was extended, with more business sponsorship and beacon schools to become examples of good practice. Estate agents reported that house prices rose near beacon schools. LEAs were to promote high standards but with reduced powers. Selection of 10 per cent of pupils by 'aptitude' for secondary schools was permitted, a distinct broken promise (see Lawton 2005). Market forces were helping to create 'failing' schools, with Blunkett declaring persistent failure would not be tolerated, and a macho language of zero tolerance, tough policy and pressure continued. It was not until October 1998 that the public humiliation of urban schools and their teachers was largely abandoned, with the head of one inner city school serving a poor, Black intake, noting bitterly that 'We have had a Herculean task to improve in a climate of hostility' (Gardiner 1997).

But as school exclusions had reached over 10,000 a year, a Social Exclusion Unit set up in the Cabinet Office aimed to reduce this, although setting no targets! A majority of exclusions, truants and those placed in schools for the Emotionally and Behaviourally Disturbed (EBD) were young Black males. An Ethnic Minority Achievement Grant replaced previous funding for minority education. There was much discussion about investing in human capital, competing in a global economy, and the need to more privatisation and business interests in state education. There was also a focus on early years and child-care facilities for all mothers to help them return to the workforce, and in 1998 a national child care strategy was launched promising more child care places paid for by public, private and voluntary sectors. Child care was treated more urgently after the torture and death of an eight-year-old child of West African origin, Victoria Climbié. This led to a public enquiry and a Children Act requiring education, health and social services to work more closely together. Sure Start Centres, the idea of Treasury official Norman Glass, were set up from 1999 bringing together professionals from all services for children 0–3 years, and these expanded into Children's Centres, although a review of the project in 2007 claimed it had failed to address the question of ethnicity with rigour or sensitivity. In one area white parents told Bangladeshi parents they could not use the Centres (Craig 2007).

Privatising education

Under New Labour education was to become less of a democratically state-funded system and more of a commodity to be bought and sold. Private companies were brought in to run national programmes from inspections to school dinners, schools were built with the Private finance Initiative (PFI), and from 2002 schools could form themselves into companies and sell goods and services to each other (see Ball 2007). A diversity of schools was encouraged, with more faith schools, including Muslim schools, alongside more Anglican. Catholic, Jewish and other faiths, specialist schools and City Technology Colleges.

But the policy which led to most fragmentation, privatisation and eventual removal of democratic accountability from schooling was the creation of academies schools. Announced as City Academies in a 2000 Learning and Skills Act, three academies opened in 2002. Enthusiastically embraced by David Blunkett, Peter Mandelson and advisor Andrew Adonis (all three later to become lords), these were to be independent state-funded schools set up as limited companies with charitable status. Sponsors from business, sport or other groups would contribute money and appoint a majority of governors to control the schools. They were outside local authority democratic influence, under central control via the Department for Education and Skills (DfES) and controlled their own admissions – an open invitation for covert selection. Blair was enthusiastic, holding 'breakfasts' in Downing Street for sponsors, including American investment bankers, and two of the early academies were under the control of evangelical creationist Christians. Blair, perhaps due to his own private education at the Empire-minded Fettes school had never, despite early utterances, really embraced non-selective education or social and racial justice. His slogan 'education, education, education' was lampooned in a cartoon by Steve Bell in 2001. This depicted Blair shouting into a megaphone, 'Education for Everyone of Excellence: you Thickies can whistle for it!' (reproduced with permission as the Frontispiece in Tomlinson 2017). Local authorities themselves were also claimed to be at risk of 'failing' and taken over by private companies. Islington, the London borough home to Blair before election (and Jeremy Corbyn for many years) became the first LEA to be taken over by the private company Cambridge Associates, and the firm Capita, which has had a chequered career of fraud and failings over the years, was appointed to take over education in Leeds. Capita was also appointed in 2001 to run an Individual Learning Accounts programme for students which eventually closed with accusations of fraud.

Controlling higher education

Following a report in 1997, a Teaching and higher Education Act ushered in a £1,000 fee for university tuition and arrangements for student loans. The success of comprehensive education from the 1970s had resulted in a wider and more diverse body of students qualifying for university entrance, but university staff pay was squeezed. Arguments as to whether private schools took a disproportionate number of places at top universities persisted, and a 2003 white paper made widening access and participation to include more working class, minorities and mature students a priority for a further Act in 2004. Although opposed by 100 Labour MPs and passed by only five votes, this Act raised fees to £3,000 a year; it set the scene for further fee increases. An Office for Fair Access (OFFA) was set up to oversee fairness in admissions, and successive governments began boasting that more working class and minority students were in higher education.

Modernising the teaching profession was a favourite theme of the Blair government, which meant more control of pay, recruitment and conditions of service. Incompetent teachers were blamed for low pupil performance, which unsurprisingly led to recruitment problems. Reports suggesting that more minority teachers might improve pupil attainments and lives were never acted on. The Teacher Training Agency, which had taken over organising teacher preparation, produced guidelines in 2000 as to how teachers should prepare for teaching in a culturally diverse society, as face-to-face courses had more or less disappeared. This mainly took the form of ticking boxes, but in 2003 a website was prepared as a resource for teachers covering some information on race, class, religion, bilingualism, Roma and Travellers. A Race Relations Amendment Act in 2000 had made it obligatory for all educational institutions to produce and monitor race equality policies, but research two years later indicated that only 20 per cent had done this. Muslim dress continued to drag on as an issue, one court case in which a 14-year old girl wished to wear a jilbad (long dress) at school taking four years to resolve (Tomlinson 2008: 153).

A 2005 Education Act increased the powers of Ofsted, the semi-privatised inspectorate, increased local authority competition for new secondary schools and extended the powers of the Teacher Training Agency to support all the 'schools workforce' including the requirement as in previous Acts, to 'promote the spiritual, moral, behavioural, social, cultural, mental and physical development of children and young people' (Education Act 2005 section 75).

There was no requirement for curriculum change to achieve these rather elaborate goals, and evidence continued to accumulate that, like the little girl questioning her teacher's dark skin, white understandings of a Black presence was not something schools were teaching.

The madness of testing

Under the Blair–Brown governments, the system was set for a future in which the madness of measurement, target setting, inspection and blame characterised education from early years to higher education. It was noted in Chapter 3 that children from colonial countries had barely had time to sit down in school before psychologists and educational researchers began to measure their intelligence and attainments, as if there had never been over 200 years of denigration of their families in colonised countries which had their own histories, languages and possible development shattered, plus Victorian eugenic beliefs in the innate inabilities of imperial subjects. Studies of the 'Empire Effect' in Britain from historical, sociological and political angles remained overdue. German sociologist Ulrich Beck, contemplating modern societies, wrote that 'the world is unhinged ... it has gone mad' (Beck 2016: 1). The madness of assuming that it was possible to compare test results of the descendants of those formerly colonised in a hostile, xenophobic society, with white young people continued, with no historical understandings as to the different modes of colonisation, or the different ways the education system treated various minorities.

Most migrant parents from former colonies were unsurprisingly concerned about the educational achievements of their children, and ambitious for them, knowing that they would be disadvantaged in employment and life chances unless they achieved at least on the same level as white children in whatever forms of schooling and testing were offered. On the whole they were and continue to be disappointed in what they have been offered, as the school systems changed, exam success became more crucial and racism continued in its various forms in and out of institutions. Declared government ambitions to overcome 'achievement gaps' between white and minority students, were rendered pointless by *Moving the Goalposts* (Gillborn et al 2007) – a redefining levels or benchmarks of what constituted success in examinations. The use of data showing differences between public examination passes of difference minority groups led to what had been noted in the USA as the creation of 'model minorities'. In England this led to invidious comparison between higher attainments of Chinese and Indian origin pupils as against Caribbean, African, Pakistani and Bangladeshi pupils, and also led to panic if any minority pupils appeared to perform better than any in what was assumed to be the whole of a white working class.

The plethora of research and collection of data on educational achievements on various groups of children and young people at all levels in education developed into a burgeoning industry. Initially, research was small scale and mainly qualitative – interviewing and observing. Later, especially since there were now large amounts of data available from, for example, the 2002 Pupil Level Annual School Census (PLASC) which collects information on individuals by achievement, ethnicity, gender and free school meals (FSM) – the proxy for poverty – large research grants were given to those who use quantitative methods and elaborate statistical analysis to demonstrate which groups are up or down in the high stakes testing.[3] The emergence of a further global industry PISA (Programme for International Student Assessment) instigated by the OECD (Organisation for Economic Co-operation and Development) created panics in governments as the results purport to show which countries were up or down in competitive tables. The PISA enthusiasts were supportive of markets, choice and efficiency in schooling, less so for democratic participation by schools, teachers, parents and the young people themselves (Meyer and Benavot 2013).

The absent curriculum

In 2005 a teacher of Ghanaian origin was asked by a five-year-old white girl she was teaching 'why is your skin like this?' (Akomaning 2018). Why was it that after several hundred years of Empire, and 60 of Commonwealth, with now around 9 million citizens from former colonial countries in Britain, did a five-year-old have to query her teacher's dark skin in 2005? The answer to the little girl could have been:

> Well dear, in 1821, your white ancestors took over my rich country, where we have dark skins. They called it the Gold Coast and made the people there slaves or working for hardly any money and they took

food and goods out to give to the white people in Britain. It was not until 1957 that the country became Ghana and got its independence from what was the British Empire. My parents and I had the right to come and live in Britain and in the 1960s my father came and qualified as an accountant and I am a teacher. I hope as you go through school you learn more about the British Empire and what happened to all the people in countries that were taken from them for so long, and perhaps why white people still keep asking why we have dark skins.

Thirteen years later criminal barrister and legal affairs journalist Afua Hirsch, of Ghanaian, German and English heritage, put it plainly. 'A lot of British people don't fully accept that you can look like me and be British' (Hirsch 2018). She noted that there is still no language to adequately describe 'What corporate-speak such as BAME and "diversity" try to hide … that this country has never had a civil rights movement, a moment of national reckoning where we grappled with the end of Empire and the disappearance of imperial words like Negro and coloured' (Clark 2018: 19).

The New Labour government was not short of ambitious targets and visions. Michael Barber, perhaps the nearest the government came to claiming a theorist or ideas man, published his vision of a 'world class education system' in 2001 (Barber 2001). The principles laid out to achieve this included a diversity of secondary schools, state and private, and demands for high standards from all, while separating out the gifted and talented. He claimed in 1999 that the numeracy and literacy hour had 'changed the face of primary education for ever' (Bower 2016: 182) with primary schools leaping in two years to be the third best in the world. In fact, the literacy hour was one-year-old and the numeracy hour had not started. Lawton later commented that his vision was a managerial, technicist approach to the delivery of a traditional education (Lawton 2005). While the New Labour government was willing to follow Conservative policies of central control of curriculum and assessment, it was similarly reluctant to encourage curriculum change to prepare all young people for life in a multiethnic society.

There were no ideas as to how the traditional curriculum could develop into an education for a multicultural democratic society. It gradually became clear that for New Labour, although they used a rhetoric of a more inclusive Britain, and had the means to direct the school curriculum into one more suitable for the 21st century, there were no plans to do this. The work of several generations of teachers, local authorities, academics, parents and communities was disregarded. There was a plea at a conference on history teaching held at the British Empire and Commonwealth Museum in Bristol in July 2004 for more teaching of Empire all through schooling, with one teacher claiming that there had been 'public awkwardness and embarrassment about our Imperial past' (Mansell 2004: 3), and a Schools History project produced a textbook on *The Impact of Empire*. But the most that was offered to all pupils was a focus on citizenship education, following a report by Bernard Crick, David Blunkett's former tutor (Crick 1998) which became mandatory in schools from 2002. Osler and Starkey, major researchers in citizenship education, pointed out that the Crick report (Crick 1998) made no mention of racism and focused mainly on cultural differences. Nothing that could really inform all pupils about the past and present nature of the society they lived in was contemplated.

Summary

This chapter has suggested that despite New Labour's declared commitment to a socially and racially just society, supporting multiculturalism and anti-discrimination, the reality turned out differently. Journalist Gary Younge suggested that initially the potential existed for the government to support an inclusive 'hybrid sense of Britishness' (Younge 2007), but positive policies in the first term of office rapidly changed as fears of supposedly segregated minorities and their religions increased. There was a continuation of anti-immigration policies, and following disastrous wars in Afghanistan and Iraq an increased threat from a small number of young terrorist Muslims which led to claims that multiculturalism had somehow failed. The implications of this was that a supposedly cohesive society was disrupted by the presence and lives of minorities. Sustained antagonism to immigrants and minorities was enhanced by the market policies and inequalities that the Labour government encouraged. Economic inequality increased and the rich got even richer, while the poor got poorer over the New Labour years (see Dorling 2017). This left low-paid workers feeling threatened by economic migrants and refugees, adding to the continuing hostility to settled former colonial people. Contradictory policies, especially in education, encouraged individual competitiveness and separation, including by faith schooling, Although the educational achievements of all young people continued to rise, as they had been doing since post-war policies actually allowed more to learn and pass public examinations, issues of the lower attainments of Black and Muslim pupils continued to be researched as though all things were equal. Politicians found it convenient to side-track the issues by reference to poor white boys and model minorities. The focus on testing and targets left the issues of what was being taught in educational institutions that might contribute to understanding how the society had been shaped by Empire and its consequences ignored. In his resignation speech in March 2007, as he handed over to Prime Minister Brown, Blair included the lyrical comment that this country is a blessed nation and the British are special and the world knows it.

Enoch Powell (and perhaps later Donald Trump in the USA) could not have put their patriotic sentiments better.

7

Not so New Labour: race and education, 2005–10

A respected author, journalist and chronicler of British politics wrote in the early 1990s that the quality of government depends on the talent inside the two Houses of Parliament and especially in the Cabinet (Sampson 1992). Since then, over the past years, the British public had been presented with a number of seemingly ineffective, quarrelling and self-interested politicians and an increasing number of equally self-interested advisers and rich lobbyists The dysfunctional relationship between Prime Minister Blair and Gordon Brown, who, full of grievance that Blair did not depart sooner than June 2007, directed attention away from crucial national issues. These included the inequalities of income and wealth that had by the early 2000s reached a high point unknown since the 1930s, the looming global financial crisis which left the Queen wondering 'why did no-one notice it coming?' (Pierce 2008), the relationships with the European Union (EU), an education system increasingly fragmented and separatist, and with racism and xenophobia fed by Blair's wars and their aftermath. It was ironic that after leaving office in 2007, one of Blair's invitations was to stand by the River Jordan while media mogul Rupert Murdoch had his daughters baptised in the holy waters.[1]

This chapter takes the story up to the defeat of the Labour government in 2010, a legacy of wars in Afghanistan and Iraq overshadowing any earlier positive race policies. There were intensified hostilities to Muslims, asylum seekers, East Europeans, including Roma, Black British citizens and others. The Prevent programme, set up after the London bombings in 2005 by young Muslims, fed suspicion and alienation among Muslims and anger from teachers expected to police young people. Discussion about the enlargement of the EU as eight more countries joined in 2004 was not on the school curriculum or debated with the general public, and much of the media remained hostile to enlargement. The inclusion of Bulgaria and Romanian workers in 2006 led to increased antagonism to immigration, despite the needs of employers. Debates about Britishness, national identity and community cohesion rumbled on, and education policy makers remained reluctant to recognise that market competition and a diversity of schools were exacerbating social and racial divisions. The encouragement of faith schools did not appear likely to diminish segregation, and on the Academies programme Colin Crouch had commented in 2003 that 'once public services are treated as commodities ... how long will it be possible to defend their being subsidised and not bought or sold in the market like other commodities' (Crouch 2003: 25). While many young people were aware that they would live their lives in a globalised world, with rapid communication and population movement, the failure to think seriously about a curriculum for a globalised future – which would need an understanding of the past – left schools either trying to ignore tensions or unable to cope with conflicts in and out of school. The continued political stress on immigration control and attempts to prevent any radicalisation of young people fed public hostility to long-settled citizens, economic migrants and asylum seekers

Significant events

2004	Lord Hutton's inquiry into the Iraq war published.
2005	Education Act. Teacher Training Agency enlarged. The Act allowed competition to set up new schools to include religious or parental groups.
2005	(May) Trevor Phillips, designate head of the new Equalities and Human Rights Commission claims 'We are becoming more polarised by race and faith and sleep-walking into segregation'.
2005	(June) New Labour elected for third time. (July) Four young suicide bombers blow up London Underground trains and a bus.
2005	Prevention of Terrorism Act. Prevent strategy initiated, to be overseen by the Home Office. Immigration, Asylum and Nationality Act (the sixth since 1990).
2006	Education and Inspections Bill. Controversy over admissions, selection and faith schools. Equality Act establishes a single Commission for all aspects of equality. (May) BNP puts up 357 candidates in local elections. Leeds University lecturer suspended for claiming white people are more intelligent than Black people and describes himself as an 'unrepentant Powellite' (Asthana and Salter 2006).
2006	(August) Blair tells his Cabinet that terrorism and immigration are two major public concerns. *The Sun* newspaper (23 August) pictures a topless page 3 girl saying she is 'very worried about immigration'. A Commission on Integration and Cohesion set up. Jack Straw publishes an article criticising the wearing of the niqab by Muslim women.
2006	(November) MPs demand an enquiry in to the Iraq war. Rejected by Foreign Secretary Margaret Hodge.
2007	(March) Celebration for bi-centenary of abolition of the slave trade. London Mayor Ken Livingstone apologises for London's role in slavery and a legacy of racism. No events organised to celebrate 50 years of the European Economic Community, despite the Union now including 400 million people in 25 countries and forming a quarter of the world economy. In local elections in May 200 Muslim councillors are elected, Muslim Bashir Ahmed the first Scottish-Asian member of the Scottish Parliament. 56 BNP councillors elected round the country. (June) Siddiqui Report on Islamic Studies in Higher Education.

2007	(27 June) Brown takes over from Blair as prime minister. (July) Attempted bombings at London and Glasgow airports. Worst floods for years and foot-and-mouth disease in livestock. Northern Rock bank in Newcastle collapses. (October) Brown declines to call a general election. (December) David Miliband, foreign secretary, signs the Lisbon Treaty in Portugal with Brown arriving later (a consolidation of previous EU treaties).
2007	Education Department split into DCSF (Department for Children, Schools and Families) and DIUS (Department for Innovation, Universities and Skills). A Children Plan aims to eradicate child poverty with ten goals to be archived by 2020.
2008	Global banking crisis. Brown worried that 'the western economy was slowing and faced collapse' (Brown 2017: 303). 850 British companies go bankrupt in three months. Education and Skills Act raises staying-on age in education/ training to 18.
2009	(April) Brown convenes G20 meeting in London to sort out the world economy. Treaty signed in Lisbon to amend previous European treaties by member states comes into force. Article 50 allows for countries to leave the EU. (May) MPs' expenses scandal. Apprenticeship, Skills and Children Act, funding for 16–18 to return to local authorities.
2009	(October) The Browne Review of Higher Education and funding set up. Michael Gove, shadow education minister, lays out plans for education at Conservative Party conference promising to 'destroy the education establishment' and return schools to a traditional curriculum and traditional British values.
2010	(May) Brown calls a general election, resulting in a hung parliament and eventual coalition between Conservatives and Liberals. Brown resigns and Ed Miliband elected shadow leader of Labour. The EU not a major issue in the election but UKIP under leader Nigel Farage takes 3.2% of vote. Future Lord Chancellor George Osborne claims spending cuts and austerity are required in the country. Browne review (November) recommends increases in higher education fees to be paid by students.

Dysfunctional politics

For New Labour, politics did not seem to work well. Political commentators agreed that the antagonistic relationship between Tony Blair and Gordon Brown affected most of the political decisions of the New Labour government, especially from 2004. Brown claimed in his memoirs that an agreement before the 1997 election that Tony should be prime minister and Brown should take over during the second term of the Parliament was made before a much quoted dinner in an Italian restaurant in Islington. By 2003 the war between the two men seemed to overshadow the war in Iraq earlier in the year. The disastrous consequences of this Iraq war were becoming apparent, despite a report by Lord Hutton appearing to excuse Blair and his team from responsibility (Hutton 2004). After Brown had attacked Blair at the 2003 Labour Conference over the war and over his privatising of public services, Deputy Prime Minister John Prescott gave a steak and kidney pudding dinner for the two men in his Admiralty House flat to reconcile their differences, but the relationship worsened and Blair announced his intention to stay on as prime minister until after the next election (Brown 2017; Rawnsley 2010). One of the contentious issues had been the increase in fees for higher education to £3,000 a year. Brown was very much against this policy and Rawnsley has described the parliamentary scene when the vote was taken and an increase in fees was agreed by five votes. 'Brown stuck up 5 fingers and thrust them into Blair's face' (Rawnsley 2010: 236). The 2005 election manifesto included a commitment to a place in school, college or training for every 16–19-year-old, and a 2008 Act raised the leaving age for all young people to remain in education or training to 18.

Disunity and diversity

Beliefs that Britain had become a disunited kingdom in which immigration and multiculturalism were the enemies became more widespread during the 2000s. Some commentators continued to claim that a once united British society had been fractured by the presence of racial and ethnic groups, and the arrival of more economic migrants and refugees. The mythical assumptions of a once cohesive society were actually nonsense in the light of the historical divisions in the society by class, wealth, gender and racial lines. It did not need Peter Mandelson's well-reported claim in a speech to computer executives in Los Angeles that New Labour was 'intensely relaxed about people getting filthy rich' adding later 'as long as they pay their taxes' to underline the disparity in wealth and income that actually characterised the period (Rawnsley 2010: 477). Despite claims that New Labour had lifted a million children out of poverty, and a New Deal for Communities had invigorated declining areas, by 2006 the Office for National Statistics recorded that the gap between rich and poor was the same as when Mrs Thatcher left office in 1990, and the richest fifth of UK households had incomes 16 times greater than the poorest. These poor household included a disproportionate number of Pakistani and Bangladeshi households, although a few of the richest included some Muslim, Sikh and Hindu households, with wealth often accrued in business in minority communities or transnational businesses.

The early Blair government assertions on respect for diversity and valuing a multiracial, multicultural society, rapidly gave way in the second and third term of Labour to promises of tougher asylum and immigration targets, fears of Islam and blaming Black youth for violence. Ruth Kelly, education secretary in 2004–06, claimed that white Britons were not comfortable seeing their shops and restaurants in town centres changing, which left the public wondering if she had ever ordered an Indian takeaway. The community cohesion and citizenship agenda supposedly supporting an ethnically diverse society, were at odds with more punitive immigration and asylum and then terrorist legislation. In 2004 David Goodhart, editor of the journal *Prospect*, made familiar right-wing claims that it was 'progressive liberals' who supported diversity and that sharing welfare benefits with diverse groups led to tension and fears. He argued that newcomers should adapt to their new country (Goodhart 2004) and was supported in 2005 by Trevor Phillips, the chair of the Commission for Racial Equality and from 2007 chair of the Equality and Human Rights Commission, who claimed that 'multiculturalism suggested separateness' and that the country was 'sleep walking into segregation' (Tomlinson 2008:161). Phillips was given a knighthood in 2022 for services to equality. Comments in the media suggested that minority communities deliberately segregated themselves, ignoring data which by then indicated that despite discrimination, outer suburbs had an increase in minority residence, and it was low incomes and/or low paid jobs, that tended to keep people in inner city areas.

In 2005 Michael Howard ran a losing general election campaign vilifying immigrants, with a Labour MP commenting that he 'escalated the dangers of immigration beyond Enoch Powell's wildest dreams' (Hattersley 2005). But in July 2005, four young Muslim men, born and educated in England, blew themselves and 56 people up in London, wounding over 700 others including Muslim citizens. Two weeks later there was an attempted London bombing by four more men, originally refugees but educated in English schools. The full force of the British intelligence and security services was then directed at gathering information on and preventing terrorist activities. In education, a Prevent programme was instigated, in which teachers in educational institutions were expected to check and report any suspicious activity on the part of children and students (Gearon 2015). This programme escalated over the years to become part of Contest – a government counter-terrorism strategy which as a *Telegraph* article pointed out 'managed to alienate just about everybody' (Murray 2010). The government commissioned a report on the teaching of Islamic Studies in British universities which reported in 2007 with suggestions for a more modernised Islamic curriculum (Siddiqui 2007). This was regarded by some students as another attempt to police Muslims. Blair changed from being relaxed about immigration – he had supported the inclusion of eight more countries into the EU in 2004, believing then that economic immigration was profitable – to telling the Labour Party Conference in 2006 that terrorism and immigration were major public concerns. In August 2005 when a young Black man was axed to death in a public park in Liverpool, he had made no comment. In October after riots in Birmingham between Black and Asian young people in which one man was killed, Blair blamed 'Black culture' especially absent fathers and a lack of Black role models. It was then disclosed that a third of all young Black men were on a police DNA data base, and a Violent Crime and Reduction Act allowed school staff to search children for knives.

During New Labour's time in office 3,600 new criminal offences were introduced and the prison population reached a record high, with an over-representation of young Black men. To demonstrate that eugenic views were still in operation, in 2006 Frank Ellis, a lecturer at Leeds University, was suspended for claiming that Black people were intellectually inferior to whites, writing in an article in the *Leeds Student* that 'multiculturalism is doomed to failure because it is based on the lie that all people, races and cultures are equal' and added that he was an 'unrepentant Powellite' (Asthana and Salter 2006). Later in the year a lecturer at the London School of Economics published a paper claiming that the causes of poverty and poor health in African states could be traced to lower intelligence (Campbell 2006). In higher education, assumptions were that students on university courses would be free from racist views despite most having come through schools where issues of Empire, race and racism were seldom discussed. This assumption was demonstrably false, as evidence (discussed in Chapter 9) began to accumulate of the racism shown by white students towards minority students. After his initial burst of enthusiasm for a multiracial multicultural society, Blair never commented on growing racial conflicts during his time in office, apart from condemning immigrants, terrorists and Black young men. It was perhaps not surprising that he was not much mourned as he left office. Marquand, as noted previously, drew attention not only to the illiberal policies around immigration and Islam after 9/11 but also the wealth gaps which tax cuts and tuition fees did nothing to alleviate as far as social inequality was concerned. Even Neal Lawson, initially an ardent Blairite, wrote that 'A decade of Blair has left the Labour Party on its knees' (Lawson 2007).

Brown's woes

While academics like to keep up with the times, it is often a mistake to rush into print while events are still unfolding. Written just before Brown finally took over as prime minister in July 2007, Labour advisor and former head of the London School of Economics (LSE) Lord Anthony Giddens, published *Over to You Mr Brown* (Giddens 2007). He was upbeat about the success of New Labour over its ten years in office, especially its market friendly policies and the benefits to citizen-consumers. He particularly extolled the City (of London) which 'Contributes a rising proportion of GDP. It is one of the great success stories of the British economy' (Giddens 2007: 5). It was unfortunate that the world was about to enter its largest economic downturn since the 1930s, the British economy would go into recession and the City banks and bankers were about to become pariahs.

Early environmental woes for Brown took the form of torrential flooding in Britain in July 2007, followed by an outbreak of foot and mouth disease.

On 29 June there had been an attempted terrorist attack at Glasgow airport by men angry at Middle East wars, but foreign policy in August meant a trip to the USA to assure George Bush that Britain was still with him in a war alliance.[2] Then home again to find that in October two discs containing the names and addresses of 25 million parents and children making claims for child benefit had been lost in the post! In the same month he decided not to call an election. In December he was so busy that he did not arrive on time in Lisbon where leaders of all the EU countries had gathered to sign the Lisbon Treaty which consolidated previous EU treaties. Foreign Secretary David Miliband did the actual signing and the Treaty came into effect in 2009. By 2009 Brown had to deal with the embarrassment of the *Daily Telegraph* revelations over MPs' expense claims which had taken some bizarre, greedy and illegal turns over the years for which taxpayers were footing the bills. Their journalists had obtained information on the expenses claimed by all 646 Members of Parliament. The most well known were claims for a duck house from Conservative Sir Peter Viggers, among his £23,083 other expenses, and claims for biscuits from Labour Austin Mitchell, among £2,300 for other expenses. The most worrying were the claims made by Alistair Darling, chancellor of the exchequer, at the time dealing with the banking crisis. He had claimed second home allowances on four properties, which led to demands that he resign. Sir Christopher Kelly was appointed to examine the claims (Kelly 2009) and improvements in the system were made. Labour Jeremy Corbyn was the only MP to make no expense claims.

The banking crisis began with the collapse of Northern Rock. From Newcastle to Surrey people queued to get their cash out this bank. Brown claimed he did not know about international banks practices and wrote in his memoirs 'I now found to my horror that a vast shadow banking system made up of banking affiliates that were not bound by the rules which applied to banks but which acted like banks – trading in dubious financial instruments' (Brown 2017: 299). He also found that during 2008, some $50 trillion dollars 'more than the entire income of everyone in the world' was pledged across financial companies without being declared. Both Brown and Chancellor Alistair Darling have documented in their memoirs the steps they took to inject money into the banks and save the careers of most of the bankers. They also both claim they saved the world from a great recession. Darling wrote that he deeply regretted that in the 2010 election the government 'failed to capitalise on our successful handling of the financial crisis' (Darling 2011: 323) but in his last budget announced that confidence had not returned to business or consumers. This set the stage for the future Coalition government to blame the Labour government for the banking crisis and instigate an era of austerity, which impacted severely on the poor and on public services, including education.

Education policy from Blair to Brown

Education under Tony Blair and his advisors continued their emphasis on improving the nation's economic competitiveness through testing, inspection and centralisation. There was more support for a diversity of secondary schools, academies being the flagship schools, with specialist schools and Trust schools added to the mix and faith schools being encouraged. As chancellor of the exchequer Brown had increased funding for education from 2002 with an extra £15 billion made available over three years, and funding per pupil increased. A Building Schools for the Future programme with money from the Private Finance Initiative was supported from 2003 and school buildings and facilities improved considerably, although at long-term cost to the taxpayer. The scheme was abandoned in 2010. An Education Act in 2005 overturned a historic funding agreement with local authorities and all funds would now come from the secretary of state to all maintained schools.

Despite constant and often contradictory policies and initiatives, public education continued its long slow improvement in terms of young people actually being taught, and entering for and passing tests and examinations, with the government taking credit for improvements and blaming schools and teachers where improvements did not occur, especially in urban schools attended by minority pupils. The language of failing was superseded by a competitive language of 'outstanding' or 'requires improvement'. Competition for 'good' schools intensified as did the increased selection of children by overt and covert means for different and unequally resourced schools. The support for faith schools of all kinds continued to create problems, with an *Observer* Comment (2007) that 'Faith has now become another word for race' (Observer 2007), and a *Times* article claiming that Church schools were used as covert forms of social and racial selection by the middle classes (Miles 2007).

The flow of reports on the comparative achievements of various minorities compared to white pupils continued, with some laudable suggestions for raising performance in tests, but as noted earlier with goalposts being moved and levels of 'success' raised. Teaching literacy and numeracy and then traditional subjects in secondary schools were a focus for debate, with reports commissioned on the National Curriculum and on primary education. But what was actually being taught and tested received minimal attention. Most publishers had by this time recognised the nature of the multicultural society and children's' books and comics contained more than the token minority presence, as did some television programmes. The question of how far schools could combat public influences continued, with MP Jack Straw criticising Muslim dress again, this time objecting to the few women who chose to wear the niqab (face covering). There seemed to be no institution willing to combat the offensive racism directed at the two tennis-playing Williams sisters, Venus and Serena, who from their arrival at Wimbledon in 2003 were subject to racist slurs from commentators and the media in England for all their careers (Jacques 2003). Ken Livingstone, as mayor of London, in 2007 did his best to raise awareness of racism by apologising for slavery on the bi-centenary of abolition of the slave trade, and HM Treasury later boasted that many years ago in 1833 it had paid reparations for the trade. It later transpired that the money, around £16 billion in today's money, had actually been paid to 46,000 slave owners to compensate them for losing their 'property'. From 2007, Labour's Harriet Harman had worked on bringing together all the various equality and anti-discrimination legislation into one Act, an Equalities Act passed in 2010. This Act consolidated 116 pieces of legislation into one Act on gender, race, disability, sexual orientation and employment.[3] Local councils in high minority areas began to be better represented with minority members elected.

Academies

The academies programme continued to develop. By 2006, 46 had open with plans for another 200. In his book defending academies, Andrew Adonis boasted that when made minister for schools in 2005 he could personally take decisions about the opening and organisation of these 'independent state schools' which would have dynamic sponsors taking control of their management. He had been grateful that he was sponsored at his private boarding school and escaped the 'vast adolescent jungle' of Borehamwood, a multiracial comprehensive school. Despite his subsequent Oxford history degree he did not apparently see any imperial connections with the jungle metaphor. The first chapter of his 2012 book was taken up with insulting Hackney Downs which had been demolished (see Chapter 5 of this book). He extolled Mossbourne, the architect-designed school eventually built on the site at the cost of £28 million. He claimed Hackney Downs was one of the hundreds of failing comprehensives which constituted a 'cancer at the heart of English society' (Adonis 2012: xii). In his book, villains opposing academies were egalitarian head teachers, teacher unions, local authorities, further education colleges, obstructive officials, some ministers and education professors, especially well-loved Professor Ted Wragg who had once referred to Adonis as 'Lord Barmy of Bedlam'. Heroes included strong head teachers, rich business-men, property developers, consultancy firms, the Churches and philanthropists (including an Evangelical car salesman). The remedy for school improvement was apparently removing schools from local authority control and any democratic accountability. A number of private schools opted to become academies and taxpayers rather than parents paid the fees. The Anglican Church's United Learning Trust quickly became a major sponsor of 20 schools. One of the donors to this Trust was multimillionaire

Muslim Mahmoud Khayani who also donated to the Labour Party. An Oasis Christian Trust, set up by the Baptist Church, planned academies based on 'core Christian values' which included opposition to homosexuality. The Catholic Church and other faiths expressed intentions to open academies, along with more business interests and sports clubs. Evidence quickly accumulated that these independent state schools were actually increasing social and racial segregation overall and not improving results when compared with similar local authority-controlled schools.

Despite his troubled agenda, Brown was more interested in real children than Blair, visiting schools in Tower Hamlets to read to Bangladeshi pupils, changing the Education Department into a Department for Children, Schools and Families, and a (short-lived) Department for Universities, Innovation and Skills and bringing in a personalised learning agenda. A Children Plan in 2007 encouraged children to enjoy their childhood and be prepared for adult life (DCFS 2007). This proposal was repudiated by future Education Secretary Michael Gove who told a conference at Brighton College in 2008 that the Conservatives would re-instate traditional styles of fact-based learning, and there would be none of this pupil-centred learning. He also began to consolidate his reputation for holding teachers and 'experts' in contempt. Although Blair in 2004 had turned down suggestions by former head of Ofsted Mike Tomlinson that all pupils work towards a Diploma at 18 which would have abolished GCSEs and 'A' levels (DfES 2004), Brown was more sympathetic to vocational education and apprenticeships. A 2006 Education Act suggested 14 vocational Diplomas be set up, although this exacerbated an academic–vocational divide and the Diplomas were another short-lived idea. His major battle was over tuition fees for higher education, but after the five-finger incident with Blair he came round to the idea of supporting student repayment of fees through a type of graduate tax. In 2009 he allowed Peter Mandelson to appoint a friend, Lord Browne, the former director of British Petroleum, to undertake a review of fees. His report suggested an increase to £9,000. Brown was relieved that after the Labour general election defeat in 2010 this was not his problem (see Brown 2017: 239).

British values and the curriculum

Whatever Gordon Brown's problems, he did demonstrate some serious thinking about the notion of Britishness. As a Scot he was aware that Britain was four nations and claimed rightly that over the past 50 years internal unity had frayed. Although he wrote that in a global era, identities were likely to be multiple, and he supported a 2007 report which suggested that cross-curricular themes in the KS 3 curriculum should include identity and cultural diversity and community participation (QCA 2007). He remained apparently unaware of the extent of racial divisions and hostilities in Britain. His remedy for conflict was a commitment to assumed British values of tolerance, liberty, fair play and social responsibility, and he suggested setting up an *Institute for Britishness* (Brown 2017: 396), a plan never implemented. In 2009 he agreed to write an introduction to a book on *Being British* edited by journalist Matthew D'Ancona, with contributors from the left and right of politics (D'Ancona 2009). Michael Gove, then shadow education secretary, contributed a chapter in which he attacked Brown for supporting Britishness to further his career and accused him of poor history and partisan politics. Brown replied that for political reasons the Conservative Party seemed determined to prevent Labour from being identified with patriotic British values. Gove's contribution did not go unnoticed, one blogger later writing that his contribution to D'Ancona's book was 'The least attractive contribution ... a tedious tone-deaf piece in which the strange little man has a go at Gordon Brown and the European Union' (Reggie's Blog 2011). Gove had previously produced a book *Celsius 7/7* (Gove 2006) in which he likened some parts of Islam to fascist and communist ideologies, but the man and his version of British values came to dominate English education once the Conservatives returned to power in Coalition with the Liberal party. He was made a lord in 2022 in later Prime Minister Rishi Sunak's resignation honours list.

An amended National Curriculum was to be put into place from 2008 with teachers to be allowed more input into the design of courses. The History curriculum was to focus less on Henry VIII and his wives and more on recent topics, including the European Union. A study of the British Empire was to be minimally covered in KS 3 and schools were to teach more foreign languages. Black History Month celebrated 20 years of reminding schools of the realities of Empire in 2007, although there were complaints that most of history was white history. Right-leaning groups had not given up their attacks on curriculum developments, the think tank Civitas claiming that 'traditional subjects have been high-jacked to promote fashionable causes such as gender awareness, the environment and anti-racism, and teachers are expected to achieve the government's social goals instead of imparting a body of knowledge' (Civitas 2007: ix).

Summary

This chapter has suggested that during the last years of a Blair government and the subsequent years of Prime Minister Brown there was little evidence of the early claims to support a multiracial and multicultural society and a fairer education system. The war in Iraq and continuing war in Afghanistan led to acts of terrorism by some young men and women, and anxiety on the part of all Muslims in Britain that they were now all regarded as the enemy within. The Prevent programme, about to be escalated by an incoming government, was regarded with suspicion by communities and teachers, and an increase in East European immigration had led to more xenophobia in all social classes. Brown did not help his claim of commitment to values of tolerance and diversity in a speech he made in 2009 demanding 'British Jobs for British Workers' to placate workers striking over the employment of more East European construction workers (Summers 2009). Young Black men continued to be regarded as less educable and more likely to be criminal. Education policy followed an agenda of choice, diversity and creeping privatisation with an escalation of social and racial segregation, and a steady removal of local authority democratic oversight. A sustained focus on testing and assessment left little room for consideration of what was actually being taught. In May 2010, after an election campaign in which Brown unfortunately called one of his supporters a 'bigoted woman', the general election delivered a hung Parliament, with the Liberal Democrats eventually joining the Conservatives in a Coalition government. Brown resigned and Ed Miliband was elected as shadow Labour leader, narrowly beating his brother David. As a final comment on the New Labour 'project', Rawnsley noted that at the last conference before the general election they sang 'The Red Flag' and 'Jerusalem' to the accompaniment of violins, and 'the melancholy strains of the strings added to the feeling that the light was fading on the project which had once had the world at its feet' (Rawnsley 2010: 679).

8

A divided society: race, class and education, 2010–16

> The materialistic and selfish quality of contemporary life is not inherent in the human condition. Much of what appears 'natural' today dates from the 1980s: the obsession with wealth, the cult of privatisation and the private sector, and the growing disparities between rich and poor.
>
> Judt 2010: 2

Even in rich developed countries inequality and the poor are apparently always with us. The Poor Laws in 1834 had one answer to poverty, people had the 'choice' to work for miniscule wages or face the workhouse. The UK in the 20th century eventually followed social democratic ideas of equality similar to those of European neighbours, and by the 1970s had become one of Europe's most equitable countries. From 1980 that all changed. Governments in the UK, led by Thatcher, Blair and Brown, and from 2010 to June 2016 by David Cameron, followed policies which increased inequalities, the justification being that free markets and privatisation encouraged enterprise and wealth creation. There was never any acknowledgment that Britain had previously become rich by exploiting the wealth and labour of the Empire. With the Empire gone, politicians claimed that the country would benefit from economic globalisation which increased flows of capital, labour, goods and services around the world, resulting in higher living standards for all. The World Trade Organization (WTO) was established in 1995 to fix fairer trade rules between countries which would supposedly solve future global trading problems.[1] As Judt noted previously, into the new century, growing disparities in wealth between the rich and poor was not a natural occurrence. What actually happened in the UK was that free markets and shrinking state institutions increased the gap between the rich and poor, and by 2016 wealth and income inequalities were the highest in Europe. As Dorling pointed out in his book *Inequality and the 1%*, by 2014 to qualify as being in the top 1 per cent a childless couple would have an income of £160,000 a year, the average income being £23,000 (Dorling 2014). The poor, as Ken Loach's film *I Daniel Blake* illustrated, could die in Job Centre lavatories after having their rightful state benefits taken away (Loach 2016). There could be no argument that the UK had become a society divided into rich and poor, with education helping this along, and with racial divisions and inequalities continuing to expand. It was not until 2016 that it became common knowledge that the Home Office, under Home Secretary Theresa May, had in 2013 instigated a 'hostile environment' policy intended to deter and deport illegal migrants, one result of which was the deportation of settled legal citizens, including some from the Windrush generation.

This chapter covers the period of the Coalition government of Conservatives and Liberal Democrats to 2015 and then Cameron's Conservative government until the June referendum on leaving the EU in 2016. It was a period dominated by claims that the only way to reduce the 'structural deficit' was by a programme of austerity, which meant cutting money for public services, including education, with higher education fee hikes, more privatisation of public services and no wage increases. The resulting inequalities and lowered living standards felt by the middle and working classes were blamed on the unemployed, benefit scroungers, European Union (EU) regulations and, above all, immigrants. Racial and religious antagonisms were fuelled by riots in urban areas in August 2011, by fears of Islam and 'extremism' as the Trojan Horse affair in Birmingham schools in 2014 demonstrated, and well before the Brexit vote, sustained campaigns against immigrant workers. One response from the DfE was a requirement to promote 'traditional British Values' in schools (DfE 2014).

The education system, with its academies, free schools and faith schools, competitive ethos and increasingly elaborate testing regimes furthered by the Blair–Brown–Cameron governments, continued to polarise children and families. An elite educated in private schools characterised the Cameron government, and most of his Cabinet had been educated privately, followed by Oxbridge. Denigration of schools and teachers in schools attended largely by poor and minority children continued. Privatisation of various kinds continued in both the school and university sectors with an unprecedented fee rise for students in higher education. A rhetoric of 'excellence', helping all children to reach their 'potential' and more social mobility were weasel words used in education documents. Poor children and students were reassigned to the intractable category of 'disadvantaged'. The entire Board of a Social Mobility Commission set up in 2011, resigned en masse in 2017, with the chair lamenting how divided the nation had become by income, geography and generation. In 2010 the Children, Schools and Families Department presided over by Labour Ed Balls reverted to being a simple Department for Education again. Michael Gove took office as education secretary, with a background of threatening the 'education establishment' and denigrating Islam. The language of diversity continued, sometimes meaning schools, mostly meaning children and young people with darker skins, non-European languages and non-Christian faiths but with white European migrants added to the mix. Yet another review of the National Curriculum further entrenched a traditional subject centred curriculum with minimal information on Empire, Commonwealth and the European Union, and no explanation as to why the society was multicultural and multiracial. Hostility towards Black and Muslim young people intensified, and those MPs and MEPs determined to force the UK to leave the European Union intensified their efforts.

Significant events

2009   Conservative leader David Cameron rules out a Referendum on EU membership.

2010   General election and Conservatives go into a Coalition government with the Liberal Democrats led by Nick Clegg. Gordon Brown resigns and Ed Miliband narrowly elected Labour Party leader. Theresa May appointed Home Secretary.

2010   (July) Academies Act. All schools allowed to become academies (October). Browne review of higher education funding published. (November) White paper *The importance of teaching* (DfE 2010) includes a chapter on bad behaviour of working class white and Black pupils. Pupil premium suggested. Free schools to be established. Building Schools for the Future programme, General Teaching Council, and the Education and Maintenance allowance all abolished.

2010   (October) Browne Review of Higher Education fees published. Cap on fees lifted. Students to repay fees when earning £21K. (December) Parliament votes and agrees fee increase. Labour opposed but Liberal Democrats agree.

2011   Education Act legislates for white paper proposals. Wolf Review of vocational education published. Review of the National Curriculum. Historians Niall Ferguson and Simon Schama advise Gove. Report by Graham Allen MP claims the deprived brains of children in dysfunctional families cost the taxpayer money.

2011   (week of 5 August) Following shooting of Mark Duggan by police, riots break out in London, spreading to Salford, Manchester, Birmingham and Nottingham. Cameron returns from his Tuscan holiday to condemn rioters. *Financial Times* article celebrates public school teenagers holidaying in Corfu.

2011   Report of the Eminent Persons Group to the Commonwealth Heads of government notes that trade between Commonwealth countries is 2.3% of world trade and Commonwealth trade preferences no longer exists.

2013   (January) Cameron gives Bloomberg speech promising a referendum after fundamental reform of the EU. (February) UKIP comes second in a by-election in Eastleigh. Home Office, under Theresa May, instigates a 'hostile environment' policy and sends vans around London boroughs telling 'illegal migrants to go home or face arrest'. Boris Johnson gives 3rd Margaret Thatcher memorial lecture and claims that ' human beings are far apart in raw ability' and 'greed is a valuable spur to economic activity'. Dominic Cummings claims that scores in National Curriculum tests show 60–70% dependence on heritability (Cummings 2013).

2014   (March) Trojan Horse affair in Birmingham. (May) Immigration Act notionally to remove illegal immigrants. In European elections UKIP wins 2.6% of vote. (November) DfE issues *Promoting Fundamental British Values* to be part of the SMSC curriculum.

2014	Michael Gove loses job after criticising Home Office slow stance on 'Islamic terrorism', replaced by Nicky Morgan but policies continue as before. Michael Wilshaw appointed as head of Ofsted. Child Poverty Action Group reports that 3–5 million children are in poverty, and forecasts 4 million by 2020.
2015	Conservatives win general election with first Tory majority since 1992.
2015	GCSE subject curriculum revisions. In English literature 20% marks for spelling and grammar. Grades A–G to be replaced by Grades 1–9. Multiplication tables and handwriting to be tested at Yr 6. Education and Adoption Bill allows more rapid conversion to academy status for schools. (December) MPs vote against lowering voting age to 16.
2016	(March) DfE *Educational Excellence Everywhere* signals end of Local Authority democratic role in English schools. A Chartered College of Teaching proposed with a National Teaching Service.
2016	(23 June) Referendum to leave EU won by 52% to 48%. (24 June) Cameron resigns as PM. (25 June) Michael Gove tells Boris Johnson he will back him for the Tory leadership, then changes his mind and stands as a candidate himself. Schools told to collect birthplace and nationality of children.

Posh politics and austerity

David Cameron, born into a wealthy family with, as he said of himself 'two silver spoons in his mouth' (Ashcroft and Oakshotte 2015: 9) took over from Michael Howard as Conservative leader in 2005. The then MP for Henley-on-Thames, Alexander Boris de Pfeffel Johnson, currently in disgrace for lying over an extramarital affair, would soon campaign to be mayor of London from 2008 to 2015, returning as MP for Uxbridge and South Ruislip in the election of 2015. In the Coalition led by Cameron his first Cabinet in 2010 had 60 percent of its members educated in private schools. He claimed that his later 2015 Cabinet was a blue-collar cabinet, but over 50 per cent of its members had attended Oxford or Cambridge universities and both cabinets included several millionaires, notably George Osborne, chancellor of the exchequer. In 2009 it was reported that Osborne had been involved in an argument with (later) Labour Lord Peter Mandelson while holidaying on the luxury yacht of a Russian oligarch Oleg Deripaska, which made the public somewhat suspicious when he and Cameron announced a programme of austerity claiming 'we are all in it together'.

The Coalition government with Cameron as prime minister and Liberal Democrat Nick Clegg as deputy, agreed that eliminating the 'structural deficit' (debt) in the country should be a major aim. Thus the first budget cut public spending by £6 billion and promised the biggest reduction in public spending since the end of the Second World War. In the 2015 manifesto another £12 billion cuts were promised. The effects of cuts in public spending have been well-documented (Atkinson 2018; Dorling 2018), and by 2015 the UK spent a lower proportion of GDP on public services than any other government in Europe.

Especially noted has been the rise in child and maternal mortality, an increase in child poverty and homelessness, a lowered life expectancy and a rise in people claiming incapacity benefits (renamed employment support allowance) but being 'sanctioned' frequently by benefit officials and receiving no money to live on. Food began to be distributed to poor people via food banks, surpassing even Victorian ideas of keeping the poor alive to work if possible. More people developed mental health issues, and suicides and drug-related deaths rose. Work became more precarious, with an increase in zero hours contracts, and spending on health and education was gradually reduced despite rising demand. There was a creeping privatisation of medical services, schools and especially universities. Even veteran Tory MP Kenneth Clarke, appointed as justice secretary in 2010, expressed surprise that as the consequences of the 2008 financial crash became more apparent, and the outrageous conduct of individuals and institutions that had led to the credit crunch and credit crash more obvious, those responsible were never held to account (Clarke 2016). People were becoming angry with their lives and feared for their children's future, but still, as in previous years blamed immigrants for taking low paid work and supposedly putting pressure on housing, education and medical services.

It could eventually be noted that 'the 2010 Government pursued austerity measures that inflicted great cruelty for no apparent economic benefit' (Dorling 2018: 16). Austerity was justified by blaming the previous Labour government for over-spending, trade unions making irresponsible demands and poor people for claiming too many welfare benefits. Geographically the country was becoming more divided than ever into richer and poorer areas, especially in London, and social class was increasingly defined by money and postcode. Meanwhile, the lives of posh politicians and their friends appeared to carry on regardless. Cameron and his friends relaxed with what eventually became known as the 'Chipping Snorton set', a reference to the fact that they lived near the country town of Chipping Norton, and drug-taking among the party-goers was a fashionable recreation. One party-goer recalled a Conservative fund-raising party held at the home of millionaire Lord Chadlington, where 'there was a huge marquee full of ladies with big hair and even bigger jewellery … Jeremy Clarkson's opening line to Dave was "come on, let's face it, no-one in this tent could care less about comprehensive schools … everyone here sends their kids to private schools"' (Ashcroft and Oakshotte 2015: 5–6).

The Camerons frequently entertained newspaper tycoon Rupert Murdoch and his family and Rebekah Brooks, an editor of Murdoch newspapers papers, although she was disowned after her paper's phone-hacking scandal. Murdoch and his papers gave considerable support to Cameron during the 2010 election campaign and a week after he became prime minister Murdoch was entertained to tea in Downing Street. Cutting taxes for the rich and welfare for the poor manufactured deep layers of inequality and poverty, and 'all of this is cloaked in the twisted language of the power elite in which the ways of the wealthy have been disguised as a service for the needs of the poor' (Davies 2014: 406).

All change on the EU

As shadow Conservative leader, Cameron was subject to continued demands from a small number of MPs and Nigel Farage's UKIP party that the country should leave the EU. Standing firm at first, Cameron announced in 2009 that there would be no referendum on the issue. But as UKIP gained votes in the 2010 election and his Eurosceptic MPs continued their pressure, he made attempts to placate the anti-EU lobby by working for changes in EU regulations. In February 2013 in a by-election in Eastleigh, UKIP came second to a Liberal Democratic win, taking 27.8 per cent of votes cast. The Conservative candidate Marie Hutchings came third, although she was on record of claiming she wanted Britain to leave the EU. Cameron made a speech at the London headquarters of the Bloomberg financial firm claiming that although as an island nation 'geography has shaped our psychology' and he was passionate about sovereignty, the EU rules needed an update. While setting out five changes that were needed, he was apparently also passionate for a single market for trade between EU states and claimed that 'Britain is at the heart of a single market and must remain so' (Cameron 2013). The speech was regarded as giving an all-clear for a referendum and by 2015 a promised referendum was in the Conservative election manifesto. His government did not appear to take much notice of a report by an Eminent Persons Group set up to report on the Commonwealth Countries and issues of trade and migration, which was finalised in 2011. Claims after Brexit that leaving the EU would make it easier to trade with the Commonwealth were already rebuffed in the Report which noted that Commonwealth trade preferences (with the UK) no longer existed. 'Many Commonwealth countries have developed close trading links with neighbouring countries and States' (Eminent Persons Report 2011: 76).

Race, class and riots

In a study of the educational experiences of Black middle class parents in their dealings with schools, one respondent, a professional woman of Jamaican heritage, was asked by a white work colleague 'Do you think that Jamaicans are genetically predisposed to violence?' (Rollock and others 2015: 27). While the study noted that the Black middle classes have relatively more power to respond to this kind of racial ignorance and covert racism, Cameron and his government continued to espouse the views that Black and white working class young people, were more inclined to violence and rioting. This was evident in the response to rioting that occurred in August 2011 in London boroughs and other cities. The trigger, as in other previous cases, was the shooting in his car in Tottenham on 4 August of a young Black man by police officers who were later exonerated from wrong doing. His family and friends went to Tottenham police station on 6 August to demand explanations and violence broke out. Rioting and looting then occurred in other parts of London and in other cities.

Cameron returned from his summer holiday in Tuscany to condemn what he called 'sickening violence' and chaired meetings of Cobra, the committee called together in cases of national emergencies (Lewis et al 2011). He gave a speech in his Witney constituency on 15 August claiming that the riots were not about poverty but bad behaviour, and 'there is a slow motion moral collapse in some parts of our country … the welfare system encourages the worst in people' (Cameron 2011). Analysis of the causes of the riots showed a complex mix of motives, but it also transpired that a majority of 'rioters and looters' were under 16 and a third had special educational needs. Despite this Cameron blamed Black gangs who earned money through drugs and announced that Home Secretary Theresa May would join with the Work and Pensions Secretary Iain Duncan Smith to 'work on gangs as a national priority', and 'no phoney human rights concerns would get in the way of action'). Former Prime Minister Tony Blair weighed in, dismissing explanations of income inequalities between rich and poor and blaming rioting on 'people from families that are profoundly dysfunctional, operating on different terms to the rest of society … many of them shaping up that way by the time they are in primary or even nursery school' (Blair 2011). Most young people were brought before the Courts for trivial offences, although prison sentences totalling 1,800 years were handed out. Fines were imposed on people who had no means of paying.

In contrast, on 6 August, while some Black and white working class young people were engaged in disturbances, the *Financial Times Magazine*, which publishes advertisements of expensive goods for rich people to buy, included an article on *The Villa Holiday* (Wry Society 2011). This detailed the exciting holiday of a family in Corfu, whose children sent out a 'clarion call for all like-minded teenagers in the area … the English public school seems a common thread' (Wry Society 2011: 57) and their swimming, boating, picnics, barbecues and other entertainments, which the young people and their parents enjoyed, their 12th year running in Corfu. Meanwhile back in London some young people are not as fortunate and some did not leave their homes in Hackney. Among the children were Candy aged 14, who sleeps under a coat on a bare mattress, looks after her mum who has depression and reports that 'sometimes' they don't have enough food. There is also Joe, excluded from school but no one has tried to get him back, and Victoria

11, playing in a small tarmac square for her holiday while keeping her eye on the younger children. Hackney had its Youth funding cut by 75 per cent and 8 out of 13 youth clubs closed (McViegh 2011). Subsequent claims by Cameron of a crusade to mend poor parenting and broken social values rang hollow with such stark evidence of inequalities (Elliot-Major 2011).

Dysfunctional families

The Labour Party under Ed Miliband did not provide much effective opposition to the Coalition austerities and appeared to support beliefs in a dysfunctional poor. Labour Graham Allen MP, who had previously written papers with Iain Duncan Smith for his Centre for Social Justice, authored a paper for the Cabinet Office on *Early Intervention, Smart Investment, Massive Savings* (Allen 2011). The cover showed a picture of a small, supposedly 'deprived brain' under a picture of a 'normal' brain. The point of the paper was to demonstrate that brains are formed by early experiences; poor dysfunctional families are not able to supply the right brain experiences and their children are thus are a cost to the taxpayer later in life. The research on which this paper was based showed no such thing. Duncan Smith, briefly Conservative Party leader, then Work and Pensions minister in the Cameron governments, was largely responsible for carrying out austerity policies and creating a universal credit system which even in early stages had left poor people poorer. He always believed that there were 'a growing number of dysfunctional families cut off from what you or I might consider the normal process of education, aspiration, and work' (quoted in Gentleman 2010), and opened a Centre for Social Justice to help reverse social breakdown, producing reports on *Breakdown Britain* (Centre for Social Justice 2006). For Duncan Smith, pathways to poverty were due to individual deficiencies rather than economic or wage policies. His plans to restrict Child Benefit to two children were intended to limit the family size of the poor. He himself had four children.

All this was and continues to be chillingly reminiscent of Victorian eugenic beliefs, when elite white men and some women in the USA and UK espoused beliefs in the inferior intelligence and abilities of lower classes and racial groups. A theme in this book is that these views never disappeared and have continued to underpin educational policies and public views. A new 'progressive eugenics' was developing, claiming evidence from advances in genetic research. Beliefs that differences in ability are largely due to genetic inheritance seemed again to be influencing policy on school selection and separation. Governments were searching for 'better brains' to enhance national economic competitiveness. Dominic Cummings, educated at Durham School and Oxford, and an adviser to Michael Gove, after three years in Russia and working for Iain Duncan Smith, produced a paper for his boss in 2013, quoting studies that supposedly showed that 60–70 per cent of success in National Curriculum tests depend on heritability. Programmes such as *Sure Start*, focusing on the health and education of children 0–3 were apparently useless (Cummings 2013). Indeed, many Sure Start Centres were later closed down in the government's austerity measures. Cummings later turned his attention to organising the *Vote Leave* campaign for the EU Referendum, being credited with inventing the slogan 'Take Back Control', and was reported in 2018 to claim that Westminster would become a smoking ruin if the Brexit supporters did not get what they wanted (see Barnett 2018). Boris Johnson, eventually a vociferous *Leave* supporter, also believed that 'human beings are very far apart in their raw ability ... as many as 16% of our species have an IQ below 85 ... while 2% have an IQ above 130.' Announcing this in the third Margaret Thatcher Annual Lecture, he also claimed that greed is a valuable spur to human activity' (Johnson 2013). He clearly believed he was in the top 2 per cent.

The enemy within all over again

While those Black and white nursery school toddlers from dysfunctional families were a worry to Blair and the Coalition government, more urgent problems were posed by the possible radicalisation of young Muslims. The demonisation of Muslims and Islam as a world religion reached peak proportions during the Coalition and Cameron governments, which discouraged sensible debate and information about national security. While British Imperial involvement in Middle Eastern countries from the 19th century has been noted in previous chapters, the anger felt by people of all faiths at the outcome of the Bush–Blair Iraq War in 2003 and the lies told in support of military intervention, was likely to be regarded as an incentive for possible retaliation.

The bombings in London in 2005, by young men educated in English schools, as noted in Chapter 7, was a catalyst for blanket condemnation of Muslims and Islam. In 2006 Michael Gove MP, future education secretary but then a journalist and writer, produced his book *Celsius 7/7* (Gove 2006) which opened with a introduction 'It's the ideology stupid'. The book detailed his views of Islam, which he claimed was a good historic faith, to be separated from Islamism – a totalitarian ideology using tactics of advancement similar to those used by fascists and communists. It included a chapter on 'The Trojan Horse' describing how fundamentalists Islamists infiltrated their ideology. As a supporter of Israel, he likened Palestinian claims for land to the 1939 Munich agreement when the then Prime Minister Chamberlain capitulated to the Nazi government in Germany The book never mentioned the historical role of the British and French in the Middle East, especially the Sykes-Picot agreement and the Balfour Declaration (see

Chapter 1 of this book). As a founder member of the Henry Jackson Society, a right-wing group set up after the 7/7 bombings, Gove lectured to the Society alongside media owner Rupert Murdoch. The assistant director of this group was journalist Douglas Murray, who later wrote that 'Europe is committing suicide' by encouraging the settlement of migrants, and claimed that multiculturalism was a failed project (Murray 2017). Given Gove's later importance as education secretary, then briefly as justice secretary, and also putting himself forward as leader of the Conservative Party in 2016, it is surprising that not more is known about his own ideologies. In 2016 a biography of Gove was withdrawn from publication.[2] Gove was eventually put in the House of Lords in 2025.

In combating the possible radicalisation of young people, the Prevent strategy, initiated by the Blair government, was extended, a review being completed in 2011 (Francis 2011). The review noted that extremism is defined as active opposition to fundamental British values which include democracy, the rule of law and mutual respect and tolerance of different faiths and beliefs. Schools and universities were expected to recognise and report signs that young people were being drawn into radical ideologies. This became more urgent with the rise (and fall) of the 'Islamic state' (Isis), and the Coalition government made Prevent one of the four elements of Contest, the government's counter-terrorism strategy. The 2015 Counter-Terrorism and Security Act extended the expectations on schools, universities, prisons and other institutions to 'prevent people being drawn into terrorism' (Geary 2015: 272). Teachers had a statutory duty to report signs of non-violent extremism, with children as young as three apparently being referred. It was also notable that cases of Islamic terrorism were matched by attacks by right-wing groups and individuals on Muslims and migrants. By 2017 a third of referrals to the Prevent strategy involved such groups.

Trojan Horses revisited

Government panic ensued over a supposed Islamic take-over of schools in Birmingham in 2014 when a letter originally sent to the City Council in November 2013 was leaked to the media in March 2014 (Shackle 2017). The letter outlined a supposed strategy named 'Operation Trojan Horse' to influence the placement of teachers and governors in 21 schools, replace head teachers and impose an Islamist curriculum. The letter was quickly discredited as a forgery, but the allegations were taken up by the media as an Islamist plot. The use of the term Trojan Horse to suggest Islamic infiltration had been used not only by Michael Gove but in other anti-Muslim writings, and was used by the neo-Nazi Norwegian Anders Behring Breivik who murdered 77 people in Norway in July 2011. The Trojan Horse affair escalated when in April 2014 Gove appointed a former head of the Metropolitan counter-terrorism division, to investigate the claims. Twenty-one schools were inspected by Ofsted and some teachers suspended. One school, Park View, had formerly been judged 'outstanding' in a previous inspection but as the school had become an academy in 2010 the local authority had no control over the school or its curriculum.

The Insted Consultancy (2014) documented the competing narratives of the affair, as did Holmwood and O'Toole (2014) and others. The outcome after legal representations was that there was no plot and teachers were unfairly sacked. The affair also raised issues of the lack of accountability in academies. A further outcome was that that at a lunch with *The Times* owners and the then Home Secretary Theresa May, Gove criticised the Home Office handling of extremist issues and was forced to apologise (Walters 2014). He was sacked as education secretary in July and replaced by Nicky Morgan. A telling comment on the issue was that 'A great deal of damage has been done by politicians who whip up hostility towards migrants coming to this country and towards the Muslim community.' One lawyer commented, 'what has the Trojan Horse affair achieved? Have great swathes of British Muslim children been saved from a path that inexorably leads to terrorism. No, Because they weren't on that path in the first place' (Faux 2017).

A hostile environment

Dealing with immigration issues had been outsourced to a Border Agency, but it had become so chaotic that in 2013 Home Secretary May took it back into the Home Office. It was not until 2018 that more information began to be made public about policies that were intended to create a hostile environment, notionally for illegal immigrants, but which eventually resulted in the deportations and denials of public services to legal and settled citizens, including those of the Windrush generation. An enthusiastic strategy of being tough on immigration was, as always, considered to be a vote winner and was embraced by Theresa May. She told the *Daily Telegraph* in 2012 that her policy was to create a really hostile environment for illegal migrants and promised to reduce immigration to the 'tens of thousands', a policy, which as Elgot later reported 'brought anguish to a generation with every right to live their lives in Britain' (Elgot 2018). It emerged that officials in Caribbean countries had alerted the Foreign Office from 2013 that older Caribbean residents were being classed as illegal immigrants but no action was taken (Gentleman 2018). The Home Office created 'Operation Vaken' curiously, named after a poem promoting fascism in 1930s Germany, and vans were sent around London Boroughs, with billboards saying 'Go Home or Face Arrest (106 arrests in your area last week) Text Home to 780070 for free help and advice'. Apparently 63 per cent of enquiries about free help were hoaxes and only 11 people left. Posters were also placed in minority newspapers, and in mosques and temples urging people to 'Go Home'.

The Immigration Act of 2014 was intended to make it easier to remove those 'with no right to be here' as the Act put it, and landlords, banks, driving instructors, NHS workers and even vicars were expected to check on people's legal status. Taylor later remarked that this Act removed legal protection from Windrush people immigrant from the 1960s and 1970s, who had no legal documentation (Taylor 2018). It later transpired that the Home Office had destroyed documents and landing cards that proved their status (Roundtree 2018). A further immigration Act in 2016 fuelled the hostile environment, with the Department of Education (DfE) instructing schools in December 2016 to collect the nationality, language and birthplace of children although claiming the data would not be sent to the Home Office to check immigration status. This led some parents who feared deportation if their status was not confirmed, to keep their children from school. As McInnery commented 'What society lets families fear deportation for sending their children to school?' (McInnery 2016). May also insisted that overseas students who came to study in Britain should be counted in immigration numbers and that, as she told the Conservative Party conference in 2015, 'far too many of them are not returning home as soon as their visa runs out' (Stewart 2017). In fact, as the Office for National Statistics (ONS) demonstrated, 97 per cent of overseas students went home and only 3 per cent overstayed.

British values

The imperial assertions that British traditions and values were somehow superior to the rest of the world had been severely shaken by the end of the Empire, the independence of former colonial countries and the inclusion of former colonial subjects with different and often denigrated culture and ways of living into the country. The imperial social system was one in which all social classes in Britain assumed the superiority of what passed for British values, which were essentially the values of elite groups and initially included the subordination and deference of lower classes. The Trojan Horse incident and fears of the radicalisation of young Muslims into pseudo-religious violence appeared to be threat to supposed British values. One response of government was the production of a policy requiring all schools to 'actively promote' Fundamental British Values (FBV). Non-statutory guidance issued by the Department of Education (DfE 2014) required schools to promote values of democracy, the rule of law, individual liberty and mutual respect and tolerance of those with different faiths and beliefs. Teachers were expected to do this through the spiritual, moral, social and cultural (SMSC) aspects of the curriculum. Ofsted was expected to police the teachers, who were told by *Teachers Standards* that they must not undermine British values. Carol Vincent studied how teachers were going about the task of producing good citizens imbued with the appropriate values. She noted that when people are asked to describe British values they are often restricted to mentions of the Queen, tea, fish and chips and queuing (Vincent 2019).

The most obvious question was whether the values to be promoted were just British values, or could also be European, Canadian, American, Australian, Indian or any other country which claimed to be a democracy. The Indian constitution of 1949 explicitly supported democracy, the rule of law, liberty and tolerance, with the added advantage of declaring the country secular, despite numerous religions. Schools in England were to be at the front line of ideological and religious wars of the 21st century, but contradictions were obvious. By 1998 faith schools of all kinds were allowed under English law – Anglican, Roman Catholic, Greek Orthodox, Jewish, Muslim, Hindu, Buddhist, but were now required to give priority to secular law while still teaching their own religious beliefs. Academy schools were free of local authority control, which gave governing bodies more opportunity to influence the curriculum, a charge made in the Trojan Horse saga.

But by 2016 a withdrawal from the European Union, possible break-up of a United Kingdom and with the end of Empire still a cause for regret, what actually constituted British values had become a crucial question. Lord Swann's 1985 report (DES 1985a) had pointed out that in a post-colonial world offering all students a relevant education would entail considerable change to a curriculum which still reflected ethnocentric values, some of which were highly questionable in terms of democracy, tolerance and social and racial justice. There were problems in explaining that in the UK democratic beliefs in racial justice are often ignored. Whether schools are actually able to overcome religious intolerance is questionable – the separate religious schools in Northern Ireland, where intolerance between Protestants and Catholics continues, suggest that this is difficult. There are problems for schools in explaining why the British government regards countries which have no regard for democracy and support punitive religious laws, as friends and allies, and even sells them arms, Saudi Arabia and the Gulf States being obvious examples. An important issue in the 21st century was soon recognised as the decline of democracy. Populist movements around the world were finding increased support, especially from those who felt they have no influence over their lives. As Mounk and others have pointed out, people had become disillusioned with liberal politics, and turn to authoritarian populists who could easily become elected dictators, and the survival of liberal democracy itself is then in question (Mounk 2018). This had become a reality by the third decade of 21st-century Britain.

Undemocratic education

Sustaining democracy in nation-states which include minorities and immigrant groups has always proved difficult in nation-states. Education in developed countries was usually regarded as a means of unifying and including diverse groups, despite disagreements about retaining languages, cultures and religions. The English education system was slowly working its way towards inclusive comprehensive schooling with partnerships between central and local government and with parents actually wanting good local schools. By 2010 the idea that education should have democratic input finally disappeared. Schooling became a 'national system nationally administered' (Ainley 2001: 457) with no input from democratically elected local councillors or teachers. Conservative policy from the 1980s was directed to ending local authority participation in maintaining local schools, teachers were to become a workforce to be managed in school businesses. The creation of a plethora of different kinds of school to be available for competitive parental choice further consolidated undemocratic advances.

Private schooling remained the choice of parents who could afford it, for around 7 per cent of children. But 26 per cent of all those taking 'A' level examinations were from private schools and also an over-representation of these students in the 'top' universities. Education services were privatised as far as possible with as much out sourcing to arms-length agencies as possible. Schools meals were supplied by private companies and supply teachers employed through agencies. University education was to be effectively privatised, the Browne Review on fees being published in October 2010 and Minister David Willetts introduced legislation to raise the fees up to £9,000 a year (Browne 2010). The assumption was that universities would obligingly sort themselves into a hierarchy of desirability with some charging lower fees. But no vice-chancellors were about to advertise their institutions as second class. The fee increase was agreed in December, which eventually ended the parliamentary career of Liberal Democrat Nick Clegg who had previously vehemently opposed fee increases. Students were to take out loans, a Student Loans company being privatised and interest charged on loans. Conservatives later claimed that despite fee increases more working class young people entered higher education, although with jobs disappearing and a loan repayment being far distant the decisions were not difficult. Top universities were consistently noted for taking fewer Black and minority students The peak of achievement apparently was to reach the universities of Oxford and Cambridge; only 40 out of 80,000 poor children on free school meals in 2010 claimed to reach this pinnacle. Gove was worried that although 'schools should engines of social mobility' more children from public schools made it to top universities than the entire population of young people eligible for that 'basic benefit'(Gove in DfE 2010: 6). Feeding children was now apparently a benefit.

Academies, free schools, grammar schools, studio schools, special schools, alternative provision schooling, remaining local authority maintained schools, sixth form colleges and university technical colleges were choices in the secondary area, with further education colleges offering enhanced vocational training and overseeing a revived apprenticeship system (Wolf 2011; Tomlinson 2013). Academies, free, grammar and maintained schools could also be faith schools. 'Choice' of school led inexorably to division and inequality by area, by social class and by ethnicity. The 164 remaining grammar schools quietly increased their intakes and the notion of expansion by allowing annexes to the schools took root. Beliefs in selective education and the social mobility of a few working class children continued to underpin policy. Money taken from other parts of the education budget, was given to schools as a Pupil Premium for their disadvantaged children but the end result of the Coalition and Cameron governments was a system with gross inequalities, heavily underfunded, assessment and curriculum centrally controlled and with children, young people and teachers experiencing unprecedented levels of poor mental health. The Institute for Fiscal Studies estimated that between 2011 and 2015 there was a 13 per cent cut in education spending and the School Cuts Organisation noted that at the end of 2015 there had been £3 billion of funding cuts per annum affecting 91 per cent of schools, with more cuts to follow (https://schoolcuts.org.uk).

Undemocratic schools

The stated policy aims of the Coalition government were to reduce attainment gaps between the rich and poor, increase social mobility, and improve England's place in international comparisons and in economic competitiveness. The 2010 white paper, presented by Education Secretary Michael Gove, claimed that what really matters is 'how we are doing in comparison with our international competitors … and for too long we have tolerated the accepted correlation between wealth and achievement at school'. But the gap between rich and poor was apparently not pre-ordained as 'Chinese girls on Free School Meals significantly out-perform the national average' (Cameron and Clegg 2010: 4). Although there were very few Chinese girls on free school meals in the cohort, the message was clear – poverty is no excuse, and if teachers smarten up, schools are made more accountable, and local authority influence removed, then scores in the Programme for International Student Assessment (PISA) tests will improve – as will economic competitiveness with other countries. Structures were to be improved by an accelerated Academies programme. These were set up, as noted in previous chapters, by the Labour government through the 2000 Learning and Skills Act, with the first academies opening in 2002.

The initial policy that academies should have external sponsors contributing funding quickly disappeared, and the Academies Act was the first Act of the Coalition government in July 2010. This allowed all schools to become academies, 'converting' without a sponsor and with no need to consult the local authority. Up to that time there were fewer than 300 academies. By 2015 there were over 4,000 academy schools, with primary schools also allowed to change their status. Academies were directly funded from central government, inspected by Ofsted and eventually eight regional commissioners were appointed by the government to oversee academies in their area. Although some schools under local authority control had developed partnerships, academies run as trusts with boards of trustees, were encouraged to form chains and eventually multi-academy trusts (MATs). By 2015 there were 846 MATs in England, with varying numbers of schools included, and with considerable scope for corruption, with unaccountable finance, large payment to CEOs of trusts, employment of family members and all the problems that big businesses exhibit.[3]

The 2010 Act also created 'free' schools which were actually state schools funded from central government and operating under academy rules. Gove had visited Sweden before the election and was impressed by the Swedish *friskolor* – private schools run with public money. By 2011 there were over 250 applications for schools, from parental, community and religious groups. The parental applications were mainly for free special schools, and religious groups included Muslim, Hindu, Sikh, Jewish and even a Maharishi school. Whether more religious schools could help heal social divisions or even raise school standards was never discussed. By 2015 some 500 free schools were in operation, but by then the Swedish free schools, many of which had become for-profit schools, were in trouble. Swedish free schools could employ unqualified teachers, and the declining Swedish scores in the OECD PISA, international comparisons were blamed on this and on the introduction of parental choice of a variety of schools (Weale 2015: 13).

By 2013 child poverty had risen in poorer areas, with fewer schools in these areas gaining the Ofsted classification of 'Good' and official anxiety was focusing on the lower achievements of white working class boys. The Labour Party, under its leader Ed Miliband, had been too embarrassed to oppose reforms, having created academies in the first place with claims that they would lead to higher standards. By 2013 Labour was becoming nervous at the lack of democratic input and the possible effects on a working class vote. David Blunkett was deputed to undertake a review of structures, funding and achievements and in 2014 made 40 recommendations for improvements. While in his opinion there was no way the current system could revert to local authority overview, he suggested community trusts to oversee groups of schools with better trained governors to avoid Trojan Horse debacles and a national director of school standards (Blunkett 2014). The Conservatives instead appointed a national schools commissioner to help along the academy agenda.

Gove's curriculum

The white paper *The Importance of Teaching* (DfE 2010) and the subsequent 2011 Act set out the Coalition's ideas for raising educational standards. A traditional subject-centred curriculum with continual assessments were the tools. The paper claimed that teachers were to be freed from bureaucracy and their professional status raised, a promise that rang hollow over the years as teachers were even more tightly controlled by assessment requirements. An English Baccalaureate (EBacc) of five traditional subjects, was to be a signal for successful schooling and further test and assessment regimes were introduced. History was to be taught chronologically, and there was to be an emphasis on facts. Especially problematic was the introduction of Progress 8, a score given to schools on the basis of improvement in eight subjects at secondary school. By 2018 vulnerable pupils – the code for working class and Black pupils with learning difficulties – were being forced out of mainstream schools due to accountability measures and a narrow curriculum (Whittaker 2018). A chapter in the 2010 paper focused on bad behaviour, suggesting that Black and working class boys were more likely to behave badly in school and be excluded or truant. Teachers were to have the power to search pupils for weapons, pornography and tobacco and head teachers given more powers to exclude pupils. Separate schooling for the problem children, if not in special schools and units, was ensured in alternative provision schooling out of mainstream schools.

The National Curriculum, although not mandatory in academies, was intended to 'embody children's cultural and scientific inheritance' but should not try to cover all human learning or 'become a vehicle for imposing passing political fads on our children' (DfE 2010: 41). It no longer needed to be spelled out that fads included discussion of race, racism, multiculturalism, immigration and gender issues. A curriculum review in 2013 resulted in an even more tightly controlled curriculum, with content and assessment published subject by subject. Gove's adviser for the History curriculum was Niall Ferguson, noted in the introduction of this book as a believer in the 'Greatness' of the British Empire. The rationale for all this was set out in a speech Gove made to the Social Market Foundation in which he claimed that a 12-subject National Curriculum, but with the five EBacc denoting high attainment, was intended for 'the cultivation of habits of proper thought' (Gove 2013a). Whether a GCSE English curriculum with a mandatory Shakespeare play, poetry since 1789 and a work from 19th and 20th century, fiction but excluding the popular book *To Kill a Mockingbird* (Harper Lee 1960) which teachers had found most useful in discussing racism, would cultivate proper thought has proved questionable. In 2018 a group of white students at Nottingham Trent University who had studied the Gove curriculum were recorded chanting racist abuse outside a Black student's room. Included in chants were 'We hate the Blacks' and 'Sign the Brexit papers' (Rawlinson 2018).

Gove did not take kindly to criticism of his curriculum plans. He described 100 professors and teachers who had signed a letter to the *Independent* paper in March 2013 as 'Enemies of promise … a set of politically motivated individuals who have been actively trying to prevent millions of our poorest children from getting the education they need'. and he 'refused to surrender to these Marxist teachers hell-bent on destroying our schools' (Gove 2013b). Grave charges indeed.[4] The last white paper produced before Cameron resigned after the EU Referendum was labelled *Educational Excellence Everywhere* (DfE 2016) which was intended to move as much teacher training as possible into schools and diminish university influence.

Summary

This chapter has documented some of the activities of the governments between 2010 and 2016, which had the effect of increasing hostility towards settled migrants from former colonial countries and immigrants from EU countries. A hostile environment which eventually encompassed thousands of legal settlers who might be liable for deportation became official policy. Young Black people and Muslims continued to be demonised. Despite a rhetoric of social mobility and helping the disadvantaged, the country became more divided than ever by wealth, income, geography and life chances through education. Poor people continued to be treated with contempt and blamed for their individual and family deficiencies. The government succeeded in its aim of removing democratic accountability in schooling, ensuring semi-privatised school structures that encouraged segregation by class and ethnicity.

The curriculum was further narrowed and testing and assessment in subjects and content decided by central government became the norm. Teachers were expected to teach 'British values' which were and are debatable. Criticism was met by accusations that critics were 'Marxists'. Schools and teachers were more intensely policed by inspection and cuts in funding for schooling defended as part of austerity measures. Private schooling for the children of richer parents continued, and an increase in fees for university education has had consequences still being assessed. There was evidence of an increase in mental health problems and suicides among students. What was learned by children and young people in schools was still influenced by historical imperial understandings. A government-controlled curriculum ensured ignorance of even basic understandings of the post-colonial past and present. Ignorance of the European Union and its actual functions was not addressed in schooling, or in the wider public, and antipathy towards the Union was encouraged by Eurosceptic politicians and the media.

9

A dog's breakfast: Brexit, 2016–19

> Comic Relief this year focused on Malawi and Uganda. I didn't see any acknowledgement that Britain had been the Colonial power in the past. 'Thanks for the gold, lads, Thanks for the diamonds. We had a whip round and got you a fishing rod.'
>
> Boyle 2015

Negotiations between the shuttle of ministers responsible for arranging leaving the European Union (EU) and EU officials dragged on for over three years. It was not until January 2020 that the then Prime Minister Boris Johnson could claim that he has 'got Brexit done'. It was becoming clear that it would take years for the reality of a Britain on its own in a globally trading world would exist, if ever. One certainty was that Britain could not rely on its imperial past or on the fidelity of a Commonwealth. Even as a divided government planned to take the country out of the EU, it became obvious that there had been a massive failure to educate several generations about both the realities of Empire or the EU. One of the few acknowledgements that former colonial countries had been stripped of their wealth under imperialism came, as noted above, from comedian Frankie Boyle. During the annual charitable Comic Relief Day he ironically commented that in exchange for extracted gold and diamonds, the countries were being offered trivial charitable aid. Despite claims of an inclusive national sovereignty long-settled citizens were still not acceptable, people from European countries no longer welcome, and refugees and asylum seekers treated with suspicion and hostility. It could also be asked how inclusive the nation was when, despite Prime Minister May asserting that she wanted 'a country that works for everyone' (May 2016), there were more food banks, an increase in homelessness, cuts to disability allowances and adult social care, with life expectancy actually decreasing in the UK compared to other European countries.

Early Brexit years

The immediate years following the Brexit vote were one of the most turbulent in British political history as parties and individuals slugged it out to present some kind of a Brexit to the British public. The British are fond of their dogs, so dog metaphors appeared to be in order to describe the Brexit negotiations by the end of July 2018, when a final deal on leaving the EU was intended to be agreed on by the following October. In the *Sunday Telegraph* on 22 July, the 'shambles' of Brexit negotiations plus a very hot summer were compared to ancient Greek times for whom the Dog Days were associated with intense heat and drought that made dogs and men go mad and 'lose their marbles' (Booker 2018). Those whose job it was to provide an exit from the European Union at first appeared to have little understanding of the future, with civil servants joking that an Empire 2.00 could be created for trade. After Labour party splits and several leadership elections, Jeremy Corbyn, although a lifelong Eurosceptic, emerged to lead the Labour Party towards what had been labelled a 'soft Brexit' – keeping the UK in a customs union with the EU, if not in a single market. A similar plan eventually devised by Theresa May and her advisors to keep a version of a customs union and solve the problem of the Irish border, was criticised almost immediately by her own 'Brexiteers', notably Boris Johnson, who resigned as Foreign Secretary over the issue on 11 July 2018. The main 'Leave' members of Parliament, Johnson, Michael Gove, Liam Fox and jumping later on to the bandwagon, Jacob Rees-Mogg, were all telling Prime Minister May that it was a hard Brexit or No Deal. Meanwhile, the USA President Donald Trump, appeared to want to start a global trade war in 2018 by putting tariffs on goods from abroad, which made more questionable assertions that British trade with the USA and the rest of the world outside the EU would be easy. The assumption that Britain and the USA were in some kind of special relationship over trade and defence, that had endured from the end of the Second World War, was now in doubt.

What the EU did for us became clearer every year since Brexit. Since the 1992 Maastricht Treaty the EU has worked its way into British politics and economy and the country has been deeply integrated with other EU states. By the second decade of the 21st century the UK shared security and defence; nuclear and other energy policy; employment and social policy; citizenship and free movement; a single market and customs union; agriculture; fishing rights; border checks; asylum and immigration; civil and criminal justice; transport; aviation agreements; tax; economic policies; health policies; university and other research including educational research and student exchange; consumer protection; industrial policy; environment issues, commercial and financial provision and much more (Geddes 2013:7). Britain also used the European Court of Justice (ECJ) which Eurosceptics had always regarded as taking legal decisions away from British courts.[1]

The negotiations between representatives of the EU and the British government over leaving the EU and the legalities and trading arrangement, started in June 2016 when a referendum to leave the EU resulted in 52 per cent voting to leave and 48 per cent to remain. Arguments ensued about which social, geographical, racial, gender or age groups voted most to leave or remain. It finally appeared that main Leavers were older Tory voters who were not necessarily from the richest of the Tory areas, some working class people in both Southern and Northern areas, and voters in coastal towns with few migrants, with young people mainly in favour of Remain. Of the whole possible electorate, only 37 per cent voted to leave the EU. The Conservative Party, never particularly united before the vote, indulged in party antagonisms more hostile than any previous internal squabbles over the Party's leadership and what leaving the EU would mean. There were no reminders of the words of the French Minister Jean Monet, sometimes described as the Father of Europe, who in 1945 forecast that 'There will be no peace in Europe if States rebuild themselves on the basis of national sovereignty, with its implications of prestige politics and economic protectionism' (Monet 1945).[2]

By 2017, contenders for the Conservative Party leadership were using imperial references to colonies and vassal states with Boris Johnson claiming that Britain should not go from a member state to a vassal state (Johnson 2017). Perhaps older people remembered 'doing the Vikings' in primary school, then learning about the Norman invaders, themselves descendants from the Vikings, who eventually managed to take over Britain, with subsequent wars to keep or take over large parts of the European continent. By the later 1500s, as the Introduction to this book noted, the process of turning over a quarter of the world into vassals of a British Empire had begun. The notion that Britain would become a vassal state of the EU was nonsense.

A negative effect of the Brexit vote in 2016 was an escalation of xenophobia, race hate and a strengthening of beliefs in a national sovereignty that excludes 'foreigners'. This included settled Black, Asian and other settled citizens; those from outside the EU; European citizens and migrant workers; asylum seekers and refugees. Even before rules to limit free movement of workers had been formulated, there were attempts to remove settled European or non-EU citizens who had been in the UK for years working and paying taxes, often married or partnered with British citizens. Colour and cultural racism was joined by Euro and global racism. While a closing of national borders was becoming common in some other European countries as far-right politicians were elected, British nationals living and working in European countries began taking their claims to remain European citizens to courts (O'Carroll 2018). The problems of Gibraltar and Northern Ireland continued, both territories having voted to remain in the EU but having borders with an EU country.

In England, while schools were constrained by the 'traditional curriculum' imposed by Gove and his fellow believers, some university students and staff were beginning to question a Eurocentric bias, demanding a de-colonisation of the curriculum. More academics and writers were demonstrating the reality of Black and minority experiences in the UK and the racism unleashed in the USA after the election of Donald Trump. The Black Lives Matter movement in the USA was influential in raising racial justice issues in the UK (McVeigh 2016). But the heirs to Enoch Powell still seemed convinced, as Conservative academic Roger Scruton wrote that 'Brexit will give us back pride in our island roots' (Scruton 2017) – roots which had been nurtured by imperialism. Moral panics over racial and cultural differences underpinned escalating antagonisms and race hate (Goodhart 2017).

Concern that universities might actually be discussing Brexit with their students was questioned by a Conservative MP, Chris Heaton-Harris who in October 2017, wrote to all vice-chancellors asking for the names of professors who might be including such discussion in their lectures. Fortunately, no vice-chancellors obliged. But the consequences of an ethnocentric school curriculum were beginning to be apparent in the racist behaviour of some white university students.

Significant events

2013	David Cameron makes the Bloomberg speech, promising reforms to the EU and a referendum on staying in the EU. UKIP comes second in the East Leigh by-election, taking 27.8% of the vote.
2014	UKIP wins 2.6% vote in European elections. Nigel Farage stays on as an MEP despite campaigning to leave the EU.
2015	(May) General election – Conservatives win a majority and Cameron promises a referendum by 2017. In October the 'Vote Leave' and the 'Britain Stronger in Europe' campaigns are launched. In December 'Labour In for Britain' campaign starts.
2015	Labour leader Ed Miliband resigns and Jeremy Corbyn wins a leadership contest and wins again after a further challenge.
2016	(February) Cameron secures an agreement in Brussels including reducing benefits for migrants. Michael Gove and Boris Johnson both back Leave. (May) They write to Cameron accusing him of 'corroding public trust'. (16 June) MP Jo Cox is murdered.
2016	(23 June) Referendum vote to leave the EU by 52% to 48% (17.4 to 16.3 million). (24 June) Cameron resigns as prime minister. Gove tells Johnson he will back him in leadership vote. (30 June) Gove says Johnson not ready to be PM and puts himself forward.
2016	(5 July) Theresa May leads in Conservative leadership campaign. (13 July) Becomes prime minister. (24 July) Jeremy Corbyn re-elected Labour leader with 62% of vote. (August) Race Disparity Unit set up. Casey review on *Opportunity and Integration*.
2016	(October) May says she will trigger Article 50 on leaving the EU by March 2019. (November) High Court rules that only Parliament, not the government has the power to trigger Article 50. *Daily Mail* newspaper calls the judges 'enemies of the people'. Donald Trump elected 45th president of USA and asks for Nigel Farage to be made British ambassador in Washington.
2017	(January) May makes a speech at Lancaster House announcing a 'Hard Brexit'. Meets and holds hands with Donald Trump at the White House in Washington. (February) Article 50 Bill passes in the House of Commons. Tony Blair urges Britons to rise up against Brexit.

2017	(29 March) May signs letter triggering Article 50. The UK to leave the EU by 29 March 2019. (April) May announces a general election.
2017	(June) Conservative lose their overall majority in general election. Labour gains 30 seats. May does a deal with the Northern Irish DUP for their votes. (13 June) Grenfell Tower fire in London kills over 70 people, many of them minority workers. (November) Black MP David Lammy's Review on minorities in the criminal justice system.
2017	(May) Boris Johnson enthuses about a trade in whisky with India while in a Sikh temple. (15 September) He publishes an article in the *Daily Mail* criticising May. (22 September) In a speech in Florence May says she will seek a two-year transition period to Brexit. (4 October) May, with a heavy cold, makes a disastrous speech to the Conservative Party Conference.
2017	(October) Tory MP Chris Heaton-Harris writes to all university vice-chancellors asking for names of professors teaching European studies with particular reference to Brexit. (November) Roger Scruton writes in *The Times* that 'Brexit will give us back pride in our island roots'.
2018	(February) Corbyn makes a speech supporting a customs union with the EU. (March) May makes a speech at the Mansion House London supporting a hard-line Brexit but with special arrangements.
2018	(March) Communities Minister Sajid Javid publishes *Integrated Communities Strategy: Green Paper: Building Stronger More United Communities*
2018	(January) Theresa May makes an poorly attended speech at Davos on Britain's proud history. (19 March) Prime Minister May and David Davis make a provisional agreement on finally leaving the EU on 31 December 2020. (First week of April) Heads of Commonwealth Meeting in London. May turns down a request to discuss Caribbean deportations with them. Home Secretary Amber Rudd denies deportation targets, then admits to them and resigns on 30 April. Sajid Javid appointed home secretary
2018	(21 June) Celebration of Windrush generation in Westminster Abbey.
2018	(Friday 6 July) May holds a Cabinet day at Chequers and thinks a 'Soft- Brexit' pro-business plan has been agreed. (Monday 10 July) David Davis resigns as Brexit secretary, Dominic Raab appointed. (Tuesday 11 July) Boris Johnson resigns as foreign secretary saying Britain is headed for 'colony status'. Jeremy Hunt appointed. (17 July) White paper published on the Future Relationship between the UK and the EU. (18 July) Johnson makes a resignation speech criticising the Brexit plan.
2018	(26 July) Parliament goes into summer recess with no plans agreed on Brexit. May takes control of Brexit negotiations. Concerns over food, medical and other supplies after a possible hard-Brexit emerge.
2018	(November) May writes an 'Open Letter' to the public claiming that 'we will take back control of our borders' if Parliament would agree to her withdrawal agreement.
2019	(January) The government loses a vote on the withdrawal agreement.
2019	(March) Still no agreement on withdrawal on the date the UK should have left the EU.
2019	(May) Conservatives lose 13,330 councillors in local elections. Theresa May resigns as prime minister on 24 May. (June) Boris Johnson elected leader of Conservative party and thus prime minister.

The politics of self-interest

Politics is a fractious business and people who enter Parliament do so with a variety of motives. The Attlee government of 1945–51, took over after a war which had decimated the economy. The country in the 1930s had reached a peak of gross economic and social inequality. Despite personal antagonisms this Labour government managed to develop a welfare state which benefited the whole society (Dorling and Tomlinson 2017). Since 2010 and especially from 2015 Britain has suffered from governments and politicians who have appeared more concerned with furthering their own careers, fighting their fellow MPs and protecting their own wealth and importance, than working for a fair and equal country. It was clear that by March 2019 when Brexit was due to occur the country was likely to continue to be economically and socially unequal.

In 2015 the Cabinet was dominated by very rich men who had attended public school, several from Eton, followed by Oxford, and who were long-time supporters of the market ideologies of Margaret Thatcher. Prime Minister David Cameron might eventually be known in history as the man responsible for the Referendum and its consequences, while walking away in 2016 with over £10 million in wealth, millions to come in family inheritance and a £25,000 garden shed in which to write his memoirs. He was noted as a man who saw the world through 'the narrowing prism of a social set and sectional interests' (Toynbee and Walker 2015: 2). In 2010, together with wealthy Chancellor George Osborne, the policy of austerity was developed, slashing spending on health, education, housing, social security and local government, which led to some £14 billion cuts in government spending over five years. This was hailed as a success in reducing the national debt, but leaving, as Pettifor put it 'our social fabric in tatters' (Pettifor 2018). Benefit recipients, apart from pensioners, were labelled as idle scroungers and 'social cohesion was subverted' as housing and other benefits were removed and low-paid jobs segregated poor people in cheaper parts of towns (Toynbee and Walker 2015). From 2015, schools were expected to make £3 billion in savings, with the ultimate irony being an announcement in 2018 that school breakfast clubs, many of which had already disappeared, would be given £26 million, but the money would come from a tax on soft drinks.[3]

Cameron never appeared enthusiastic about the EU, but a referendum to leave the EU had been in the 2015 election manifesto. He was worried by the rise of the UKIP vote in European elections in 2014. Nigel Farage, then their Party leader and an MEP (Member of the European Parliament), financed by rich donor Arron Banks, was determined to split the UK from the EU. Cameron was apparently surprised to win the 2015 general election, and he did his best to prevent a referendum by travelling in Europe to persuade the European Commission to change some of the rules on migration and benefits. He did manage to negotiate a temporary brake on welfare benefits for EU migrants, but that was not sufficient to placate his increasingly Eurosceptic colleagues. Theresa May, as home secretary, had suggested migrants should be refused entry to the country unless they had a job, while Sajid Javid, then business secretary, suggested only migrants from richer countries as measured by their gross domestic product (GDP), should travel freely. Visas were available for rich people. A Tier 1 visa allowed an immigrant to settle permanently in the UK if they invested £10 million. In early 2018, wealthy Chinese had been given 146 out of 355 investor visas. The referendum went ahead on 23 June 2016, although there were subsequent suggestions, notably from former Prime Minister Blair, that the referendum could be run again and might produce a different result. But the 'Committee for Exiting the European Union' had already started negotiations, work towards leaving the EU continued, the arguments, demands, conciliations and insults documented daily in all newspapers and on social media.

Brexit lies and wishful thinking

The political arguments and campaigns before the referendum, the outright lies told during the campaign and the jockeying for leadership of the Conservative Party after June 2016, have been presented in detail in two books by the political editor of the *Sunday Times* (Shipman 2016, 2017) and in other books produced quickly after the Brexit vote.[4] The Leave campaign, led by former education adviser Dominic Cummings, who had spent three years in Russia and perhaps knew something about disinformation, posted an online video which claimed 'every week the United Kingdom sends £350 million of tax-payers money to the EU … Vote leave, let's take control' (Shipman 2016: 55). The money claim was a lie but appeared on the Leave bus which toured the country in 2016, with Boris Johnson loudly supporting the claim that the money would go to the NHS. Michael Gove, former education secretary and a key figure in the 'Vote leave' campaign, claimed during the campaign that Turkey and four other countries would soon join the EU, leading to a possible 5.2 million more migrants into Britain with visa-free travel open to 77 million Turkish citizens This claim was a lie. In 2018 he admitted the Leave campaign should not have 'stoked up fears' about Turkish migration (Sabbagh 2018). On 27 July the House of Commons Digital, Culture Media and Sport Select Committee (DCMS) published a report on their enquiries into the misinformation used by the Vote Leave campaign through the use of social media, notably Facebook, and concerns about the funding of the Leave campaign. The committee concluded that data abuses and the disinformation spread, constituted a risk to democracy (Waterson 2018).

The 'Stronger In' campaign found it hard to combat the lies and present a positive view of the EU. The subsequent negotiations over the way the country would leave the European Union was eventually described as a 'war', with the ministerial group meeting to decide the future of the country described as a 'War Cabinet' (Montgomerie and Pancevski 2017). The way ministers and their advisers actually conducted themselves between June 2016 and the 2017 general election and subsequently, was perhaps more reminiscent of toddlers fighting, with a great deal of bad language and insults. Boris Johnson had made no secret of his wish to become Tory leader and prime minister, and his friend Michael Gove promised to support his candidacy when Cameron resigned on 24 June 2016 and a leadership contest ensued. Colleagues opposing Johnson had previously formed an 'Anyone but Boris' group (Shipman 2016: 508). On 30 June Gove suddenly announced he was not supporting Boris but standing himself for the leadership. In the event, Theresa May was elected leader and became prime minister, with family money in an offshore tax haven left over from the Empire.[5]

May and Machiavelli

As prime minister, May had grasped that any discussion of the future of Britain after Brexit must depend on new trade partners, if the £44 billion trade done annually with the EU was to disappear. Her first foray was to the USA, to congratulate President Donald Trump on his election in November 2016, then to rush over as his first overseas visiting prime minister to beg for trade deals, and inadvertently be photographed holding his hand. Other ministers, notably Liam Fox, were sent off to attempt to make trade deals with India and China. Selling arms had long been a major trade for Britain and this was to continue, often to countries with poor records of human rights and little regard for civilian populations, In March 2018 the Crown Prince of Saudi Arabia was welcomed by May and deals to sell more fighter planes and other arms agreed, although Saudi Arabia was at war with Yemen, a former British protectorate.

Other problems were likely to be with the Commonwealth countries, noted in the previous chapter as being less enthusiastic over trade deals. Much was to be made of hosting the Commonwealth Heads of Government Conference in London in April 2018, where it was hoped trade would be an important topic. The Commonwealth countries were actually less interested in trade deals than in their debts and especially in climate change. The Conference was originally scheduled to meet in Vanatu (colonised 1887, independence 1980) but had to move as tropical storms and floods affected the island. The countries had also given notice that in the event of the Queen's death they wanted to discuss her successor as head of the Commonwealth as it was by no means agreed on her heir (Aing-Roy and

Bowcott 2018). Eventually, it was reported that at the prompting of the Queen, the heads of governments agreed that Prince Charles should take over as head after her as indeed he did.

May had a particularly difficult time as prime minister, although following Italian nobleman Machiavelli's advice from the 16th century, she endeavoured to keep her enemies closer by appointing them to her Cabinet, while aware that he also said, 'one can make this generalisation about men: they are ungrateful, fickle, liars and deceivers, they shun danger and are greedy for profit' (Machiavelli in Bull 1961: 96). Her foreign secretary, Boris Johnson, was regarded with amazement by the global diplomatic world for his gaffes and ignorance, and his eventual resignation from the post in July 2018 was reported to have been greeted with cheers and champagne in the Foreign Office. She gave in to the campaign led by Gina Miller, noted in the introduction to this book as being vilified as a 'bloody immigrant', when High Court judges ruled that Parliament should eventually have a vote on the terms of leaving the EU. An independent judiciary was apparently in some danger when the *Daily Mail* newspaper denounced the judges as 'enemies of the people' (Slack 2016). May seemed concerned enough about racial inequalities to order the creation of a Race Disparities Unit in Augus 2016. This Unit produced a report on Ethnic Disparities which put a somewhat skewed interpretation on its collection of race and ethnic statistics (Gov.UK 2017). Although mentioning in her memoir after leaving office her concerns over women's treatment and child sexual abuse, May did not mention race and ethnicity or this Unit (May 2023). On 29 March 2017, May finally signed the letter triggering Article 50 in the 2009 Lisbon Treaty, which allowed for withdrawal of a member state from the EU. Despite speeches at Lancaster House and in Florence, suggesting a 'Hard Brexit' and more plotting by her colleagues to remove her from office after she made a poor speech at the Conservative Party conference in October 2017, by March 2018 she and Brexit Secretary David Davis signed a provisional agreement with the EU over leaving terms. Michael Gove, now environment minister, was immediately upset about the fate of British fish in the agreement.

The politics of exclusion

There were many reasons why 17.4 million people voted to leave the European Union. As this book has suggested, one reason was a mindset of Empire, a nostalgia for an imperial past nurtured by a desire for a British national sovereignty unencumbered by the presence in this country of those 'black and brown inferiors' that Victorian England tolerated providing that they toiled oversees. But around 13 per cent of the population are the descendants of these 'toilers' who came post-war to build up the economy as well as take the jobs the white workers did not want to do. As Afua Hirsch eloquently noted, colour of skin or a foreign-sounding name brings the question 'where are you from?' to which in their imagination is 'a mythical darkie country' (Hirsch 2018: 32). The language of a 'Great' Britain spoke of a colonial past when a quarter of the world 'belonged to us'. As noted, the doctrine of what became 'Powellism' – Enoch Powell's views of national sovereignty, anti-immigration and Euroscepticism – surfaced regularly over the years (Tomlinson 2018). It nurtured the assumption by governments and the public that a Great Britain with a former Empire had no need of closer union with its European neighbours, even as that Empire was disintegrating. This book has also recorded that there has been a massive failure in the education system to teach truthfully about Empire and its consequences or about the EU.

By the 21st century the UK had become deeply integrated with other member states, especially in trade and investment and security issues.[6] But public opinion surveys, as Geddes noted in 2013 'show that British people declared less knowledge of interest in and confidence in the EU than citizens of the other EU states' (Geddes 2103: 6). Claims that leaving the EU would result in less immigration, led to settled citizens, EU workers, refugees and those 'foreigners' being targeted for open and covert hate crime and that familiar message 'Go Home'. The most shocking hate crime happened the week before the Brexit vote on 16 June, when Labour MP Jo Cox was murdered in her Yorkshire constituency by a man with links to the far-right neo-Nazi group 'Britain First'. The police recorded a 57 per cent rise in reported race crime incidents after the vote, including the murder of a Polish man in Harlow, Essex, in September 2016. The Polish Ambassador visited the town and expressed shock at the murder and the rise in xenophobic attacks following the Brexit decision (Weaver 2016).

In education, the organisation 'Reclaiming Schools' documented children being subject to racist abuse by adults and other children, with five-year-olds asking their teachers when they would 'be forced to leave' (Reclaiming Schools 2016). While journalists, and academic and voluntary organisations quickly collected evidence of racial and xenophobic attacks, especially on Muslim women,[7] journalist Aditya Chakrabortty encapsulated the situation in an article 'After a campaign scarred by bigotry it is now OK to be racist in Britain' (Chakrabortty 2016). He also noted that during the campaign Boris Johnson and Michael Gove had falsely claimed that Turkey and its 77 million Muslims would join the EU, Nigel Farage claimed that Syrian refugees would put British women at risk of sexual assault, Polish school children were given cards calling them vermin and telling them to leave the EU, and people made such comments as 'we've got the country back' and 'blow up that f*****g mosque' (Chakrabortty 2016: 33). The history of the previous 120 years demonstrated that immigration had always been a persistent and often vicious topic of discussion (see Dorling and Tomlinson 2020: 7–9).

After the 2017 general election Prime Minister May expressed horror at the racist, sexist and anti-Semitic attacks on candidates. Long-serving Labour MP Diane Abbott received racist abuse every day, and Conservative candidate Ameet Jogia found graffiti in the voting booths reading 'keep Pakis out of politics' (Mason 2017). On 13 June 2017 a horrendous fire engulfed Grenfell Tower, a London Tower Block of flats with over 70 people killed. Although the block was in one of the richest boroughs in London, the residents were mainly poor and/or minority. The resulting lack of assistance to the survivors or acceptance of responsibility by the local council or national government led to the conclusion in a national newspaper 'Behind this disaster lies a brutal indifference to the lives of the poor' (Observer 2017) and to the lives of minorities. After years of attempts to 'kick racism out of football' open racism against Black, minority and European footballers and referees surfaced again with the Chairman of the Football Association and the Technical Director accused of failures to tackle racism and sexism in the game (Taylor 2017) and a Northern Irish footballer apologising for his wife's racist tweet against the Romanian Referee, 'Romanian Gypsy c★★t, to actually think Northern Ireland has probably homed one of his smelly relatives' (Hunter 2017). Some targets for hate were off limits. Meghan Markle, the mixed race fiancé of Prince Harry, later his wife, was certainly not to be targeted by racist slurs, as the *Daily Mail* announced in January 2018, after the partner of Henry Bolton, the current UKIP leader, claimed that 'Meghan's seed will taint our Royal Family' (Owen 2018). Bolton lost his job and he was forced to apologise. With the documentation of such hate, indifference and exclusion, government pronouncements on social integration rang hollow.

Integration all over again

But governments over the years have persisted in producing papers and policies examining the barriers to an ill-defined notion of integration. Chapter 3 showed that post-war immigration from former colonial countries was met with much hostility, despite the migrants filling labour needs. A plethora of government and academic literature on the themes of assimilation, integration and living in culturally plural societies had appeared, much of it naïve and lacking a historical context. Eventually the language of integration became the favourite way of complaining that Black and ethnic minorities and recent migrants were reluctant to be absorbed into what was assumed to be a homogeneous majority culture and way of life. The 2011 census showed 81 per cent living in the country defining themselves as white British or white Irish. Most settled minority citizens lived in London, Manchester and the West Midlands and also in northern towns where owners of textile mills had used their labour then closed the mills as they became unprofitable. The settlement of newer migrants and refugees was largely determined by government policies of dispersal, to Glasgow and Gloucester for example, while EU migrant workers went where the work was – potato picking in Lincolnshire – or moved into urban areas where other minorities lived in low cost housing. The familiar and untrue complaints surfaced continually over the years, that migrants took jobs, houses, medical services and overwhelmed schools. By the early 21st century and after the events of 9/11 in the USA, particular hostility was directed at Muslim communities, and as Abbas noted, politicians, the media and public views across the political spectrum, blamed Muslims for cultural separatism and self-imposed segregation (Abbas 2005). The idea spread that 'politically correct' multiculturalism had fostered fragmentation rather than integration and 'Britishness'.

The successive reports blaming minorities for segregation continued to lack background history. Riots in Northern towns in 2001 were blamed on Asian segregation in the reports by Ted Cantle and others and in 2005 Cantle set up an Institute for Community Cohesion and an ICOCO Foundation, which was claimed as the leading authority on community cohesion. In 2016, at the instigation of David Cameron, Dame Louise Casey published a review *Opportunity and Integration* (Casey 2016) which again with no historical context, complained that people felt overwhelmed by demographic shifts in their communities and blamed harmful community practices and possible terrorism. Communities with poor English and not enough adherence to 'British values' were blamed again. In 2017 Ted Cantle worried that the government had not responded to the Casey review and chaired another group reporting on *Integration and Demonisation* (APPG 2017). His All Party Group included Chukku Umunna MP and the Bishop of Oxford and it acknowledged the demonisation and xenophobia that were impediments to integration. The government eventually responded to the Casey review with a Controlling Migration Fund, and in 2018 produced yet another *Integrated Strategies* Green Paper (HM Government 2018a). Sajid Javid, then Housing, Communities and Local Government Minister, complained in a foreword that his Pakistani mother and elderly ladies like her, could not speak English. This report also noted there was a lack of social mixing, high unemployment among minorities, more in prison – as a report by David Lammy MP had indicated – and there was a need to promote 'the values that unite us'. Evidence seemed to suggest that these values were more connected to exclusion, xenophobia and racism than to democracy, tolerance and even the rule of law.

Windrush and a hostile environment again

It was noted in the previous chapter that in 2010 Theresa May was appointed home secretary, and Prime Minister Cameron decided that 'a tough stance on immigration was a flagship party offering'. Although this had been Party policy for years, it was enthusiastically taken up by May (Malik 2018). She promised in 2012 to create a 'really hostile environment' to illegal migration and reduce legal migration to what became a mantra of 'the tens of thousands'. As noted she insisted on counting international students as immigrants, insisting that many did not return home after their studies. Even when research demonstrated that 97 per cent of university students coming to study did return to their home countries, she continued this policy. But immigration Acts in 2014 and 2016 fuelled a hostile environment, with policies restricting healthcare, bank accounts, renting, marriage and other rights for suspected illegal migrants, with landlords, doctors and NHS staff, teachers, vicars and others expected to check on immigration status. Schools were told in December 2016 to collect the nationality and birthplace of migrant, refugee and asylum-seeking children, although told the information would not be sent to the Home Office. Campaign groups challenged this and eventually the DfE announced collection would cease in September 2019 but the collected data retained.

All this helped fuel a scandal when it became clear that many people without regular documentation, which included Caribbean arrivals as children from the Windrush generation, had been targeted for deportation. The issue was raised in 2013 in response to a Parliamentary question and the government admitted there was a problem with undocumented migrants. (Gentleman 2018a). By April 2018, the treatment of many of the Windrush generation was reported daily in the media during April 2018. Cases included the denial of cancer treatment to a man who had lived and worked in England for 44 years, and the attempted deportation of a woman who had lived in the country for 50 years and worked as a cook in the House of Commons (Gentleman 2018b).

It emerged that people arriving as children from Jamaica had been deported back to the island if they had no regular documentation, the *Jamaican Gleaner* reporting in 2016 that over 9,000 people had been sent back to the island, mainly from the UK. A National Organisation for Deported Migrants (NODP) had been set up in Jamaica in 2016, supported from the British High Commission, and booklets given to deported arrivals (in a country they had never lived in) with such nonsensical instructions as 'try to speak Jamaican' and 'keep your wallet safe' (Saunders 2016). As noted, the Home Office had actually destroyed thousands of landing cards and other documents of Caribbean migrants that would have proved entitlement to citizenship (Roundtree 2018). Amber Rudd MP, appointed as home secretary after May became prime minister, first denied the Home Office had targets for deportation, then had to resign her job after admitting she had 'misled' Parliament over deportation targets (McCann 2018). She issued an apology for the 'appalling' actions of her own department towards Windrush citizens.

Sajid Javid was appointed home secretary in her place and together with the prime minister, attended a celebration of the contribution of the Windrush generation and their descendants in Westminster Abbey on 22 June. Despite all this a YouGov poll in the last week of April 2018 found a majority of those polled supported a 'hostile environment' policy towards immigrants (Nevett 2018).

Schools, universities and the curriculum

The curriculum in England from the 1980s, and especially from 2010, had largely become a vehicle for government – approved learning, obsessed with a traditional model of transmitting approved 'knowledge'. In 2018 'A' level History candidates were presented with a module in which post-war history began in 1951 and ended in 1997, thus missing out the Attlee government creation of the welfare state and ending before the first Blair government (Abrams 2018). The curriculum was in no way changed to overcome the dishonest presentation of the past and present history of colonialism and its consequences, or relationships with Europe and the rest of the world. Book publishers, having realised from the 1980s that books should include some minority characters, were found in 2018 to produce only 1 per cent of children's books with a main Black or minority character (Flood 2018). While there was limited research on how Michael Gove's curriculum, imposed in 2013, has affected schools, the consequences can be assessed by examining the views of students in higher education who have experienced the recent curriculum. The picture to 2018 was bleak. The director of the South Asian Centre at the LSE noted that:

> Students arrive at university completely ignorant about the Empire, that vital part of history. When we talk of Syria they have no knowledge of Britain's role in the Middle East over the last century … they have no clue about the history of immigration. They don't understand why people of other ethnicities came to Britain in the first place, they haven't learned about it in school. (Mohsin 2016)

Perhaps this is why 32 medical students were suspended at Cardiff University in 2017 for a play in which they mocked one of their lecturers by blacking up and wearing a dildo portraying him as a 'stereotypical hyper sexualised black man'. When African students complained, they were told they were unduly sensitive (Morris 2017). The university produced a report which included the familiar rhetoric that issues relating to equality and diversity were taken very seriously. At Exeter University a law student posted screenshots of his fellow law students calling people 'p**i' and 'n***a sluts' and signs saying 'Rights for Whites' had been found on the campus (Motavali 2018). Those

Nottingham students chanting 'We hate Blacks' and 'Sign the Brexit papers' were noted in Chapter 8. In May 2018 11 students at Warwick University were suspended for their rape and racist 'jokes' being found on a Facebook 'chat'. These included comments such as 'rape 100 girls' and 'Love Hitler … hate Jews and Corbyn' (Bushey 2018). Comments on the incidents by other students included claims that free speech was being eroded by private conversations being criticised.

Not all students have succumbed to such stupidity, although objecting to a racist past or present would never be easy. Attempts by students at Oxford to remove the statue of Cecil Rhodes from Oriel College and at Cambridge to return a golden cockerel stolen from Nigeria were frowned on by the university administrations. Suggestions that the English curriculum at Cambridge could be 'decolonised' by including a diversity of literature was met with racist and sexist abuse, especially directed at Lola Olufemi, the Cambridge Student Union woman's officer, with the *Daily Telegraph* claiming white authors would be replaced by Black authors (Khomami and Watts 2017). At least the *National Geographic* magazine acknowledged, on the 50th anniversary of the assassination of Martin Luther King Jr in the USA, that in the past its coverage of Black and ethnic minorities in the magazine had been historically racist, by promoting caricatures of the noble savage and presenting 'White teenage boys with pictures of brown bare breasts' with westerners always fully clothed (Greenfield 2018).

During the Brexit negotiations there was apparently some suspicion in government that universities were actually discussing Europe and the vote to leave the EU. Chris Heaton-Harris, MP for Daventry and a former MEP and Chair from 2010–16 of the Eurosceptic European Research group, wrote to all university vice-chancellors in the UK. He wanted to know the names of academics lecturing on Brexit. His request was described by Lord Patten, Chancellor of Oxford University as 'idiotic and offensive Leninism' and no VCs obliged (see Private Eye 2018). In July 2018 after the Brexit secretary David Davis and his deputy had resigned, Dominic Raab was appointed as the new Brexit secretary with Heaton-Harris as the new deputy.[8]

Summary

By July 2018 politicians, journalists and the public were tired of hearing about Brexit and worried about what a *Telegraph* journalist described as 'The glaring shambles of the Brexit negotiations' (Booker 2018). Negotiations went from bad to worse and although May wrote an 'Open Letter' to the public in November 2018 (BBC News 2018) attempting to explain her Withdrawal Agreement, she lost another vote in Parliament in January 2019. By March 2019, worried about trade, people were stockpiling toilet rolls and baked beans, and hospitals stocked up on medical supplies. In local elections in the spring the Conservative Party lost some 1,330 seats, and Theresa May gave up and resigned on 24 May 2019. Thirteen hopeful candidates vied to be the next prime minister, and 91,153 paid-up members of the Conservative Party (0.3 per cent of all citizens) voted Boris Johnson in as leader of the party and thus prime minister in July. Theresa was the second female prime minister to leave Downing Street shedding tears, but she then set about writing a book in which she blamed a variety of individuals and groups who had opposed her efforts to get Brexit done. She directed vitriol especially at the speaker of the House of Commons, John Bercow, who she claimed had abused his powers to 'thwart the delivery of Brexit' (May 2023: 44), and she blamed Jeremy Corbyn and the Labour Party who had 'scuppered' her withdrawal agreement. She even blamed Keir Starmer, only elected an MP in 2015, for 'playing to those in the Labour Party who wanted a second referendum' (May 2023: 58)

The persistence of post-imperial ideologies and claims that a post-Brexit future will 'give us back our island roots' and make Britain 'Great' were directed at populations already ageing, angry at their economic situation and willing to blame immigrants and 'foreigners' for their situation. *Financial Times* writer Stephens wrote that 'Today's nostalgia (for the past) has become an engine of nationalism, it thrives on the economic and cultural insecurities thrown up by globalisation, we look backwards for a safe identity' (Stephens 2018). The evidence suggested it would be a 'white' identity. Despite limited attempts over the years to develop a more realistic education system that presented young people with the realities of the past and present of their country's position in the world, and leave behind the whitewashing of the past which still imbues schools and higher education curricula, those in government, their advisers and their academic supporters, persisted with the myths and delusions. As a third prime minister since the Brexit vote took office the ideological commitment of those currently in power prevented any serious debate on what kind of future Britain could look forward to in a world in which popularism, nationalism and protectionism in trade were challenging democracy and global engagement. The overt racism and xenophobia, always there but unleashed after the Brexit vote, continued to damage the country.

10

Boris, COVID and educational chaos, 2019–22

There have been many politicians and prime ministers in Britain who were moral hazards in terms of their personal lives and self-interest, but the election of Alexander Boris de Pfeifle Johnson as leader of the Conservative Party and thus prime minister on 24 July 2019 was of a different order. Newly elected prime ministers usually have to deal with unexpected and often dramatic events, and Johnson was no exception. History usually gives a verdict on how events are dealt with and to date there are few plaudits for the period to 2022. In his first year in office in 2020, 81,795 people died of COVID-19 related illness in England and Wales (ONS 2021), with Black men three times more likely to die than white men and a generation of children have had their lives affected by the pandemic. Much has already been written on Johnson, his life and his effect on the country as prime minister. Well known for his stunts as London mayor for two terms from 2008 (and for making it back into Parliament in 2015), he cultivated his ruffled blond hair and a shambling gait to appear 'lovable', although it had long been noted that Johnson was actually known for duplicity, lies and adultery. He 'had long been aware that he could get away with not only extramarital affairs, gratuitous insults and even racist, sexist and homophobic comments that would have killed of most political careers' (Dorling and Tomlinson 2020: 362 and see Bower 2020; Seldon and Newell 2023). These included referring to African children as Piccininnis with watermelon smiles and to Muslim women wearing the burka as looking like letterboxes. Theresa May had been well aware of his ambition to take her place and in appointing him foreign secretary had attempted to follow the politic rule of 'keep your enemies close'. In a final comment on the Johnson administration, Rawnsley (2025) referred to the 'grim chaos' of the period which demonstrated that stunts and wheezes do not make a state smarter.

Johnson won the leadership election in July 2019 out of 13 candidates, 6 of whom like him had attended Eton and Oxford University. He had a sixth child in April 2020 with his then fiancé Carrie Symonds while still married to his second wife, with whom he had four children, and was now divorcing. He went on to marry Symonds in a ceremony paid for by rich supporter and owner of JCB Diggers Anthony Rampton and in a general election campaign in November 2019 triumphantly drove a JCB machine through a wall of Styrofoam bricks with the label 'Get Brexit done' (Bale

2023). He had two more children with Carrie while in office, and having appointed Dominic Cummings as his chief advisor, found life difficult when she and Cummings disagreed on policy. He finally sacked Cummings in November 2020.

Despite a promise to 'do or die' in delivering Brexit by October 2019, he did neither and instead sacked 21 unsupportive Conservative MPs and attempted to leave the EU by unconstitutional means. He planned to stop Parliamentary scrutiny of a Withdrawal Bill by proroguing (suspending) Parliament and persuaded the Queen to agree. The move was challenged in the High Court and Supreme Courts in London and Scotland. Lady Hale, chief of the Supreme Court judges, delivered the verdict that the move was unlawful. Parliament opened again in October and his Attorney General Suella Braverman, threatened to reduce the powers of judges, presumably having forgotten that in democracies no one is above the law, even prime ministers. The political parties agreed on a general election on 12 December and the Conservatives won with an 80-seat majority. Jeremy Corbyn, Labour leader, was vilified during the campaign as being anti-Semitic and supporting a two- state solution for the Israeli–Palestine conflict, ongoing since the British gave up overseeing the territory in 1948. Johnson promised, as May had, to reduce immigration numbers. The trials of Brexit had overtaken issues of Empire and Commonwealth, although identity, nationalism and fear of immigration continued to be important during the 2019 election campaign. Booth pointed out that 'Conservative voters were almost twice as likely as Labour voters to yearn for Britain to still have an empire', although a number of older Labour voters also appeared to hold nostalgic views of Empire (Booth 2020). Johnson claimed to have 'got Brexit done' and officially banged a gong on 31 January 2020. But by then it became clear that a global virus was spreading in the UK and the Scientific Advisory Committee for Emergencies to the government (SAGE) met on 22 January. The UK finally followed other European countries in telling the public to stay at home on 23 March and schools closed. Although a Civil Contingency committee, COBRA, was set up, Johnson missed five meetings while finalising his divorce and in April becoming ill with COVID-19 himself. Although he survived the virus, the following two and a half years were disastrous for a generation of children as the pandemic affected their education and their parents' and carers' lives. It had taken over two centuries to get almost all children to attend a school in a building away from their homes, and this was an interruption in the formal way young people received current 'knowledge'.

The murder of George Floyd in May 2020 in the US was a catalyst for young people worldwide to protest against racial injustices past and present, including toppling statues of imperialists. Right-wing politicians quickly turned this into a 'war on woke', which led Johnson to appoint a Commission on Ethnic Disparities, chaired by Tony (later Lord) Sewell, who in previous research had blamed phallocentrism, rap and reggae for Black youth problems (Sewell 1997). The Conservatives and Nigel Farage's Brexit, later known as the Reform Party increased media attacks on minorities, immigrants and anti-racists despite the Conservatives eventually boasting in this government a chancellor of Indian origin, Rishi Sunak, and an equalities minister of Nigerian origin, Kemi Badenoch. Hostility to immigration, especially the immigrants who arrived on small boats across the Channel continued, and pandering to this Johnson agreed to a scheme to deport asylum seekers to Rwanda[1] in April 2022. This scheme was declared unlawful by the UK Supreme Court in 2023.

This chapter briefly documents some of the chaotic government policies and actions over this period, with failures of those supposedly in charge of the country failing to follow their own rules, a mismanaged economy, health and education and a final scandal which led to his own MPs telling him to resign, marked the end of a Johnson administration. It did not mean an end to chaos, as the following competition for a successor had eight MPs in contention, with Liz Truss emerging the victor, but lasting only 49 days in the job.

Significant events

2019	(24 July) Boris Johnson becomes prime minister. Dominic Cummings as Chief adviser.
2019	(September–October) Attempts to prorogue Parliament declared unconstitutional.
2019	(12 December) General election won by Conservatives. Dominic Raab deputy PM, Sajid Javid chancellor of the exchequer, Matt Hancock health secretary, Gavin Williamson education secretary.
2020	(22 January) First meeting of a Scientific Advisory Group for Emergencies (SAGE) to discuss the COVID virus spreading globally, initially in China. Chief scientific advisor Patrick Vallance, chief medical officer Chris Whitty.
2020	(6 January) Donald Trump, having lost the election to be president of the USA again, encourages his supporters to attack Congress in Washington who were meeting to confirm Joe Biden as president. He then spends four years asserting the election was 'stolen'.
2020	(31 January) UK leaves the European Union. Cummings puts out an advertisement for 'weirdos and misfits' to work in Whitehall.
2020	(23 March) First COVID 'lockdown'. Johnson announces on all TV main channels 'You must stay at home'. Schools closed (apart from those taking in children of key workers and the vulnerable).
2020	(27 March) Dominic Cummings drives family to Durham despite lockdown, and 'tests his eyesight' driving to Barnard Castle before returning to London. (20 May – Police investigate this.)
2020	(5 April) Johnson hospitalised with COVID. Back to work on 26 April.

Education and Race

2020	(25 May) George Floyd, a Black man, is killed by a white policeman in Minneapolis, USA. Resurgence of a Black Lives Matter (BLM) movement and woke agenda from right-wing politicians and activists.
2020	(7 June) Statue of slave trader Edward Coston pulled down and thrown in the river in Bristol England by BLM protesters.
2020	(15 June) Johnson appoints a Commission on Race and Ethnic Disparities, chaired by Tony Sewell.
2020	(June/July) Lockdown lifted. Some schools reopen. Exams take place with teacher assessments and 'the algorithm'. Concern over 'A' level marking.
2020	(15 August) Rishi Sunak, new chancellor of the exchequer, announces an 'eat out to help out' plan, which causes an increase in COVID cases.
2020	(October–November–December) Lockdowns in regional tiers, including over Christmas.
2020	(November) Equalities Minister Kemi Badenoch says teaching Critical Race Theory (CRT) in schools is illegal. New Ofsted inspection framework affects equality and diversity providers. Cummings sacked as Johnson adviser.
2021	(January) Lockdown again until February– March. Britain is 15th out of 28 EU countries in terms of excess deaths from COVID.
2021	(March) Commission on Race and Ethnic Disparities (Sewell report) published.
2021	(9 April) Prince Phillip, the Queen's husband of 55 years, dies and 16 April Johnson apologises to the Queen over parties held in Downing Street the day before Phillip's funeral.
2021	(June) Home Secretary Priti Patel introduces a Nationality and Borders Bill, further criminalising illegal migrants. It becomes law on 6 July 2021. (9 Sept) Gavin Williamson sacked as education secretary but given a knighthood in March 2022. Nadhim Zahawi new education secretary.
2021	(30 November) *Daily Mirror* reports that ten 'gatherings' took place in or around Downing Street over Christmas 2020 and Allegra Stratton press secretary seen on video joking about parties. Reports of parties over 2020 denied by or minimised by Johnson.
2021	(December) Civil servant Sue Gray appointed to inquire into 'Partygate' and Metropolitan police begin an inquiry.
2022	(22 February) President Putin's Russian troops invade the Ukraine, calling it a 'special military operation'.
2022	(April) Johnson announces a 'Migration and Economic Development Plan' to deport asylum seekers and other migrants to Rwanda.
2022	(May) Sue Grey's report published saying there was 'excessive drinking' at parties illegally held during lockdowns. Johnson and other staff receive penalty notices from police. He is accused of lying to Parliament about parties.
2022	(June) Vote of no confidence in Johnson is won by him but several Cabinet members including Rishi Sunak resign from government. 9 June Boris Johnson resigns as prime minister.
2022	(6 September) Liz Truss elected prime minister, resigns 49 days later. A churn of education secretaries are appointed, Michelle Donelan (two days), James Cleverly (two months), Kit Malthouse (49 days).
2022	(25 October) Rishi Sunak elected prime minister. Gillian Keegan education secretary.

COVID lockdowns

The lack of preparation for a global pandemic was probably not surprising, since the last pandemic that people remembered was the 1918 flu illness which killed millions worldwide. Despite various scares related to outbreaks of cross-species-related illnesses most health planning had assumed a flu-like virus which could be contained by ordinary nursing or achieving herd immunity if enough people suffered. The arrival of the COVID-19 virus which had been spreading in the UK since early 2020 came as a shock to government and the public. Tim Shipman recorded an account of a text message to PM Boris Johnson from his advisor Cummings on 12 March 2020 as 'We've got big problems coming. The Cabinet Office is terrifyingly shit. Totally behind the pace. We must announce today. Not next week. If you feel ill with cold or flu, stay home' (Shipman 2024: 294). It took over a week for Johnson to announce what became described as a lockdown on 23 March. Johnson and the experts on SAGE – the scientific advisory group for emergencies, were proved wrong in their assumptions that one short lockdown, with the whole country 'staying at home' would get rid of the virus. Several lockdowns followed, as three 'waves' of the virus spread a calamitous health emergency, accompanied by personal tragedies and an economic crisis. Dominic Cummings who in early January had put an advertisement out for 'weirdos and misfits' to work in the civil service and hired Andrew Sabiski, a friend with dubious views on race,[2] drove to Durham with his family on 27 March and made a ludicrous attempt to defend this and a trip to 'test his eyesight' before returning to London.

The rapid development of vaccines initially in Oxford laboratories mitigated much illness but a count by the World Corona Virus Tracker reported that by April 2024 over 7 million people worldwide had died of the virus in its various mutations. The UK seemingly lost interest in how its former Empire was doing in terms of COVID deaths, although the World Health Organization published numbers dead or ill from the 54 Commonwealth countries, 27 of them small island states. In the UK a COVID inquiry reported in 2023 that some 227,000 people had died with COVID mentioned on their death certificates (BBC News 2023). Amnesty International reported that in the UK 60 per cent of health and social workers dying of the virus were Black, Asian or other minority workers. Old people were more likely to die, especially in care homes, Health Secretary Matt Hancock having agreed to sending them back from hospitals with no testing for the virus. Johnson did not endear himself to older Conservative voters when he told his advisers that as many of those dying from the virus were aged 82–85 'that is above life expectancy, so get Covid and live longer' (Bale 2023: 167). Black men were more as likely to die than white men. Black and especially Muslim women were three times more likely than white women to die. Although children and young people were less likely to fall ill, in the long term the largest groups to suffer from the haphazard way the government dealt with the virus were children and young people in their future lives.

Educational chaos

Schools had remained open during the Second World War and plans made for post-war schooling. Nothing like this happened over the COVID emergency. Although a Coronavirus Act was passed on 25 March 2020 with sections giving Ministers powers to close schools after taking advice from public health officials, plans for the future of some 4.7 million children in primary schools, 3.41 million in secondary schools, over 140,000 in special schools or alternative provision and 576,000 in private schools (Gov.UK 2020) were largely non-existent. Funding for education had been cut by around £28 billion from 2015 with staff and resources reduced, and schools were in no position to cope with the virus. An Education Summit was held in March 2021 at a Conservative-backed Foundation for Education Development, but 'new' ideas seem to have been tried before. During the pandemic, divisions between the rich and poor increased and the ultra-rich increased their wealth by a third. Johnson claimed that his government had introduced a 'levelling up' agenda when it became clear that around 45 per cent of children in the north of England were 'in poverty'. But even in supposedly genteel Cheltenham over 4,000 children were estimated to be living in poverty and parents were unable to sustain the intended home learning that followed school closures (Enfield 2023). Those families in overcrowded housing, on benefits or working for low wages had higher rates of infection and death. This particularly affected households of Pakistani and Bangladeshi origin.

Johnson appointed Gavin Williamson as education secretary, an MP who had been sacked by Theresa May for a possible leak of defence information but who supported Johnson's bid to be PM. He claimed to support vocational education but regarded some vocational courses as a 'second rate qualification'. As noted, he managed to upset both football and rugby fans when he confused Black footballer Marcus Rashford, who led a campaign for free school meals for children over the holidays, with Black rugby player Mario Itoje who had campaigned for free school laptops for disadvantaged children (Tomlinson 2022: 156). There was less comment as to why footballers were drawing attention to educational disparities and the learning deprivation of poor children rather than those in charge of education. Williamson conducted a feud with Health Secretary Matt Hancock over closing of schools, a number of their emails being published later. Hancock had attempted to by- pass the education secretary in December 2020 and have schools closed. In an exchange of emails they also insulted the teaching unions; Hancock described them as 'absolute arses' and Williamson replied 'they just hate work' (Cooney 2023). On average, children and young people aged 4 to 18 would have lost 25 weeks in school or college in 2020 and 14 weeks in 2021. It was largely left to head teachers to decide what to do to protect children and staff from the virus by rules for social distancing, wearing face masks and also arranging home schooling and digital learning. An inadequate test and trace system, lack of any protective clothing for staff, lack of promised laptops, debate over whether and when children should be vaccinated against the virus, which led to arguments with parents, and deteriorating children's mental health were all issues ministers did not seem able to attend to. Savage and Ferguson (2020) documented much of this in an article on 'How Ministers made a shambles of English schools'. Williamson appeared to have little sympathy for parents or children, complaining after lockdowns that children needed 'Behavioural Hubs' to teach them how to behave in schools again.

Among other people disappointed with Williamson's performance, the online group NetMums were especially angry over the chaos over examinations in both 2020 and 2021. Having first cancelled then reinstated GCSE examinations, in 2020 the 'A' level exams (Highers in Scotland) went ahead and were marked by teachers and standardised by computer algorithms (sets of rules followed by a machine after information is fed in). This led to a significant downgrading in marks and around 40 per cent of young people, first in Scotland, then in England, and especially those from poorer backgrounds found they had lost out on promised university places. Williamson, who was on holiday when exam results were published, blamed his officials and Jonathan Slater, permanent secretary in the Department for Education (DfE) and Sally Collier, CEO of the exam regulator Ofqual, resigned. Mary Bousted, secretary of the National Education Union, wrote that 'it's scorched earth policy for civil servants. Ministers refuse to take responsibility … the unfortunate fall guys for Ministerial incompetence' (Langford 2020). Meanwhile, Boris Johnson told children at Castle Rock School in Leicestershire that exam results had been derailed by a 'mutant algorithm', speaking (unobserved by him) in front of a book display of *The Twits*. More students in private schools were graded 'A' and the gap between advantaged and disadvantaged children increased. The government announced a National Tutoring Programme to help children whose learning had fallen behind. The contracts for this went to a Dutch firm, Randstad, and many schools never received the promised cash. In June 2021 an Education Recovery Plan was announced and Sir Kevan Collins put in charge. He estimated that £14 billion was needed for education at all levels to recover from the effects of the pandemic. The government offered £1.4 billion and Collins resigned. He wrote that the minimal support offered by government to schools and colleges risked the failure of hundreds of thousands of children and young people to catch up with their learning.

By June 2021 Matt Hancock had been dismissed from his job as health and social care secretary, having been caught on camera embracing his female aide in defiance of lockdown social distancing rules. Sajid Javid, chancellor of the exchequer, became health secretary, his former job going to Rishi Sunak. By September 2021 after four teaching unions had called for his sacking, Williamson was replaced as education secretary by Nadhim Zahawi, born in Bagdad, MP for Stratford on Avon and loyal to Johnson. Zahawi had become notorious in the expenses scandal of 2008, when he claimed expenses for electricity for his horses stables. He lasted almost a year as education secretary but managed to pay attention to high levels of spending for Special Educational needs (SEND) and Alternative Provision (AP) which was causing much anguish for families claiming special resources, with local authorities left with large debts. The concept of 'inclusion' of all children in mainstream schools continued to be contested, with special schools, units and a variety of AP developing and school exclusions increasing (Tomlinson and Johnston 2024). Black boys continued to be over-represented in the more stigmatised categories of 'special educational need' and alternative provision, and in school exclusions. Parents of all social classes, worried that their children could not thrive in the competitive orientation of schools, were demanding resources, especially for Education and Health Care Plans, which if obtained meant that local authorities were legally entitled to provide the places or resources, some costing up to £90,000 annually. In particular, claims for autism and Attention Deficit and Hyperactive Disorder increased, with numbers of adults and especially celebrities suddenly discovering they suffered from the symptoms. After a review and consultation and three more short-staying education secretaries in post, the government produced a *Special Needs and Improvement Plan* (DFE 2023) and a road map for changes, the debt for SEND/AP in all local authorities now around £4.9 billion, much of the money having gone to private providers.

Black Lives Matter

In the chaos of COVID in the UK, hostility to minorities appeared to decrease slightly, especially when it became apparent that many of the medical NHS staff Johnson encouraged the nation to clap for every week were predominantly from Black, Asian and other minority groups. This did not last long. Into the third decade of the 21st century Britain was not well served by governments presiding over a society increasingly multiracial, multicultural and multifaith. It was slowly becoming more generally acceptable that this was an inevitable consequence of Empire. But there continued to be hostility from right-wing groups, lobbies and parties, especially the newly constituted Reform Party. The racism directed at settled citizens, asylum seekers and refugees after Brexit and the antagonism to 'immigrants' encouraged by a right-wing media continued. Despite this the 2021 Census demonstrated that numbers of people identifying as 'white' in the UK was slightly down – 81.7 per cent including white Irish and Roma, with those identifying as visible 'ethnic minority' up to 18.3 per cent. This last presumably included the members of Johnson's government who he was proud to claim were from minority groups, despite his own record of racist remarks and behaviour. Numbers of 'mixed race' households increased, love taking precedence over politics.

Johnson was in no position to deal with the resurgence of a Black Lives Matter movement and anti-racist protests in the UK. This was, as noted previously, a political movement started in the USA in 2013 by activists appalled at the number of deaths of African Americans, especially those killed by police.[3] In May 2020 some 20 million people around the world protested after a white policeman in Minneapolis, USA, was seen on camera murdering Black man George Floyd by kneeling on his neck. There were widespread protests in England, and the most senior minority police officer in the Metropolitan police, Neil Basu, resigned in disgust at this and at the catalogue of racial crimes committed or overlooked by his colleagues in England. In June 2020 it was mainly young people in Bristol who pulled down the statue of Edward Colston, a 17th-century slave trader, responsible for the trading and possible deaths of some 80,000 African people but who had given money and become a respected person in the city. Protests in London threatened a similar fate for a statue of Winston Churchill, Johnson's hero, his response being to set up a Commission on Race and Ethnic Disparities in the UK, chaired by Tony Sewell.

The members of the commission were chosen by Johnson's close aide Munira Mirza, herself a Muslim of Pakistani heritage born in Oldham Lancashire. She was already well known for her objections to the idea of institutional racism and multiculturalism. An adviser to Johnson when he was London mayor, she had written that 'anti-racism is becoming weaponised', criticised a report by shadow Home Secretary David Lammy into judicial inequalities and claimed a culture of grievance was emerging among minorities (Walker, Siddique, Grierson 2020). The commissioners were mainly all 'successful' minority people[4] and a major conclusion by Sewell was that 'We no longer see a Britain where the system is deliberately rigged against ethnic minorities … the impediments and disparities do exist but are ironically very few are directly to do with racism. Too often racism is a catch-all explanation' (Commission on Race and Ethnic Disparities 2021). This view and the Commission's use of evidence was widely critiqued, the Runnymede Trust concluding that:

by denying the evidence of institutional racism … the Government has insulted not only every ethnic minority in the country – the people who continue to experience racism on a daily basis, but the vast majority of the UK population that recognises racism as a problem and expect their government to contribute to eradicate it. (Runnymede 2021: 5)

Comedian Sir Lenny Henry and Marcus Ryder assembled a group of 'successful' minority contributors to a book *Black British Lives Matter* (Henry and Ryder 2021) demonstrating that racism was indeed a problem to be overcome to achieve success in a variety of areas.

Both before and after these events in both the USA and the UK, individuals and organisations working against discrimination and racism had been accused by a right-wing media, politicians and others of being 'woke', a word initially associated with Black communities in the USA in their awareness of injustices. Claims that a 'woke' culture was inhibiting free speech and action led in the USA to assaults on a half century of civil rights measures and legislation, restricting teaching at all levels of education of race, gender and sex issues, including removal of textbooks. In England institutions including universities had been reevaluating the UK's colonial history –especially slavery – and in February 2021 the culture secretary Oliver Dowden sent a letter to the National Trust and other institutions, telling them that 'countries should not run from or airbrush the history on which they were founded', especially critiques of slavery. The National Trust had bravely been placing information about the original owners of their properties, many having become rich and building the houses with money from slavery and indentured labour overseas. The DFE appointed a 'Free Speech' advocate for universities, and the often vitriolic discussions of 'free speech' became entangled with issues of sex and transgender. The Equalities Minister Kemi Badenoch, later to be leader of the Conservative opposition, was a prominent critic of anything 'woke', especially asserting that Critical Race Theory (CRT) should not be taught in schools (it is not, apart from a mention in 'A' level Sociology). Seldon and Newell noted that Johnson let her do the critiques while being 'hailed as the leader who would take on woke' (Seldon and Newell 2023: 347). A full account of racism, education and CRT has been documented by Gillborn (2024). Footballers were again in the news and accused of being 'woke' when in July 2021 before the European championships players copied American players by 'taking the knee'– kneeling in support of Black Lives Matter campaigns before matches. Gillian Keegan, then a skills minister in Johnson's government, claimed that English players were creating new divisions and BLM was all about 'defunding the police and the overthrow of capitalism' (Bale 2023: 203). In reality, the BLM in the USA and the UK continued to be a matter of life and death for Black people. In May 2022, an 18-year-old white youth killed 13 people, 11 of them Black, in Buffalo New York, leaving a note that he 'wanted to kill as many Blacks as possible' and describing his engagement with race hate and white supremacist sites on-line (Stanley 2022). In England the case of murdered student Stephen Lawrence in 1993 continued to be a focus for justice and for police practices. Two men had been gaoled for his murder, but the name of a further suspect was revealed in 2022, although the man had died the previous year.

Cronies, parties and lies

The years 2020–22 were undoubtedly crisis years in the UK and continued to be the subject of much comment (Tomlinson 2022). Bale described Johnson's government even before the COVID emergency as one of 'bullying, babies and balls' (Bale 2023: 149), the last referring to Johnson's attendance at a Conservative ball where a Russian billionaire helped pay an auction price of £90,000 for a game of tennis with him. Accusation of sleaze and cronyism surfaced referring to ministers taking lucrative second jobs or being paid to lobby Parliament on behalf of business. Johnson attempted to defend his friend Owen Patterson, MP for North Shropshire, who was suspended from Parliament accused of breaking lobbying rules, and then lost his seat in a by-election. In addition, the behaviour of Dominic Cummings, whose arrogance and bullying had finally caused his dismissal as chief advisor in November 2020, upset former colleagues. After leaving his £140,000 plus salary, Cummings started up a technology consulting firm, Siwah Ltd, and devoted a blog with the on-line *Substack* to attacks on his former boss. The overt cronyism during COVID with ministers directing lucrative contracts for personal protective equipment (PPE) and other goods towards their friends was soon noted. BBC *News* on 20 April 2020 detailed a *Timeline of covid contracts and accusations of chumocracy*, which revealed contracts given without the required competition, including a contract for PPE given to the company Public First run by a former aide to Michael Gove – James Frayne and his wife, Rachel Wolf, who was credited with writing the Conservative party election manifesto in 2019. As a man who had and continued to have great influence over the school system Gove, with Cummings, was eventually ruled by a judge to have acted unlawfully. Lord Agnew, the academies minister, was reported as recommending three firms for contracts worth some £876 million. In Parliament Angela Raynor chaired a debate examining government contracts, including the £4 billion spent on unused and faulty equipment (Hansard 2022: vol 724) and the saga of £200 million being handed to Baroness Michelle Mone and her husband for PPE which was never used, dragged on for several years. Mone, a peer well known for a successful underwear business, was given a peerage by David Cameron in 2015 and first denied, then admitted, that she was in the 'VIP Lane' for contracts, with the National Crime Agency still checking two years later (Conn 2023).

Seeking fresh advice, after having sacked Cummings, Johnson made some new appointments as advisers early in 2021: Dan Rosenburg as chief adviser, who lasted over a year in post, and the ubiquitous Sir Michael Barber who had worked for Tony Blair on delivering government targets in institutions and for the May government. He was appointed in January 2021 for a year, but there were few signs that even he could deal with the man who interviewer Laura Kuenssberg called a 'chaos machine' (Cooke 2023). As noted, there was a further lockdown in January to March 2021 as another wave of COVID arrived, and in March 2021 the Sewell report caused the reported controversy, denying the continuation of racism in the country. The news that there had been 'gatherings' and parties in Downing Street, while the public was ordered to minimise contacts with other people, was being documented daily by the media. These revelations that there had been parties in defiance of lockdown rules in Downing Street and elsewhere trickled on for over a year, with pictures surfacing on social media of Johnson, family and others drinking in the garden in May 2020. It was claimed that this was a work event, as was a drinks party for Johnson's birthday. There was even a report of a drinks event in the Department for Education on 14 December. Shaun Bailey, the first Black chair of the Police and Crime Commission, reigned his post in December after admitting being at a party in December (he was later made a peer in the resignation honours list).

At the end of 2021 Johnson lied to Parliament asserting that there were no parties and lockdown rules had always been followed, even claiming that on his birthday he was 'ambushed by a cake' produced by his staff. Despite this the report by civil servant Sue Gray in May 2022 recorded a succession of parties, including one where participants had been told to 'bring your own booze' and even after Johnson's resignation as prime minister and later as an MP, a Parliamentary Committee recorded that he had 'misled Parliament'. Johnson received some plaudits in February 2022 when he supported Ukraine after Russia under Putin invaded the country – a war still in progress in 2025. But overall the political view was that the Johnson government had 'ushered in a debasement of democracy' (Reed-Langan 2024). In chapters aptly named 'Things fall apart' and 'End of the road', Bale (2023) described some of the events which led to Johnson's resignation as prime minister in June 2022. This included the final scandal that Johnson had supported his Deputy Chief Whip Chris Pincher who was accused of being a 'sex pest' (Bale 2023: 259). Bale wrote that on leaving Downing Street Johnson made 'what will surely rank as one of the most graceless resignation speech ever made by a British Prime Minister' blaming others for all the mistakes (Bale 2023: 260). But Johnson, having witnessed the short rise and fall of

Liz Truss, returned from another holiday in October apparently prepared to put himself up for the leadership of the Conservative Party again. This time the offer was rejected.

Summary

It was unfortunate for both Johnson and the public that no sooner had he finished banging a gong for Brexit than the COVID virus began to spread. It did not at first affect him as in January 2020 he disappeared on a holiday to Mustique in the Caribbean, apparently in a villa paid for by David Ross, wealthy owner of Carphone Warehouse who was in charge of an academy trust with 34 schools. This trip and a subsequent holiday paid for by Zac Goldsmith, made a lord by Johnson after losing his seat as an MP in 2019, were subject to an investigation by the Parliamentary Standards Commission (Standards and Publications Committee 2021). The country and its institutions, especially education and young people, were not well served by Johnson and his ministers. He claimed in an article in *The Times* in 2021 that 'Britain is not remotely a corrupt country' but the unconstitutional behaviour and near corruption both before and after the pandemic was undeniable, even to some of those who were Conservative supporters. Peter Oborne, a chief political writer for the *Telegraph*, wrote without compromise that ' The British Prime Minister has repeatedly lied. About economic policy, about Brexit, about borders, about the Covid pandemic' (Oborne 2021: 165). Brexit negotiations, especially with EU countries, paled into the background after 2020 when attention was concentrated on the virus. But even five years after Brexit, a newspaper headline could read 'Brexit a key factor in worst medicine shortage in four years, report says' (Campbell 2025) – a comment on the negative impact extra rules and costs have had on importing goods and working with the EU. The Empire also took a back seat during these years, with little interest demonstrated in how the Commonwealth was doing in a global pandemic. The slogan 'Take Back Control' was becoming a 'populist racialised dog whistle' against immigration and minorities, despite the attempt of the Commission on Ethnic Disparities to persuade otherwise (Elkins 2022: 680). Although he put Tony Sewell and Dambisa Moyo, another member of the Sewell Commission, into the House of Lords, neither Johnson's nor the following three prime ministers and their governments diminished the racialised world view based on white biological, economic and cultural superiority.

11

Multiracial Britain, Brexit and the end of Empire, 2022–25

> In fact the idea of race has been one of the most important ideas in the modern world. It has underpinned centuries of enslavement, justified genocide, and has been used as the demarcation line between those who lived and those who died.
>
> Akala 2019: 34

Lord Rosebury, as noted in Chapter 1, was clear at the start of the 20th century that the British 'race' was directed by God who had looked kindly on the creation of a British Empire covering a quarter of the world at the turn of the 20th century. Into the 21st century, this Empire had diminished into a Commonwealth of countries not particularly keen on close links with Britain but which had made the 'Mother' country multiracial, multicultural and multifaith, however much this was deplored by diminishing numbers of the population. The musician Akala, noted previously, offered a succinct rebuttal to Lord Rosebery and his views of race. Joining a European Union (EU) and making closer economic, trade and population links with nearby countries made sense but was derailed by a Brexit which, fuelled by nationalist myths and lies, lost the country £27 billion in trade in the first two years of leaving. Global war and religious conflicts exacerbated immigration as more people left or were forced from their homes, and Western countries created more border controls with more anti-immigrant hate rhetoric. The political chaos caused by Boris Johnson and his resignation, with three more prime ministers up to 2025, was joined that year by a global chaos caused by the election of Donald Trump, sworn in for a second term as president of the USA. Trump, who declared he was 'saved by God to Make America Great Again' (Trump 2025) seemed to be keen on modelling an American Empire on the lines of the 19th-century British Empire, with protectionism in trade, making rich people even richer and hostility to any policies for racial equality. Like Britain in the 19th and into the 21st century, this included using the education system for propaganda and ignorance, re-writing or banning textbooks, but with the added use of a social media to spread lies and misinformation.

This chapter covers the problems of three prime ministers in the three years following Johnson, facing unprecedented events at home and abroad. The ending of the British Empire had left a residue of nostalgic pseudo-patriotism in a public wedded to flags and songs and a familiar undercurrent of racism. The young British musician Sheku Kannah-Mason, watched by 2 billion people as he played at the wedding of the Duke and Duchess of Sussex, was subject to an 'uprising of racist bile' when he politely disagreed that the song 'Rule, Britannia' (commissioned by German King George I) should be played at the Last Night of the BBC Proms concert (Higgins 2025). Brexit was proving a trade and service disaster not helped by Liz Truss's brief premiership in the autumn of 2022. Shipman's view was that she became a bold advocate of Brexit and Britain as 'a buccaneering nation, cutting taxes and regulations at home while championing free markets abroad' (Shipman 2024: 690), none of which was realistic. Her Northern Ireland secretary was Chris Heaton-Harris, noted in Chapter 9 as regarding university lecturers who discussed Brexit as unpatriotic. On taking over government Rishi Sunak[1] managed to sort out Northen Irish trade relations via the 'Windsor Framework' but claimed he would 'stand up to the lefty woke culture that seems to want to cancel our history, our values and our women' and present a radical plan to stop migrants coming on small boats (Bale 2023: 290). Failure to fix Brexit and woke, stop boats and losing local councillors in the May 2024 elections, led him to announce his resignation in pouring rain outside No. 10 Downing Street. A general election in July ushered in a Labour government after 14 Tory years, with Keir Starmer as prime minister,[2] and in November Kemi Badenoch as the first Nigerian heritage leader of the Conservative Party in opposition.[3] Starmer was immediately faced with race riots and immigration problems following the murder of three small girls in Southport by a British-born boy of Rwandan heritage, plus unpopularity over policies to reduce debt and raise money. By 2025 he was grappling with wars in Ukraine and the Middle East, the policies of Donald Trump and the rise of the Reform Party in the UK, headed by Nigel Farage.[4] In the political search for immigration control, Starmer appeared to be adopting the Farage anti-immigrant rhetoric but was also searching for ways to move closer to the EU again. The chapter covers some of the negative education policies over these years, an inspection system that led to a head teacher suicide, an academies structure demolishing a maintained national system that resulted in some debt and corruption, a 'broken' special needs system and a continued failure to rethink a curriculum struggling to present a truthful account of the past and present and a possible different future.

Significant events

2022	(6 September) Liz Truss becomes prime minister. Kwasi Kwarteng appointed chancellor of the exchequer. Supports Johnson Rwanda plan.
2022	(8 September) Queen Elizabeth II dies. Ten days of mourning.

2022	(14 October) Truss Mini Budget crashes markets. *Daily Star* asks if a lettuce will outlive her term in office. 20 October she resigns.
2022	(25 October) Rishi Sunak appointed prime minister by King Charles III.
2023	(8 January) Ruth Perry, primary school head teacher kills herself after an Ofsted inspection. Coroner says the manner of the inspection contributed to her death. Amanda Speilman, CEO of Ofsted, is replaced (but given a peerage in 2025).
2023	(February) The Windsor Framework presented to Parliament. A reset of Brexit trade arrangements with Northern Ireland. Finally accepted by all parties and came into effect October.
2023	(July) Illegal Migration Act makes it easier to deport illegal migrants, especially those arriving on small boats.
2023	(7 October) Palestinian Group Hamas[5] make a surprise attack on Israelis living near Gaza and young people at a music festival, killing 1,200 and taking 250 hostages. Israel invades Gaza in retaliation.
2023	(November) Supreme Court rules that the Rwanda plan to send migrants there is unlawful.
2024	(May) Conservatives lose seats in local elections. Sunak announces a general election for July. Tory MP Les Anderson defects to Reform.
2024	(July) Rishi Sunak resigns. Labour wins the general election with Kier Starmer as prime minister. Bridget Phillipson as education secretary initiates a curriculum review.
2024	(29 July) Axel Rudakubana, Cardiff-born Christian boy, aged 17 kills three small girls, injures 10 others in Southport Lancashire. Rioters attack the Southport mosque. Racial violence is spread to other towns and cities: London, Liverpool, Hartlepool, Manchester, Aldershot, Hull, Liverpool, Leeds, Nottingham, Stoke on Trent, Rotherham. Police are attacked and make 1,600 arrests.
2024	(4 August) Rotheram. Rioters try to burn down a hotel housing asylum seekers.
2024	(September) A seven year-long enquiry into the Grenfell fire disaster published. Business and greed blamed for the fire but Starmer apologies on behalf of the State.
2024	(November) Kemi Badenoch takes over as leader of the Conservative opposition. She has a history of opposing teaching critical race theory in schools (it isn't) having in 2020 said she did not want her blackness seen as victimhood. Donald Trump wins USA presidential election and plans to set up a Department for Government Efficiency (DOGE) run by billionaires Elon Musk and Vivek Ramaswamy.
2024	(17 December) Children, Well-being and Schools Bill introduced. Academies required to follow National Curriculum and local authorities to propose new schools.
2025	(January) Borders, Security, Asylum and Immigration Bill introduced in Parliament. More border control to deter criminal gangs organizing illegal immigration, especially on small boats. Changes to visa fees and citizenship application.
2025	(January) Trump sworn in as President and begins to change world trade rules and global expectations of America. He suggests the USA take over Canada (a former British Dominium), Greenland and Panama.
2025	(March) Trump claims tariffs are forcing world leaders to negotiate with him, reportedly claiming 'countries are calling us up, kissing my ass. They are dying to make a deal.' He argues with President Zelensky on a visit to the White House over US aid to Ukraine.

2025	(March) Kier Starmer calls for a 'Coalition of the willing' of European leaders to aid Ukraine and increase defence spending. EU leader Ursula von de Leyden supports this.
2025	(2 April) Trump declares Liberation Day and signs Executive order 14257 listing tariffs other countries would pay to import their goods. UK and EU 10%. Lesotho which he said is 'an African nation no one has ever heard of' 50%. Tariffs imposed on Heard and McDonald islands in the Antarctic, populated mainly by penguins.
2025	(30 April) Parliamentary seat of Runcorn and Helsby lost to Reform Party by 6 votes. Reform Party takes 677 local council seats out of 1,650 up for election in England. 30% turnout of voters.
2025	(9 May) White paper 'Restoring Control Over the Immigration System' and Border Security Asylum and immigration Bill in final stages. Starmer suggests 'return hubs' overseas for failed asylum seekers. Children Bill in committee stages in Parliament.
2025	(17 May) UN Office for Coordination of Humanitarian Affairs reports that 52,828 Palestinian people have been killed in Gaza with nearly 20,000 wounded. The office also reported 43,000 civilian casualties in Ukraine with 12,000 dead, plus soldiers on both sides in the war started by Putin on 24 February 2022.
2025	(19 May) EU 'Reset'. Starmer meets EU leaders and 'puts Britain back on the world stage'.

The politics of unexpected events

The post-Johnson political scene certainly lived up to previous Prime Minister Harold Macmillan's comment that politics could be derailed by 'events, dear boy'. Liz Truss had the misfortune to visit 96-year-old Queen Eliabeth II to be appointed prime minister on 6 September 2024, with the Queen dying two days later on the 8th. After this difficult start, she and her new chancellor of the exchequer, Kwasi Kwarteng, devised a budget which included £45 billion of tax cuts with little hint of how the nation would fund its public services. She sent Kwasi off to Washington to explain this to the Americans but had to recall him quickly when the financial markets and the nation panicked. She was forced to resign after 49 days in office, her tenure sadly being compared to the life of a lettuce. She blamed the Treasury, Bank of England and the Office of Budget responsibility for the financial problems and later started up a social media platform 'Truss Social' blaming the 'deep state and the elite' for her sacking (Williams 2025). In 2025 there were reports that, having attended Nigel Farage's 60th birthday party, she was keen to join the Reform Party.

But in October 2022 there was a transfer of power to Rishi Sunak, appointed by the new King George III. Sunak, of Indian (Hindu) origin, came from a relatively modest family compared to Cameron or Johnston, but had the familiar prime ministerial background of public school (Winchester), Oxford and Stanford in the USA. He then worked for Goldman Sachs banking and finance and having married the daughter of a billionaire, he became richer than the King. Tim Shipman recorded that despite taking on the problems left by the Truss government 'the best part was that Sunak was Britain's first non-white prime minister – and almost no one regarded it as remarkable at all' (Shipman 2024: 711). What was also remarkable was the energy that this son of immigrants expended in pursuing would-be immigrants, especially those coming over the channel in unseaworthy rubber boats. Under Boris Johnson the number of immigrants, both legal and illegal, into the UK had risen to the high level of 900,000 in 2023. Sunak adopted the familiar rhetoric about reducing the numbers. Both Truss and Sunak supported the plan initiated by the Johnson government, to send asylum seekers arriving in the UK to Rwanda in Africa, a country which only joined the British Commonwealth in 2009. Rwanda, a former German, then Belgium colony, was known in the UK for a genocide in 1994 when some 800,000 ethnic Tutsi and moderate Hutu people were murdered by the then dominant Hutu ethnic peoples. The country continued to be unstable until 2003 when President Paul Kagame brought some order and was later pleased to accept a reported £700,000 which came with plans to send asylum seekers to his country notionally for 'processing' their applications. Only four people went voluntarily and the scheme was abolished by Keir Starmer in July 2024. In opposition both the Conservatives and Reform Party claimed they would reinstate the policy, but by 2025 Donald Trump had made a trade treaty with Rwanda over mineral rights and the country was not so keen on taking in illegal migrants from the UK.

Sunak's major aim was to sort out the Brexit trade negotiations, especially over the Northern Ireland issues. He was helped by a friendly relationship with Ursula von de Leyden, the EU European Commissioner, both having studied at Stanford University in the USA. After much negotiation, a legal agreement between the UK and the EU was agreed in February 2023 known as the Windsor Framework. Relations with the recalcitrant Democratic Unionists were sorted, and he claimed that he had abolished 1,700 EU laws affecting Britain. His Home Secretary Suella Braverman, another child of immigrant parentage, was annoyed that the agreement still left Britain susceptible to challenges from migrants in the European Court of Justice. While it was becoming clear that leaving the EU had damaged British business and the service industry – no friendly European young people at hotel desks and care workers only from outside the EU – discussion of Brexit and its consequences faded from British politics. Rawnsley pointed out that as an election drew near in the summer of 2024 there was a 'conspiracy of silence' from the Tories as the golden age post Brexit had not happened, and from Labour as the party needed the support of working class people who voted to leave the EU (Rawnsley 2024). Another unfortunate 'event' occurred as Sunak managed to annoy voters of all social classes by leaving a

Second World War D-Day commemoration ceremony in France early on 6 June 6 – a most unpatriotic action!

Sunak had no more luck in his dealings with the two major wars in progress during his leadership. His government promised support for Israel in what was turning out to be a genocide of Palestinian people as a response to the killing and hostage taking of over a thousand Israeli citizens by Hamas in October 2023. He sent military aid to Israel and abstained from UN resolutions on a ceasefire. When he left office some 42,000 Palestinian people had been killed, the majority women and children. On the Ukraine war, when Russian President Putin's invasion of February 2022 was ongoing, he met Ukraine President Volodymyr Zelensky and promised £2.5 million in aid over 2024, but the war continued. After the Conservatives lost local councils in the May 2024 elections, Sunak supporters were drifting away and colleagues were plotting to replace him as leader. Not wanting to be seen as a 'wally with a brolly' (Shipman 2024: 812), he stepped out in Downing Street into what became a deluge of rain and announced his resignation through a torrent of water.

Whatever happened to education

In the hiatus between Boris Johnson's resignation and the Liz Truss brief premiership in the autumn of 2022, teachers were bemused to find they were working under four education secretaries in three months. Nadhim Zahawi departed Education in June and Michelle Donelan, who had been a junior minister, was appointed education secretary but only stayed for 36 hours in post before resigning. James Cleverly was appointed but was supplanted two months later by Kit Malthouse, appointed by Liz Truss in September and departing the post with her in November. Sunak appointed Gillian Keegan, who did remain in post until 2024, although her frustration with her many problems caused her in one interview to remark 'does no-one ever say you've done a f*****g good job' (Boulton 2023) for which she had to apologise. One immediate problem was the revelation that many schools were literally crumbling from dangerous concrete. While renovation of 147 was in progress she authorised £34 million to improve the Westminster Education Department, and £1 million was paid into her husband Michael Keegan's IT company from the schools rebuilding programme (Forest 2023).

There was no change in the undemocratic, divisive and fragmented school structural arrangements with schools as businesses run for some eight million children and by a million staff. From 2010 a Coalition then Conservative government had overseen a familiar divide between private and state maintained schools, a divide between remaining selective grammar schools and comprehensive schools, a divide between those in mainstream schools and in special or alternative provision and a divide between those attending schools and unknown numbers who were lost to the system. By 2023 there were some 2,400 academy trusts, 1,250 of them single schools, and by 2024 some 81 per cent of secondary, 41 per cent of primary schools and 40 per cent of special schools were in trusts with the rest still with local authorities. Academy schools, exempt from the national curriculum, were intended to improve test results by removing them from local authorities, apart from in the contested areas of special educational need and alternative provision, children in care and school exclusions which remained local authority responsibility for all schools. Although there had been some attempts to cut down the high salaries paid to Trust CEOs – the CEO of the Harris Trust Sir Dan Moynihan was paid over £500,000 a year, Sir Hamid Patel of the Star Academies over £300,000 – the money spent on these semi-privatised schools continued to be pointless. Despite attempts to suggest achievements were higher in academies, evidence concluded there was no difference in test results overall between local authority-run schools and academies (McGlade and Kelly 2025). The main differences between school performance continued, as always, to be connected to the social class and economic status of parents.

The school achievements of minority children and young people continued to be contested, with 'model minorities' – Chinese, Indian and Black African students presented as more successful with those of Caribbean and Pakistani origin doing less well. Specious arguments that 'white working class boys' were the real victims of poor schooling were presented in the media (Gillborn 2024). In reality, comparisons are unreliable and shifting. For over 50 years:

> researchers had tended to assume the experiences of majority society pupils and the different minority groups was roughly comparable and that comparison of performance was fair ... given the different colonial, cultural, linguistic and class backgrounds of the children and the different attitudes of educators towards minorities, this may be an unwarranted assumption. (Tomlinson 1984: 132)

Research over these years has also continued to discover the over-representation of Black boys in school exclusions, in stigmatised categories of special education and relegation to 'alternative provision'. A new low was reached in 2020 when a Black girl was strip searched by police in a Hackney school with no teacher or parent present and while menstruating. She was thought to be carrying cannabis but none was found, and it took the police two years to apologise (BBC News 2022).

There was also to be no change in the inspection system Ofsted, apart from removal of learning about race issues in inspector training. The inspectorate and its simple grading system had long been the focus for criticism from teachers and parents, and in January 2003 the suicide of a head teacher of a primary school, Ruth Perry, worried about the demotion of her school after an inspection, led to the coroner noting that anxiety over the inspection had contributed to her death. The head of Ofsted, Amanda Speilman, left after denying any responsibility. Despite her influential post, Spielman had no teaching experience, only moving from a career in finance to education in 2002, and managing the Ark Schools trust. She had been accused of racism by the National Education Union in 2018, when she refused to support the wearing of hijab by Muslim girls in school, and there was some anger when in 2025 she was nominated for a peerage by Badenoch and Sunak (Fazackerley 2025). In March 2025 Sir Hamid Patel, having first been an interim chief, was appointed as CEO of the inspectorate, the first person of the Muslim religion to take the post.

The years following the COVID pandemic had affected all children and young people in education from nursery to university and undoubtedly caused many to suffer from mental health issues. The increase in parental, teachers and others claiming children had some form of special educational need or disability increased dramatically, especially those requesting an Education, Health and Care Plan (EHCP) which brought a legally specified place in a special school or special resources, and the possibility of claiming disability benefits. Local authorities were responsible for this area and were legally bound to use private provision if requested. A review of Special Educational Needs and Disability (SEND) reported in 2022 that the pandemic had exposed existing difficulties in SEND and alternative provision (AP) and a glut of media articles complaining that the system was 'broken' ensued. The review noted that around 1.4 million school pupils identified with some form of special need and 82 per cent of those in alternative provision had a special need, especially the stigmatised category (social, emotional and mental health) which mainly comprised white and Black working class boys. Costs mounted with local authorities combined eventually recording nearly £5 billion of debt, much due to costs of private provision (Tomlinson and Johnston 2024). Gillain Keegan complained that the system was 'lose, lose, lose' (Whittaker 2023) and proposed linking funding and organisation of SEND and AP. This was in progress when Keegan lost her seat in the general election and Bridget Phillipson took over for Labour. An early contested change the new government announced was the intention to charge 20 per cent VAT on private school fees. The schools, holding charitable status, had previously been exempt from this tax. It was estimated that this would bring in some £1.7 billion to the Exchequer, but private schools claimed they would have to raise fees and some would close.

Starmer and change

Kier Starmer, prime minister in waiting until Labour won the 4 July election, announced that there would be 'Change' and a vote for Labour would be a vote to stop chaos. His chief adviser was Morgan McSweeney, an Irishman who had worked to promote Starmer as leader since 2015. Morgan was a change from Sue Gray, who had previously been the major Starmer advisor. His wife, Imogen Walker, was elected in 2024 as a Labour MP for a Scottish constituency. There was no change in the suspicion that the Labour Party was not totally committed to anti-racism, and there were complaints that the Labour election posters attacking Rishi Sunak and his wife for her non-domicile status were marginally racist. Faiza Shaheen, the Labour candidate for Chingford and Woodford Green in Essex was deselected on the grounds that she had claimed there was a campaign of racism, islamophobia and bullying against her. Her view was that Labour 'had a problem with black and brown people' (Stewart 2024). Another candidate was hastily found who was defeated by Conservative Ian Duncan Smith, who had once defended Boris Johnson's mendacious attack on USA President Barak Obama as disliking Britain on account of his part-Kenyan heritage.

Labour also had problems with Diane Abbott, the first Black woman to be elected to Parliament (in 1987). She had been a consistent champion of anti-racist organisations and supported Jeremy Corbyn as Party leader in 2015. In March 2024 Frank Hestor, a business man who had donated £10 million to the Conservative Party, claimed that Diane 'made him hate all black women … and that she should be shot', but she had no official support from the Labour government. Hestor apologised, admitting his comments were 'reprehensible' (Sky News 2024) As the election approached she was suspended from the Labour Party for comments on Jewish people and banned from standing as a Labour candidate. After much debate, she was allowed to compete and won her seat in Hackney and Stoke Newington again, becoming the 'Mother' of the House of Commons. Over her Parliamentary career she had suffered more racist hate messages and personal attacks than any other member of parliament over the past 50 years. In addition, Nigel Farage, having tried and failed to become an MP seven times, decided to stand for the Reform Party in Clacton, where he attracted many Conservative votes and won the seat, claiming that as a Hindu Sunak was a man who did not understand 'our' history and culture. Keir Starmer and Labour won the 2024 election with a large majority and many of the Conservative politicians who have been discussed in previous chapters of this book lost their seats and departed from Parliament – Jacon Rees-Mogg, Grant Shapps, Jeremy Hunt and former education Secretaries Michelle Donelan and Gillian Keegan among them. The Reform Party won five seats and Nigel Farage announced that he intended to build a mass national movement and win a general election for Reform in 2029, later adding that he would be prime minister. As the history of his Party had been one of fascism and racism, it would seem that reversal rather than change was to be expected, especially as Kier Starmer eventually moved towards a more hostile anti-immigrant policy.

The Southport tragedy

There was no change in familiar British racist rioting following a tragic event that happened just a week into Starmer's premiership. A 17-year-old boy, Axel Rudakubana, entered a Taylor Swift-themed dance class in Southport, Lancashire, with a knife, and killed three small girls aged six, seven and nine, injuring ten others. It emerged that the boy was born in Cardiff, Wales, the son of evangelical Christian parents who had migrated from Rwanda before the genocide there, and had settled first in Cardiff then Southport. He had been excluded from school the previous week, returned to threaten staff, and he was known to professionals and other pupils as being a mentally ill threat and even reported to the Prevent anti-terrorist programme. Lies and propaganda began to circulate almost immediately on social media that he was a Muslim asylum seeker and race riots ensued around the country, notably in London, Liverpool, Nottingham, Rotherham, Hull, Hartlepool, Stoke on Trent and near the Aldershot military barracks. A vigil for the children held the day after the killings led to the Southport mosque being attacked and police injured (Vinter 2024).

There are still questions as to who organised these riots as the scale of the violence and the participation by young children astonished police and politicians, especially when a mob attempted to burn down a hotel housing asylum seekers in Rotherham on 4 August. People were trapped inside while rioters shouted anti-Muslim and racist slogans. Some 1,600 arrests were made nationwide, with the Metropolitan commissioner noting that most of those arrested in London already had criminal convictions and were 'racially motivated thugs' (Dodd 2024). The participation of so many children, from a variety of backgrounds, was harder to explain. But the ignorance exhibited by some of the children about migration and minorities suggested failures in the education system (Halliday and Pidd 2024). Nigel Farage, for Reform, attempted to make political capital out of the tragedy, claiming the police were 'covering up' events. The CEO of Sefton, Southport, where the killings took place, wrote later that he had been happy to see an anti-racist protest on 7 August but that to be forever connected to the summer racist violence would take a long time to overcome. Astonishingly, in March 2025 Tony Sewell, chair of the much-criticised Commission on Ethnic Disparities, and made a lord by Boris Johnson, told a debate at the Oxford Literary Festival that the riots were caused by '*Guardian* editors' as apparently *Guardian* readers wanted only to hear about racism and terrible white people oppressing Black people (Godwin 2025). It also fell to Starmer, just two months into his office, to apologise for the 2017 Grenfell Tower fire tragedy, when a seven-year long national enquiry into the deaths of 72, mainly minority working people, was published. In an apology 'on behalf of the British State' he promised justice for the victims and their families, as the fire had been caused by the greed and dishonestly of multi-million dollar firms who had failed to make the Tower safe (Booth and Sinmaz 2024).

Trump makes America great again

A major issue for Starmer in the first months of his premiership was forming a relationship with new US president Donald Trump. Having spent four years complaining that he had really won the 2020 election which Joe Biden won, Trump was actually successful in the presidential election of November 2024. He took office or a second time in January 2025, seemingly determined on revenge against people and institutions whom he thought had offended him. He pardoned the gaoled rioters whom on his behalf had attacked the White House in January 2020, appointed billionaire Elon Musk as head of a Department of Government Efficiency (DOGE) and declared war on institutions supporting diversity, equality and inclusion (DEI). He continued a trade war which destabilised trade in the world and in foreign policy threatened to withdraw American support for wars 'against dictators', although by May 2025 he was making friends with authoritarian leaders in Saudi Arabia and the Arab Gulf States (Roth and Christou 2025). His immediate claim that he would make Canada the 51st state of the USA led to the newly elected Liberal Prime Minister Mark Carney politely repudiating any such nonsense. Trump also claimed he would 'buy Greenland' – a country overseen by Denmark – an echo of 19th-century European imperial ambitions. He also threatened to take back Panama and its canal, through which international trade passed.

In his first term of office Trump had questioned the rules governing global tariffs and trade. These rules had developed out of a 1934 reciprocal trade agreement devised by President Roosevelt and were regarded as one of the USA's great achievements. In his second term he set out to demolish this achievement and destabilise world trade. In 2025 he began an extension of tariffs on goods from countries globally, singling out China for special negative treatment, and on 2 April he declared 'Liberation Day' for America, showing a list of countries with increased tariffs on their imports to the USA. This caused some amusement when it was noted that he had included the Norfolk and Heard islands – overseen by Australia – and almost totally inhabited by penguins. He also managed to insult Lesotho, previously Basutoland – a former British protectorate from 1866 to 1966 – declaring it a country no-one had ever heard of. Although Trump's 'Kiss my ass approach towards long-standing partners of the US has staggered, alienated and sown distrust among them' (Rawnsley 2025) Kier Starmer made several visits to the White House, passing on an invitation from the King to visit Britain and emerging in May 2025 with a trade deal lauded by the British government as 'a Landmark economic deal that saves thousands of jobs in the car and steel industry' with much more to follow (Gov. UK 2025). A White House fact sheet also praised the deal and claimed that the USA/UK trade was worth $148 billion in 2024. In reality, not many people in the USA buy expensive UK cars or need much British steel, and it was chicken washed in chlorinated water that the media focused on as a 'dangerous' import to Britain.

A second major Trump project which was copied by the right-wing opponents of the supposed woke agenda in Britain, was his determination to demolish any legislation, institution or activity which could be associated with racial and ethnic equality, diversity and justice. In his first term of office some states had begun banning school textbooks referencing race and gender issues, and this increased during his second term. A list of his accomplishments in the first hundred days of his presidency included closing the Office of Civil Rights and Civil Liberties, the Office for Equity, Inclusion and Diversity, abolishing Diversity and Equality offices in the US military, prohibiting the flying of flags for Black Lives Matter and Gay Pride, withdrawing from the UN Human Rights Council, withdrawing funding from the World Health Organization, cutting the US budget for international disaster aid and cutting off government contracts for institutions with a 'woke' agenda supporting diversity in hiring staff or teaching particular courses. This included ending contracts with universities. Harvard University, which had $2.2 billion of funding withdrawn, took legal action against the government and other universities joined the protest. In England, Oxford University academics sent a letter supporting Harvard which was published in the *Financial Times* on 12 May 2025.

Immigration all over again

Starmer and his trade secretary Jonathan Reynolds also managed to make a trade deal with India in May 2025, after negotiations that had begun three years previously under the Johnson government. Whisky and frozen prawns were safe in trade agreements, although Starmer was criticised for deals with the Indian premier Modi and the detail in the agreement that, as in all companies with people working in overseas trade, Indian business people temporarily in the UK for these companies would not pay national insurance. Trade with India was due to rise to over £25 billion over the year, but any detail which might provide evidence that Starmer was 'soft' on immigrants was seized on by opposition parties.

There was actually no need for such criticism as over the years the major political parties have vied with each other to claim that immigration was out of control and measures were needed to control numbers, and Kier Starmer continued with this fiction. Academics from all disciplines, political commentators, journalists, writers and artists of all kinds had either wearily abandoned retelling the anti-immigrant story from post-war Britain to the present or were still producing evidence that whether a person was a judge or politician, a shop assistant or construction worker – if they had a different physical appearance to 'white' they were likely to be labelled as 'immigrant' and subject to racism (Mills 2007; Rollock 2022). Starmer's policy in May 2025 resonated with Labour in 1965 when Richard Crossman MP announced in Cabinet that 'It has been quite clear that immigration can be the greatest potential vote loser for the Labour Party if we are seen to be permitting a flood of immigrants to come in and blight the central areas of our cities' (Crossman 1975: 73). This was mendacious then and later when politicians repeated the lies, usually in pursuit of office and influence, Enoch Powell being the most influential liar (Tomlinson 2018). In 1965 there were some 190,000 'non-white' immigrants into Britain, mainly from former colonial countries, necessarily living in cities which had been blighted by years of neglect and war. But the possibility of losing votes over the issues lived on. In introducing a white paper on immigration in May 2025, Kier Starmer told a press conference that if there were no further rules on immigration the country risked becoming an 'Island of strangers'. Adopting the language of Brexit, he claimed that Labour would 'take back control of our borders'. Castigating employers for bringing in low-wage cheap labour, he added that as there were fewer apprenticeships on offer 'Is it fair to young people … to miss out on these apprenticeships … and to see colleges in their community almost entirely dedicated to one-year courses for overseas students' (Gov.UK 2025; Sylvester 2025). There is no evidence that fewer apprenticeships are due to immigration, and it is untrue to suggest that colleges run English language courses to the detriment of other students.

There was some public and media outrage at what Crace (2025) described as a 'race to the bottom with Farage on immigration' and disquiet in Labour circles as to why Starmer was attempting to outdo Reform promises. By the spring of 2025 there was debate as to whether the Reform Party would merge with the Conservative Party or take votes from it in elections. Collins (2025) and others have documented the far-right policies which Farage endorses and both Conservative and Labour policies would contend with. These include taking control of universities and controlling a 'woke' agenda, defunding the BBC and attacking opposition party finances, abolishing overseas aid, allowing the government to appoint judges, mass deportation of immigrants after abolishing the Human Rights Act and leaving the European Convention on Human Rights.

By May 2025 Starmer and Chancellor Rachel Reeves were anxious to 're-set' relations with the EU, while resisting suggestions that they were attempting to rejoin. They were also conscious that suggestions for simplifying trade relations and a Youth Mobility scheme to allow young people to travel and study in respective countries would be attacked by both the Conservative Party and Reform. Closer ties with Europe on defence, security and policing might be harder for a right wing to attack, but fish in the channel might worry that they would become English fish rather than French as fishing rights were debated again. On 19 May the prime minister met with EU leaders in London, the first time since Brexit in 2016, for this re-set and Starmer claimed that the 'EU deal puts Britain back on the world stage' (Elgot and O'Carroll 2025), but there was no agreements on immigration policies.[6]

Still no curriculum for the 21st century

A constant theme in this book has been failure of education at all levels to prepare all children and young people for their future as a British Empire ended. Britain actually became more like a majority of countries in the 21st century – multiethnic and multiracial, with all the implications for cultures, faiths and language and relationships that go along with that. In the restructuring of education in post-war Britian there were few challenges to underlying imperial values despite the arrival of migrant workers and families from former colonial countries. The unpreparedness and ignorance of schools and teachers as the children of migrants entered schooling and the collusion of all political parties in regarding the children as problems rather than the system, has been well documented. There is a growing literature describing the racist treatment of minorities over the years written by those who suffered over the years, as many adults and children still do. The ignorance of why there is anti-migrant rioting and hostility towards immigrants from children as young as ten, observed in the summer riots of 2024, must be traced back to the failure in the school curriculum to explain the realities of migration and the presence of minorities as fellow citizens. Although into the 1970s there was some government, teacher, Her Majesty's Inspectors (HMI) and union support for creating multiracial schools, from the 1980s the traditionalists views dominated. Roger Scruton, editor of the *Salisbury Review* and praised on his death by Boris Johnson, encouraged the belief that western civilisation was at stake if there was curriculum change. This view is perpetuated in the current focus on the pretence that there are culture wars and a 'woke' mindset. The Sewell commission on Race and ethnic disparities (Commission on Ethnic Disparities 2021: 83) briefly discussed what teaching an inclusive curriculum might look like, but this was restricted to teaching about classical civilisations, the European enlightenment and new arrivals after the Second World War with no mention of the Windrush scandal when new arrivals found themselves deported years later. Sewell himself suggested an official textbook for all schools to teach 'the truth' about modern Britain but did not specify whose truth. Two examples of inclusion quoted were 'inspiring people in Black history' and local history artefacts. In reality, there are already many thoughtful examples of curriculum projects through which all subjects in a national curriculum could be examined and changed.[7] Although one of the first actions that the Labour education Secretary Bridget Phillipson took in July 2024 was to initiate a review of curriculum and assessment, there did not initially appear to be concern about race issues, although gender and sexuality received early mention. Having received over 7,000 responses to this review the chair, Professor Becky Francis, CEO of the Education Endowment Foundation, noted the limitations of including all issues in the curriculum, although an interim review noted on page 28 that 'one of our strengths as a nation is our diversity' (Curriculum and Assessment Review 2025). What is becoming clearer is that without schools, teachers and teacher educators becoming involved in creating a national curriculum for all students, that goes beyond 'decolonising the curriculum' the future of a conflict-free multiracial society will be in jeopardy.

Summary

The 14-year dominance of the Conservative Party, with its five prime ministers, attempting to deal with catastrophic wars, floods, pandemics, inequalities, alienation and disenchantment through policies of neo-liberalism, privatisation and marketisation, came to an end in July 2024. In the first half of that year, with a prime minister and a several Cabinet ministers from former imperial countries, it seemed as though, despite continued hostility to 'immigrants', acceptance of a multiracial Britain was less of an issue. A government report on *Inclusive Britain*, published in May 2024 under the Conservative ggovernment began with the sentence that 'Our country is a multi-ethnic, multiracial and multifaith success story' (Inclusive Britain 2024) and in July there seemed to be a promise of change to reliable government by a temperate leader of more centrist Labour party. But once again events proved problematic. This chapter covered some of the issues facing the three prime ministers following Boris Johnson's chaotic regime, with global disarray following the election of Donald Trump in the USA and continuing war in Ukraine and Gaza. The election of a Labour government in July 2024 introduced more antagonisms, as efforts to pay debts and raise taxes meant cutting welfare support, and there were attempts to make friends with autocratic leaders to manage global trade deals and move closer to European countries and their leaders without upsetting the vociferous politicians of the right. But despite promises of change and some success with authoritarian leaders abroad there was up to 2025 capitulation to right-wing parties over immigration and overseas workers and even visitors. There were few signs of real change in school structures, the curriculum and the education system as a whole that might lead to more acceptance of a multiracial Britian.

Conclusion

> What are the biggest fears we have about the future ... people in similar situations tend to share the same fears, which leads to a collective anxiety-visions of decline, even despair ... a wider education helps us live together and be less fearful of each other.
>
> Dorling 2025: 6, 37

This book, a revised edition to that published in 2019, gives an account and critique of the time from the dominance of a British Empire, through Brexit – the shorthand for leaving the European Union – to the possibility that ties with the EU may be increased again. A quarter of the way into the 21st century the British Empire has continued to disintegrate[1] – with more diplomacy but still some violence, a right-wing authoritarianism again threatened democracy in Britain and Europe, and an American president ushered in a period of chaos and instability to world trade and democracy in the USA. Wars, post-imperial conflicts and economic conditions continued to bring more migration, although the majority of migrants stayed in their own or nearby countries. In the circumstances, as Danny Dorling points out as mentioned previously, it is natural for people to feel anxious and fearful. So is the choice to sink into despair or to study how the situation came about and how it will be changed in the future?

Two major arguments made in the book are first that as a consequence of Empire Britain has become multiracial, multicultural and multifaith and that there is no way this will be reversed, no matter what nostalgic, racist and fascist attempts are made to revert to a mythical romantic imperial past. Other countries – the USA, Russia and China – have increased their imperial ambitions. The second argument is that those in charge of both the state-maintained and private education systems over 150 years, have failed to develop an equitable and just post-imperial 'Education For All' that would inform and include all children in current and future generations. The predominance in government of mainly privately educated people, whose confidence in their right to rule was often matched by their inability and ignorance, is slowly being replaced by those with more enlightened outlooks, some of whom may even have been educated in state-maintained multiracial schools (Helm 2024). It is more widely understood that many politicians and policy makers of all ideologies can be more concerned with personal self-interest than with social and racial justice, and they can appoint their friends and colleagues to carry on ideological battles, as has been documented in chapters here. The British Empire still has its defenders. In

London on 22 May 2025 Prime Minister Starmer formally signed off the Chagos islands in the Indian Ocean, one of the last of the British Overseas Territories, to Mauritius, although keeping the island of Diego Garcia with its military bases. This action was challenged hours later by the High Court as response to two citizens who wanted the island to remain under British sovereignty.[2] There have been no grumbles from those wealthy individuals and the multinational corporations that use some of the remaining British Overseas Territories for tax evasion. *Tax Justice* (2024) records that some £338 billion, a quarter of all annual global tax dodging 'is enabled by British overseas territories'. In what is still notionally the United Kingdom those first internal colonies, Ireland and Scotland, are still demanding full cessation from their colonisers, there is a Council of the Nations and Regions in England, and there is a view that 'the UK risks falling apart' through geographical, political, economic and social divisions (Kettle 2025).

One conclusion drawn from this discussion of the Empire, decolonisation, immigration and the presence in Britain of people from the Global Majority who are 'not white' is that it is *not* falling apart due to what is currently called diversity. Britain, thankfully having become more normal than 'Great', is now multiracial, multicultural and multifaith, and despite the efforts of right-wing politicians there will be no return to a 'keep Britain white' mentality. Rather than the malicious story that 'immigrants', especially from former colonial countries, caused hardships for the native population, the reality was that having helped to make Britain a wealthy country through looted land and labour, it was post-colonial labour into Britain and the talents of their next generations that have helped keep the country functioning. This was clearly demonstrated during the COVID-19 pandemic. It is now no secret that some institutions in the country are overtly or covertly racist, that the many reports and recommendations over the years intended to eliminate racism have not been acted on and that it will take years to achieve race equality. An older generation, brought up and schooled to believe in the glories of the British Empire (of which I am one) will die off, and younger people, brought up in a different kind of society, are mostly demonstrating more realism and understanding. Global and national protests over the George Floyd murder, the persistence of a Black Lives Matter Movement, the groups dedicated to opposing anti-racist and anti-fascist movements and the still predominant decency and humanity of a majority of the whole population were and are helping to overcome notions of white supremacy (Okundaye 2025). In 2024 a British social attitudes survey reported that pride in Britian's history had fallen over the past decade and the country had become less nationalistic and jingoistic and more reflective of the place of Britian in the modern world (National Centre for Social Research 2024). The rise of populist, authoritarian and neo-Nazi parties will continue to be opposed, as will messages and riots of hate and exclusion. Even the use of 'immigrants' by all political parties as a catalyst for hostility to gain votes will eventually be dealt with by political action, other countries seemingly tired of Britain trying to unload their failed asylum seekers onto them (Hymas 2025).

The major divisions in Britain, as in much of the world, continue to be connected to inequality and poverty – the World bank recording in 2023 that there is currently the biggest increase in global inequality and poverty since the end of the Second World War. Despite the country being labelled as the sixth richest in world rankings of wealth 'The UK is now home to the largest concentration of children living below or on the poverty line across the entire continent of Europe – far more poor children than the poorest parts of Eastern Europe' (Dorling 2024: 4). Race, ethnicity and gender are clear indicators of who lives in poverty. In London, children of Pakistani, Bangladeshi and 'other Asian' are more likely to be living in poverty, as are households headed by single women. The bright golden Brexit future promised by the Leave campaign, its 'European Research Group' which never produced actual research, and the Conservative and Reform parties, never materialised. The effects of leaving the EU on business, finance and services has proved disastrous in many cases. There have been no apologies, and the major players in this disaster are still either very rich or making money.[3]

A second conclusion from the historical record documented in the book is that a hierarchical education system, dominated from the 19th century by 'public' schools for the upper classes with mass education developing for the middle and working classes, incorporated racist and xenophobic values from the outset. The imperial beliefs of public schools were disseminated into grammar and elementary schools and all social classes were encouraged to believe in their superiority over imperial subjects and the legality of imperial conquests. The nationalistic narrative of a brave island repelling invaders and incomers, despite a royal family of German origins, underpinned by an ethnocentric school curriculum made it difficult for generations of white people in particular to accept the realities of Britian's place in a post-colonial and post-Brexit world. If education includes the ability to think rationally, reason and make judgements based on evidence and distinguish truth from lies, generations have been ill-served by education and what passed for knowledge of Empire and the realities of current society

But there are signs of the change. There is a belated recognition that at all levels from early schooling to higher education what is taught and learned is actually running behind public understanding of the changing nature of society. There are few changes to be noted in the structure of the system, with the pointless and expensive academies and their trusts left to operate, and a sub system of 'included' but separate arrangements for those designated as special or in need of alternative provision. It has been noted that it took the suicide of a head teacher to bring about change in the inspection judgements, but curriculum change is now on offer. The Labour government in 2024, with

Bridget Phillipson, a younger (40) education secretary, initiated a review of the national curriculum which referred specifically to 'diversity of content' (Curriculum and Assessment Review 2025: 28) and took evidence from pupils who 'told us that not being able to see themselves in the content they learn or encountering negative portrayals, can be disempowering and demotivating'. While this may lead to change in content, especially from the narrow range of texts offered by the Gove regime, the reviewers have been careful to point out that a broad and balanced curriculum should be inclusive. Academies will also be required to teach the National Curriculum, although most have been mainly doing this over the years. Formal schooling will certainly need to attend to the misinformation on what is turning out to be an 'anti-social' media that young people are now subject to. There can be no social or racial justice in the society if the crucial institution of education perpetuates ignorance or misinformation to coming generations. Education, not ignorance, is crucial if we are to live in a less fearful and more humane world.

The racialised view of the world, developed as the British Empire expanded and which saturated political, social, educational and economic institutions, is necessarily giving way to a global majority that does not function on the assumptions of white biological or cultural superiority. The imperial world was subject to change, as is the current world. There are moral choices to be made by political people with power, by groups and organisations and by individuals. The world can be remade by demagogs and charlatans, or by those who want all humanity to live without despair, in a humane and just world.

Notes

Introduction

1. There is a large internation literature on concepts, descriptions and debates over the meanings of race and ethnicity from the pseudo-science of the 19th-century to 21st-century writers. This book does not attempt to review this literature, but see Gould (1981), Rex (1986), Rose and Rose (2012), Saini (2019), Warmington (2014) and Gillborn (2024).
2. Donald J. Trump was elected the 47th president of the USA in 2024 and took office on 20 January 2025. He had previously been president in 2016–20. His career as a property developer was funded by his father, and he was the subject of many lawsuits concerning sexual and financial improprieties, being convicted of a sex crime in 2023. Trump made Elon Musk, reputedly the 'richest man in the world' and in control of space, automobile and social media companies, for a time an unelected adviser in charge of a new Department for Government Efficiency. Musk was brought up in South Africa under the apartheid regime.
3. 'Woke' originated in African American descriptions as being woken up to racial injustice and discrimination. It was used more after a Black Lives Matter movement developed in 2014 in the USA (after the murder of a young Black student, Trayvon Martin). It is currently used positively by the political left and negatively by the political right.

Chapter 1

1. 'Of the whole cost of constructing a railway, 5/7 is held in shares, and the remaining £400,000 borrowed on mortgage at 5%. Find what amount of gross annual receipts – of which 40 per cent will be required for the working expenses of the line, and 8 per cent for a reserve fund – will yield to the shareholders a dividend of 4.5 per cent on their investments' (Question 24, p 206, Colenso 1892). (The answer was given as £125,000.)
2. Rudyard Kipling (1865–1936) poet, novelist and imperialist, wrote poems describing Africans and Asians as 'lesser breeds without the law' and urged his readers to 'take up the white man's burden' (Kipling 1940). He was awarded the Nobel prize for literature in 1907.
3. UCL/Institute of Education University of London has created an archive of old school textbooks. Special Collection University College London (UCL) University of London, is creating an archive of old school textbooks.
4. Kipling, born and later working in India, spent only three days in Burma. He subsequently wrote the poem 'The Road to Mandalay' depicting a British soldier thinking about his Burmese girlfriend.

Chapter 2

1. Cobain (2017) noted that in 2013 the government disclosed that it had been unlawfully hoarding 1.2 million files on controversial aspects of 20th-century British history in a high security compound in Milton Keynes. The Foreign Office admitted that they had withheld thousands of colonial era files, including those relating to the detention and torture of Kenyans during the Mau Mau insurgency in the 1950s.
2. Glasgow, one of the first cities to give up its slave trade in the 1840s, also experienced race violence in 1919. An English left-wing journalist, E.D. Morel, brought Germany into the race and sex wars, asserting in 1920 in the *Daily Herald* that Black soldiers deployed by the French on the Rhine were oversexed rapists spreading venereal disease (Reinders 1968). Refugees in Germany in the 21st century have been accused of similar behaviour.

Chapter 3

1. Canada and its various territories gained independence as a (white) dominion in 1847–71, Australia 1852–90, New Zealand 1852 and South Africa 1872–1910. By the 1960s these countries were referred to as the old (white) Commonwealth. More recent de-colonised countries were the New Commonwealth.
2. The Rose et al study was the largest carried out by the Institute of Race Relations, an organisation founded in 1958. From 1971 conflict in the Institute and a 'revolution' among the staff led to funding being withdrawn and the Institute becoming a smaller Marxist organisation headed by Ambalavaner Sivanandan. The Institute's journal *Race* became *Race and Class*, edited by Darcus Howe, later a TV producer and documentary maker.
3. The policies here refer to England and Wales. Scotland had some control of its education system from 1945 and Northern Ireland had partial control. After devolution in 1997/1999 Wales and Northern Ireland controlled their education systems.
4. The author had her first teaching job in Wolverhampton during the time Enoch Powell was making his racist speeches 1968/69. He had been a Minister for Health in 1962 and responsible for encouraging women from the Caribbean to come and work in the local hospital. Some came to the school alarmed and sad that 'this man who asked us to come, was now telling us to go away'.

Chapter 4

1. A list of former British colonies, dependencies and overseas territories gaining their independence in the 1970s and 1980s is in the appendix to this chapter. By 2017 there were 3 dependencies and 14 small overseas territories (several of them tax havens) left over from the British Empire.
2. A white boy with two adopted Black brothers remembers how he and his brothers were subjected to racial taunts and abuse at school in Oxford in the 1970s and 1980s. He is now Professor of Human Geography at Oxford University (Danny Dorling).
3. In 1973 Asian women workers at Imperial Typewriters in Leicester led a strike over pay, and in 1977 a strike by Asian workers at the Grunwick Laboratories in North London led to fights between police and pickets.
4. The National Front became the British National Party (BNP), a forerunner of UKIP and other far-right parties, for example Britain First.
5. As the government in Grenada was Marxist-orientated the USA was determined to end this and invaded the island. Bernard Coard was accused of involvement in the killing Prime Minister Maurice Bishop. He spent 19 years in prison and is still fighting to clear his name (see John 2010).

Chapter 5

1. The Eurosceptics at that time, although not named in his interview, but recorded in Stephen Castle's article, were Michael Howard (Home Secretary), Peter Lilley (Social Security), Michael Portillo (Chief Secretary to the Treasury) and John Redwood (Secretary of State for Wales).
2. The East London Mosque was eventually recognised as a centre for radicalising young Muslim men, influenced by the cleric Omar Bakri, who was eventually deported from Britain.
3. The 1991 Census categories were white, white Irish, Black Caribbean, Black African, Black Other, Indian, Pakistani, Bangladeshi, Chinese, Other Groups. Birthplace was also requested.
4. Asylum seekers become refugees when they are given the right to remain in the country.

5   Michael Barber by 2018 was chair of an Office for Students (OfS) with power over universities
6   The failing schools legislation was set out in the Education Act 1993.
7   The National Curriculum was intended to 'promote the spiritual, moral, mental and physical development of pupils at school and in society: and prepare pupils for the opportunities, responsibilities and experiences of adult life' (Education Act 1988 section 1.2). A National Curriculum was legislated for via the 1988 Education Reform Act.
8   Tomlinson was a member of this Task Group.

Chapter 6
1   The British justice system is supposedly independent of Parliament. In 2017, judges were attacked in the media as 'enemies of the people' for supporting the right of MPs to vote on a final Bill to leave the European Union.
2   On 12 November 1998, a paper entitled 'Iraq's Weapons of Mass Destruction' was presented to Parliament. Further developed, this was to be used as justification for the invasion of Iraq in 2003.
3   Other large datasets include the Longitudinal Study of Young People in England (LSYPE) and the Millennium Study of young people born at the turn of the 21st century.

Chapter 7
1   The ceremony dates back to the days of John The Baptist. The subservience of British prime ministers to Rupert Murdoch, owner of influential right-wing newspapers and described as 'one of the most powerful people in the world' (Davies 2014: xiii) was well known. He and his companies survived a phone-hacking scandal after 2011, and continue to influence politics and politicians.
2   The Alliance had been at war in Afghanistan since 2001. It was Britain's 4th Afghan War. The three previous wars in 1839–42, 1878–80 and 1919, all ended in humiliating defeat. Brown regretted sending more troops to fight the Taliban after 2006. Continuing conflict is the major reason for Afghan asylum seekers arriving in Britain, often trying to enter illegally from Calais.
3   The 2010 legislation brought together the 1970 Equal Pay Act, the 1975 Sex Discrimination Act, the 1976 Race Relations Act and 2000 Race Equality Act, the 1975 Disability Discrimination Act, the 2003 Employment Equality (religion) Act and the 2006 Employment (sexual orientation) Act.

Chapter 8
1   The World Trade Organization (WTO), grew out of GATT, the General Agreement on Tariff and Trade 1945–94. On 1 January 1995, it became the WTO and met in Doha in 2001 to try to agree world trading rules. The organisation itself notes that making trade agreements are complex and lengthy as they are legal texts. In 2018, President Trump in the USA declared tariffs on certain goods coming into the USA and supported a protectionist agenda. China and other countries retaliated in kind.
2   A book *Michael Gove: A Biography* by Alistair Cathcart Sloan, was under contract with Biteback publishers in 2016, when the book contract was cancelled. The book purported to suggest that Gove was part was part of a right-wing group linked to British intelligence services. Gove's views are changeable. In *Celsius* 7/7 he complained that the Saudi Royal Family were funding London's central mosque and encouraging Islamists and extremist ideologies (Gove 2006: 113). By March 2018 he was part of a government welcoming the Crown Prince of Saudi Arabia, which is a major importer of arms manufactured in Britain, and at war with Yemen, a former British Protectorate.

3   The expanding academy agenda, intended to semi-privatise all schools, had only been in operation since 2002. Research collecting evidence on the rapidly changing school structure has necessarily been limited. Journalists have provided much of the evidence of malfunctions and corruptions especially in multi-academy trusts, for example the work of journalist Warwick Mansell, and those writing in the journal *Schools Week*.
4   Gove likened the 'enemies of promise' who signed the newspaper letter (I was one signatory) to those quoted in a book by writer Cyril Connelly, who in the 1930s had complained that Enemies of Promise stopped him from working. If Gove had read the book he would have found that Cyril's enemies were his rich friends who distracted him from his writing. Gove described the signatories as 'the Blob', a label first used by Chris Woodhead, the unpopular head of Ofsted in the 1990s.

Chapter 9
1   The EU European Court of Justice (EJC) is often confused with the European Court of Human Rights (ECHR). The latter is overseen by a Council for Europe, which was founded in 1949 after a suggestion by Winston Churchill that all countries in Europe should work more closely together. There are currently 47 member states (as against the 28 [27 after Brexit]) in the European Union. The Council for Europe oversees a European Court of Human Rights enforcing a European Convention on Human Rights.
2   Events between 2013 and 2017 are documented in a timeline in Tim Shipman's two books (Shipman 2016, 2017).
3   In 2014 a school in Cardiff, with funding cut and the head having to close the club which fed children who came without breakfast, stayed open because the 'dinner ladies', on low wages themselves, decided to pay for the breakfast food out of their own money (McInch 2018).
4   Several dozen books quickly appeared in bookshops in the years following Brexit. See, for example, Bennet (2016); Clegg (2017); Macshane (2017); Seidler (2018).
5   In 2017, the *Paradise Papers*, a series of documents held by a law firm in Panama, showing the use of tax havens by wealthy people, including many Conservative ministers and party donors, were leaked to newspapers. Beneficiaries of those finding (legal) ways to minimise their tax payments in the UK by using off-shore accounts included David Cameron's father, Philip May, Arron Banks, Michael Ashcroft, Jacob Rees-Mogg and many others (see Garside et al 2017).
6   The importance of security links with the EU were demonstrated when in March 2018 a former Russian spy living in Salisbury, England, was poisoned with a nerve gas thought to come from Russia.
7   Some of the organisations collecting evidence of racism and xenophobia were the Oxford Centre *Compass*, the Institute of Race Relations, the Runnymede Trust, Tell Mama, Stop Hate UK, True Vision, Breaking Views and the Huffington Post.
8   In 2012 Dominic Raab co-edited *Britannia Unchained: Global Lessons for Growth and Prosperity*. The book claimed that British workers were the worst idlers in the world and that small business owners should be exempt from paying the minimum wage. He also chaired the Eurosceptic European Research Group.

Chapter 10
1   The Rwanda scheme, titled the Migration and Education Development Partnership Scheme, was devised to send asylum seekers to Rwanda in Africa to live and have claims for asylum processed. It was intended to deter those crossing the Channel in small boats. It cost the government some £700,000. Four people eventually went of their own accord before it was declared unlawful and cancelled in 2024 by Keir Starmer.

Notes

2   Andrew Sabiski had apparently worked for a USA company that offered political forecasting to the CIA among others. He had written articles suggesting couples should select their frozen embryos for 'intelligence', Black people were less intelligent than white, and there should be compulsory contraception for the working classes to reduce their numbers (Johnston 2020).

3   The murder of 17-year-old Trayvon Martin in 2012 in Florida USA launched the Black Lives Matter movement. He was shot by George Zimmerman who was found not guilty in court. President Barak Obama said that 'it could have been me 35 years ago'. BLM led to Black civil rights groups being set up in Britian and other countries, including South Africa. In 2016 Zimmerman sold the gun he had used in the shooting for $250,000.

4   The 11 Commissioners included Sir Martyn Oliver, then CEO of Ofsted, and ten minority members, including Dr Maggie Aderin-Pocock, an astrophysicist and space scientist, Dr Dambisa Moyo, Zambian-born macroeconomist and business women, Dr Samir Shah, broadcaster and later appointed chair of the BBC by Johnson, whom he had advised when working for Goldman Sachs, and Aftab Chughtai, business man and Founder of Muslims for Britain, an organisation which supported Brexit.

Chapter 11

1   Rishi Sunak: MP for Richmond and Northallerton from 2015. He was born in Southampton in 1980 with parents of Indian (Hindu) origin who migrated from East Africa to England in the 1960s. His father was a doctor and his mother a pharmacist. He supported Leave in the Brexit vote, was chancellor of the exchequer in the Johnson government, took over from Liz Truss as PM in November 2022 and resigned in July 2024. His wife is Akshata Murty, daughter of a billionaire, who initially claimed 'non-domiciled' status and exemption from tax on overseas earnings.

2   Kier Starmer: MP for Holborn and St Pancreas from 2015. He was born in London, raised in Surrey and attended Reigate Grammar School. His father was a toolmaker with his own small company, and his mother was a nurse. He had law degrees from Leeds and Oxford Universities, worked as a human rights lawyer before becoming head of the Crown Prosecution Service, and he was knighted in 2014. He supported Remain in the referendum and campaigned for a second one. He served in Jeremy Corbyn's Shadow Cabinet in 2016 as shadow minister for exiting the European Union, was elected leader of the Labour Party in 2020 and became prime minister in July 2024. His wife, Victoria, is Jewish, and he had previously marched against the 2003 Iraq war, supported the Black Lives matter movement and 'took the knee' at an event in Westminster after George Floyd's funeral in June 2020.

3   Kemi Badenoch: Olukemi Badenoch, MP for Saffron Walden 2015, then North West Essex from 2017. She was born in London in 1980 when her mother, a professor of physiology, travelled from Nigeria for her birth, which gave her British citizenship. She was educated in Lagos and a further education college in south London, then gained a computer systems engineering degree at the University of Sussex and a law degree from Birkbeck, London. She is married to Hamish Badenoch, a banker. She supported Johnson and the Brexit vote, and she was minister for equalities and for trade and business under Sunak where she was accused of bullying subordinates. She eventually beat Robert Jenrick in the contest to be leader of the opposition and took over in November 2024.

4   Nigel Farage: he was born in 1964 in Farnborough Kent with a wealthy stockbroker father. Educated at Dulwich private school, he did not attend university but became a commodities trader in the City. He has a long history of populist nationalistic views, and he is anti-immigrant and Eurosceptic despite a second marriage to a German national and currently has a French right-wing politician Laure Ferrari as a partner. He joined a

UKIP party in 1993, which became a Brexit party in 2019 and Reform UK in 20121. Although a European Parliament MP from 1999, he stood eight times to be an English MP, succeeding in 2004 to become MP for Clacton, He holds a 53 per cent share in Reform UK Party Ltd and stood down as leader in 2021, billionaire Richard Tice taking over. He survived an air crash in 2010 while the plane flew a UKIP banner. The pilot was found dead at home in 2013.

5   Hamas emerged in 1987 as part of the worldwide Muslim Brotherhood and opposed to the existence of an Israeli State. The group had ruled Gaza from winning an election in 2007. By 2025 the UN reported that some 50,000 Palestinian people had been killed by Israeli troops and 2.3 million people displaced from their homes.

6   The meeting in Lancaster House London om 19 May 2025 was attended by the president of the European Council, Antonio Costa, the European commissioner Ursula von der Leyden, the EU high commissioner Kaja Keller and Keir Starmer. Agreements were made on trade, defence and security, youth mobility, fishing rights and other issues.

7   For example, Jason Arday, now a Cambridge professor, produced with others an outline of Black British history in the National Curriculum (2020); Jason Todd and Katherine Burns, from the Education Department at Oxford, have led projects on producing a diverse history curriculum; Lavinia Sennett in Hackney has some 700 schools signed up to her diverse curriculum project; Vini Lander, at the Centre for Race, Education and De-coloniality at Leeds Beckett University is a leader on teacher education for racial diversity; the NEU has edited a collection of articles by global majority academics on curriculum change entitled *Thinking Beyond the Box* (National Education Union 2025).

Conclusion

1   For example, the Caribbean island of Barbados, gaining independence in 1966, removed the Queen as head of state in 2021, electing Dame Sandra Mason as its first president.

2   The Chagos challenge was actually funded by the *Great British PAC* – an organisation funded mainly by rich Americans. It is supported by several Conservative MPs and peers and former prime minister Liz Truss has also endorsed past campaigns.

3   *Celebrity Net Worth* claimed in 2023 that David Cameron had a net worth of £50 million. Also in 2023 *The Sun* newspaper claimed on 11 June 2023 that Boris Johnson has net worth of £67 million.

References

Abbas, T. (ed) (2005) *Muslim Britain: Communities under Pressure*. Zed Books.

Abrams, F. (2018) 'A-levels: If history starts in 1951 did the Tories "blue-wash" the syllabus' *The Guardian (Education)* 19 June.

Adonis, A. (2012) *Education, Education, Education: Reforming England's Schools*. Biteback.

Aing-Roy, E. and Bowcott, R. (2018) 'Commonwealth will discuss Queen's successor' *The Guardian* 13 February.

Ainley, P. (2001) 'From a national system locally administered to a national system nationally administered: the new leviathan in education and training' *Journal of Social Policy* 30: 457–76.

Akala (Kingsley Dalee) (2019) *Race and Class in the Ruins of Empire*. Two Roads Press.

Akomaning, L. (2018) *The Educational Experiences of Young People of Ghanaian Origin in England*. PhD thesis. Anglia-Ruskin University.

Albright, M. (2108) *Fascism: A Warning*. William Collins.

Allen, G. (2011) *Early Intervention, Smart Investment, Massive Savings* (2nd report). HM Government.

APPG (2017) *Integration and Demonisation*. Report of the All Political Party Group on Community Cohesion. House of Commons.

Apple, M. (1999) 'The absent presence of race in educational reform' *Race, Ethnicity and Education* 2/1: 9–16.

Archbishop of Canterbury (1985) *Faith in the City*. Church House Publishing.

Arday, J. (2020) *The Black Curriculum: Black British History in the National Curriculum*. The Black Curriculum.

Ashcroft, M. and Oakshotte, I. (2012) *Call Me Dave: The Unauthorised Biography of David Cameron*. Biteback.

Aspden, P. (2018) 'The Art of War' *Financial Times* 7 July.

Astbury, K and Plomin, R. (2014) *G is for Genes: The Impact of Genetics on Education and Achievement*. Wiley.

Asthana, A. and Salter, J. (2006) 'Campus storm over racist Don' *The Observer* 5 March.

Atkinson, A.B. (2018) *Inequality: What Can Be Done?*. Harvard University Press.

Attlee, C. (1960) *Empire into Commonwealth (The Chicele Lectures)*. Oxford University Press.

Avon National Union of Teachers (1980) *After the Fire*. NUT.

Bale T. (2023) *The Conservative Party after Brexit: Turmoil and Transformation*. Polity Press.

Ball, S.J. (2007) *Education plc*. Routledge.

Barber, M. (1995) 'The school that had to die' *Times Educational Supplement* 22 November.

Barber, M. (1996) *The Learning Game*. Gollanz.

Barber, M. (2001) 'High expectations and standards for all, no matter what: creating a world class education service in England' in Fielding, M. (ed) *Taking Education Really Seriously: Four Years Hard Labour*. Routledge/Falmer.

Barnett, A. (2018) 'How to win the Brexit civil war: an open letter to my fellow remainers' *Open Democracy* 6 June.

BBC (2018) 'The women who saved the NHS' BBC 4 2 July.

BBC News (2002) 'Blunkett stands by swamping remark' BBC 24 April.

BBC News (2022) 'Met apologies for strip-search of Hackney Schoolgirl' BBC 15 March.

BBC News (2023) 'Covid Inquiry: the UK pandemic in numbers' BBC 5 July.

Beck, U. (2000) *What Is Globalisation*. Polity Press.

Beck, U. (2016) *The Metamorphosis of the World*. Polity Press.

Beckett, F. (2007) *The Great City Academy Fraud*. Continuum.

Benewick, R. (1969) *Political Violence and Public Order*. Allen Lane.

Benn, C. and Chitty, C. (1996) *Thirty Years On*. David Fulton.

Benn, T. (1974) *Years of Hope 1940–1962*. Arrow.

Bennett, O. (2016) *The Brexit Club*. Biteback.

Best, N. (1979) *Happy Valley: The Story of the English in Kenya*. Secker and Warburg.

Bew, J. (2016) *Citizen Clem: A Biography*. Riverun Press.

Bhambra, G. (2016) *European Cosmopolitanism: Colonial Histories and Post-colonial Societies*. Routledge.

Bhopal, K. (2018) *White Privilege*. Policy Press.

Biggar N. (2023) *Colonialism: A Moral Reckoning*. William Collins.

Bishop, A.J. (1993) 'Culturizing mathematics teaching' in (eds) King, A.S. and Reiss, M.J. *The Multicultural Dimension of the National Curriculum*. The Falmer Press.

Blair, T. (1996) *Twentieth Anniversary Lecture*. Ruskin College, University of Oxford.

Blair, T. (1997a) *Speech to the Labour Party conference*. October.

Blair, T. (1997b) *Speech to the European Socialists Congress*. Sweden 6 June.

Blair, T. (1998) *The Third Way: New Politics for a New Century*. The Fabian Society (pamphlet no. 588).

Blair, T. (1999) The Prime Minister's New Year Speech given at Trimdon Community Centre. *Durham, County Durham*. 29 December.

Blair, T. (2003) Meeting with President Bush. The White House. Washington DC, USA.

Blair, T. (2007) Resignation Speech. 10 March.

References

Blair, T. (2010) *A Journey*. Hutchinson.

Blair, T. (2011) 'Blaming a moral decline for the riots makes good headlines but bad policy' *The Observer* 21 August.

Bloom, J. (2017) 'Free trade area, single market, customs union – what's the difference' *BBC Business News* 14 August.

Blunkett, D. (2014) *Education Structures, Funding, and Raising Standards for All (Policy Review)*. The Labour Party.

Booker, C. (2018) 'The last word: the ever more glaring shambles that is the Brexit negotiations is now entering its dog days' *The Sunday Telegraph* 22 June.

Booth, M. (1993) 'The foundation subjects: History' in King, A.S. and Reiss, M. (eds) *The Multicultural Dimension of the National Curriculum*. The Falmer Press.

Booth, R. (2017) 'The ambassador, Kipling and Johnson' *The Guardian* 30 September.

Booth, R. (2020) 'UK more nostalgic for empire than other ex-colonial powers' *The Guardian* 11 March.

Booth, R. and Sinmaz, E. (2024) 'Grenfell a disaster caused by dishonesty and greed' *Guardian* 5 September.

Borger, J. (2025) 'In imperial mode Washington and Moscow sharpened their carving knives in Riyadh while outside everyone had to wait' *The Guardian* 19 February.

Boulton, A. (2023) 'The revolving door of education has created an environment as stable as crumbling concrete' *SKY News* 10 September.

Bourke, D. and MacBride, I. (2016) *The Princeton History of Modern Ireland*. Princeton University Press.

Bower, T. (2016) *Broken Vows: The Tragedy of Power*. Faber and Faber.

Bower, T. (2020) *Boris Johnson, The Gambler*. Ebury Publications.

Boyle, F. (2015) 'Britain's criminally stupid attitudes to race and immigration are beyond parody' *The Guardian* 20 April.

Brace, A. (1994) 'Is this the worst school in Britain?' *The Mail on Sunday* 20 March.

Bratton, J.S. (1986) 'Of England, Home and Duty: the image of England in Victorian and Edwardian juvenile literature' in MacKenzie, J.M. (ed) *Imperialism and Popular Culture*. Manchester University Press.

Breathnach, D. (2018) 'White Paper a starting point for meaningful Brexit Negotiations' *Statement by Declan Breathnach. Ireland Spokesperson for North-South Bodies and Cross Border Co-operation. Dublin, Ireland*.

Brendon, P. (2007) *The Decline and Fall of the British Empire 1781–1997*. Jonathan Cape.

Bright, M. (1999) 'The loves and lies of Chris Woodhead' *The Guardian* 11 April.

British Trades Alphabet (1955) British Trades Alphabet Publications.

Brown, G. (2017) *My Life, Our Times*. Bodley Head.

Brown, G. and Al-Othman (2025) 'Nothing happens here: how atrocity rocked a town and a nation' *The Guardian* 21 January.

Brown, P., Lauder, H. and Ashton, D. (2011) *The Global Auction: The Broken Promises of Education, Jobs and Income*. Oxford University Press.

Browne, Lord J. (2010) *Securing a Sustainable Future for Higher Education: An Independent Review of Higher Education Funding and Student Finance*. Department for Business, Innovation and Skills.

Bull, G. (1961) *Niccolo Machiavelli: The Prince* (Translated Bull). Penguin Books.

Bullock, Lord A. (1985) *A Language for Life*. HMSO.

Burnham, A. (2016) *Speech to House of Commons. 7 December.*

Burroughs, E.T. (1919) *Tarzan the Untamed*. Methuen.

Bushey, E. (2018) 'University of Warwick suspends 11 students over rape jokes and racist slurs' *The Independent* 9 May.

Cameron, D. (2011) Speech given in Witney Constituency. Witney. 15 August.

Cameron, D. (2013) *Speech on the European Union (Given in the headquarters of the Bloomberg Company)*. 23 January.

Cameron, D. and Clegg, N. (2010) 'Foreword by the Prime Minister and Deputy Prime Minister' *The Importance of Teaching* (cmd 7980). Department for Education.

Campbell, A. and Stott, R. (eds) (2007 *The Blair Years*. Hutchinson.

Campbell, D. (2006) 'Low IQs are Africa's curse, says lecturer' *The Observer* 5 November.

Campbell, D. (2025) 'Brexit a key factor in worst medicine shortage in four years, report says' *The Guardian* 22 March.

Cannadine, D., Keatman, J. and Sheldon, N. (2011) *The Right Kind of History: Teaching the Past in Twentieth Century England*. Palgrave-Macmillan.

Casey, Dame L. (2016) *Review into Opportunity and Integration*. Department of Communities and Local Government.

Castle, S. (1993) 'Major says three in Cabinet are "bastards"' *Independent* 24 July.

Castle, S. (2017) 'Defence Secretary quits over inappropriate conduct' *New York Times* 1 November.

CEA (Conservative Education Association) (1992) *Reply to the White Paper 1992*. CEA.

Centre for Contemporary Cultural Studies (1982) *The Empire Strikes Back*. Hutchinson.

Centre for Social Justice (2006) *Breakdown Britain*. Centre for Social Justice.

Chakrabortty, A. (2016) 'After a campaign scarred by bigotry it is now OK to be racist in Britain' *The Guardian* 28 June.

Chantiluke, R., Kwoba, B. and Nkopo, A. (2018) *Rhodes Must Fall: The Struggle to Tear Out the Racist Heart of Empire*. Zed Books.

Civitas (2007) *The Corruption of the Curriculum*. Civitas.

Clarendon Commission. (1864) *Report of the Public Schools Commission* (4 vols). HM Government.

Clark, A. (2018) 'Shared experience' *The Observer* 4 February.

Clarke, K. (2016) *A Kind of Blue: A Political Memoir*. Macmillan.

Clegg, N. (2017) *How to Stop Brexit*. The Bodley Head.

Coard, B. (1971) *How the West Indian Child is Made ESN in the British School System*. New Beacon Books.

Cobain, I. (2016) *The History Thieves: Secrets, Lies and the Shaping of a Modern Nation*. Portobello.

Cobain, I. (2017) 'Files on Britain's most controversial episodes vanish from archives' *The Guardian* 26 December.

Cole, M. (2016) *Education. Equality and Human Rights* (4th edn). Routledge.

Colenso, J.W. (1892) *Arithmetic: Designed for the Use of Schools* (2nd edn). Longman Green and Co.

Collingham, L. (2017) *The Hungary Empire: How Britain's Quest for Food Shaped the Modern World*. The Bodley Head.

Collins, M.L. (2025) *Hate: My Life in the British Far Righ*. Biteback.

Collins, P. (2025) 'Could it happen here?' *Prospect* June: 12–21.

Commission for Racial Equality (1988) *Learning in Terror: A Survey of Racial Harassment in Schools and Colleges*. CRE.

Commission on Race and Ethnic Disparities (2021) *The Sewell Report*. CRED report Gov.UK.

Commonwealth Immigrants Advisory Committee (1964) *Third Report* (cmd 2458). HMSO.

Conn, D. (2023) 'Michelle Mone admits involvement with VIP lane PPE company' *The Guardian* 6 January.

Conn, P., Lewis, P. and Dodd, V. (2022) 'Michelle Mone's home raided as PPE firm linked to Tory peer investigation' *The Guardian* 24 April.

Connolly, S.J. (2007) *The Oxford Companion to Irish History*. Oxford University Press.

Cooke, A. (2012) 'Enoch Powell and Ulster' in Lord Howard of Rising (ed) *Enoch at 100: A Revaluation of the Life, Politics and Philosophy of Enoch Powell*. Biteback.

Cooke, R. (2023) 'Laura Kuenssbergs's state of chaos: a parade of strange and idiotic people' *New Statesman* 18 September.

Cooney, C. (2023) ' Matt Hancock: leaked messages reveal battle over Covid and schools' *BBC News* 2 March.

Cosslett, R.L. (2017) 'How sad that English-speaking parents fear their children being taught in Welsh' *The Guardian* 27 June.

Coupland, R. (1954) *Welsh and Scottish Nationalism*. Collins.

Cox, B. (1991) *Cox on Cox: an English curriculum for the 1990s*. Hodder and Stoughton.

Cox, C.B. and Boyson, R. (1977) *Black Paper 1977*. Temple-Smith.

Crace, J. (2025) 'Starmer fires starting gun on race to bottom with Farage' *Guardian* 13 May.

Craig, G. (2007) *Sure Start and Black and Ethnic Minority Populations*. DfES Publications.

Crick, B. (1998) *Education for Citizenship and the Teaching of Democracy in Schools*. Report of an Advisory Group on Citizenship. DfES Publications.

Crossman, R. (1975) *Diaries of a Cabinet Minister 1964–70*. Hamish Hamilton and Cape.

Crouch, C. (2003) *Commercialisation or Citizenship: Education Policies and the Future of Public Services* (Fabian ideas 606). The Fabian Society.

Cummings, D. (2013) *Some Thoughts on Education and Political Priority. Paper presented to the Secretary of State for Education*. October.

Curriculum and Assessment Review (2025) *Interim Report*. Department for Education. April.

Currie, E. (2002) *Diaries 1992–1997*. Biteback.

Curtis, L.P. (1968) *Anglo-Saxons and Celts*. Bridgeport Press.

D'Ancona, M. (2009) *Being British: The Search for Values That Bind a Nation*. Transworld Publications.

Dalrymple, W. (2015) 'The original corporate raiders' *The Guardian* 4 March.

Darling, A. (2011) *Back from the Brink*. Atlantic Books.

Davies, N. (2014) *Hack Attack: How the Truth Caught Up with Rupert Murdoch*. Chatto and Windus.

DCSF (2007) *The Children's Plan: Building Brighter Futures*. The Stationary Office.

Derbyshire, H. (1994) *Not in Norfolk: Tackling the Invisibility of Racism*. Norfolk and Norwich Racial Equality Council.

DES (1965) *Circular 10/65*. Department of Education and Science.

DES (1971) *The Education of Immigrants. Education Survey 13*. HMSO.

DES (1974) *Educational Disadvantage and the needs of immigrants*. Department for Education and Science.

DES (1977) *Education in Schools: A Consultative Document*. HMSO.

DES (1978) *Special Educational Needs: Report of a Committee of Inquiry into the Education of Handicapped Children and Young People*. Department for Education and Science (The Warnock Report).

DES (1981) *West Indian Children in our Schools*. Department of Education and Science (The Rampton Report).

DES (1985a) *Education for All: Report of a Committee of Enquiry into the Education of Children from Minority Groups*. Department for Education and Science (The Swann Report).

DES (1985b) *Better Schools* (cmd 9469). HMSO.

DES (1991) *History in the National Curriculum (England)*. Department for Education and Science.

DfE (1992) *Choice and Diversity: A New Framework for Schools*. Department for Education.
DfE (2010) *The Importance of Teaching* (Cm 7980). Department of Education.
DfE (2014) *Promoting British Values as Part of SMSC (Social, Cultural, Spiritual and Moral Values) in Schools*. Department for Education.
DfE (2016) *Educational Excellence for All*. Department for Education.
DfE (2023) '*Special Educational Needs and Disability (SEND) and Alternative Provision (AP) improvement plan*. Department for Education.
DfES (2004) *Curriculum and Qualifications Reform 14–19: Final Report (Mike Tomlinson Report)*. DfES.
DoE/Home Office (2003) *The Victoria Climbie Inquiry. Report of an inquiry by Lord Laming*. The Stationary Office.
Dodd, V. (2024) 'Rioters after Southport attack, largely racially motivated thugs, Met Chief says' *The Guardian* 19 September.
Donegan, L. (1995) 'Muslim leaders warn of other cities on verge of violence as police give up' *The Guardian* 16 October.
Dorling, D. (2010) *Injustice: Why Social Inequality Persists*. The Policy Press.
Dorling, D. (2014) *Inequality and the 1%*. Verso.
Dorling, D. (2017) *The Equality Effect Improving Life for Everyone*. New Internationalist Publications.
Dorling, D. (2018a) *Peak Inequality: Britain's Ticking Time Bomb*. Policy Press.
Dorling, D. (2018b) *Personal Communication*. August.
Dorling, D. (2023) *Shattered Nation, Inequality and the Geography of a Failing State*. Verso.
Dorling, D. (2024) *Seven Children, Inequality and Britain's Next Generation*. Hurst and Co.
Dorling, D. (2025) *The Next Crisis*. Verso.
Dorling, D. and Thomas, B. (2016) *People and Places: A 21st Century Atlas of the UK*. Policy Press.
Dorling, D. and Tomlinson, S. (2017) 'Is Corbyn as lacking in drive and personality as Attlee? Let's hope so '*The Guardian Online*' 9 May.
Dorling, D. and Tomlinson, S. (2020) *Rule Britannia, Brexit and the End of Empire* (2nd edn). Biteback.
Dorras, J. and Walker, P. (1988) 'Two-way culture shock' *The Times Educational Supplement* 19 February.
Duncan-Smith, I. (2012) 'Foreword' in Lord Howard of Rising (ed) *Enoch at 100: A Re-examination of the Life Politics and, Philosophy of Enoch Powell*. Biteback.
Eddo-Lodge, R. (2017) *Why I'm No Longer Talking about Race*. Bloomsbury.
Edgerton Commission (1889) *Report of the Royal Commission on the Blind, Deaf, Dumb and Others, of the United Kingdom* (4 vols). HMSO.
Education Act (2005) London Gov.UK.

Elgot, J. (2018) 'How May's "hostile environment" for migrants brought anguish to a generation with every right to live their lives in Britain' *The Guardian* 18 April.

Elgot, J. and O'Carroll, L. (2025) 'EU deal puts Britain back on the world stage, says Starmer' *The Guardian* 20 May.

Elkins, C. (2022) *Legacy of Violence: A History of the British Empire.* The Bodley Head.

Elliot, L. and Atkinson, D. (2007) *Fantasy Island: Waking Up to the Incredible Economic, Political and Social Illusions of the Blair Legacy.* Constable.

Elliot-Major, L. (2011) 'Do wrongs make a riot' *Society Now Autumn: 6.*

Eminent Persons Group (2011) *Report of the Eminent Persons Group to the Commonwealth Heads of Governments.* Commonwealth Secretariat Perth. Scotland. October.

Enfield, L. (2023) 'Shocking extent of child poverty in Cheltenham' *Punchline Business* 4 August.

Evans, A. (2017) 'Evans apologises for wife's racist outburst at referee' *The Guardian* 11 November.

Evans, R. and Lewis, P. (2013) 'Their son was killed by racists: so why did the police spy on them?' *The Guardian* 24 June.

Eysenck, H.J. (1971) *Race, Intelligence and Education.* Temple-Smith.

Faux, F. (2017) 'How Gove's "brain flip" poisoned the extremist debate' *The Guardian* 4 July.

Fawcett, R. (ed) (1948) *Empire Youth Annual 1948.* P.R. Gawthorne.

Fazackerley, A. (2025) 'Peerage for Ofsted chief at time of Head's suicide would be an insult' *Observer* 30 March 2025.

Ferguson, N. (2003) *Empire: How Britain Made the Modern World.* Penguin.

Field, F. (1990) 'Britain's underclass: countering the growth' in Murray, C. (ed) *The Emerging British Underclass.* Institute for Economic Affairs (IEA Health and Welfare Unit).

Finnemore, J. (1902) *Men of Renown: King Alfred to Lord Kitchener.* A. and C. Black.

Fletcher, C.R.L and Kipling, R. (1911) *School History of England.* Oxford University Press.

Flood, A. (2018) 'Only 1% of children's books have BAME main characters, study finds' *The Guardian* 17 July.

Foot, P. (1969) *Immigration and Race in British Politics.* Penguin.

Forest, A. (2023) 'Gillian Keegan's department gave £1 million from schools rebuilding to company linked to husband' *The Independent* 6 September.

Francis, M. (2011) '2011 Prevent Strategy'. HM Government. www.radicalisationresearch.org/research/2011/

Fremeaux, J. and Maas, G. (2015) 'Colonization and globalisation' in Nicolaidis, K., Sebe, B. and Maas, G. (eds) *Echoes of Empire.* I.B. Tauris.

Fryer, P. (1984) *Staying Power: The History of Black People in Britain.* Pluto Press.

Galton, F. (1869) *Hereditary Genius*. Macmillan.

Gardiner, J. (1997) 'Blunkett to continue shaming' *Times Educational Supplement* 14 November.

Garside, J., Osborne, H. and MacAskill, E. (2017) 'The loud voices of the Brexit campaign who put their money offshore' *The Guardian* 10 November.

Garton-Ash, T. (2018) 'A humiliating deal risks descent into Weimar Britain' *The Guardian (Journal)* 27 July.

Gaskell, E. (1855) *North and South* (1995 edn). Penguin Books.

Gaythorne-Hardy, D. (1977) *The Public School Phenomenon*. Hodder and Stoughton.

Gearon, L. (2015) 'Education, security and intelligence studies' *British Journal of Educational Studies* 63/3: 263–79.

Geddes, A. (2013) *Britain and the European Union*. Palgrave-Macmillan.

Gentleman, A. (2010) 'Life on the edge' *The Guardian (Society)* 11 April.

Gentleman, A. (2018a) 'Warnings of Windrush scandal date back to 2013' *The Guardian* 19 July.

Gentleman, A. (2018b) 'Rudd tells MPs: we were wrong over Windrush citizens' *The Guardian* 17 April.

Giddens, A. (2007) *Over to You, Mr Brown*. Polity Press.

Gillborn, D. (2007) 'Tony Blair and the politics of race in education' *Oxford Review of Education* 34/6: 371–25.

Gillborn, D. (2010) 'The white working class: racism and respectability: Victim, degenerates and interest convergence' *British Journal of Educational Studies* 58/1: 2–25.

Gillborn, D. (2024) *White Lies, Racism Education and Critical Race Theory*. Routledge.

Gillborn, D., Demack, S., Rollock, N. and Warmington, P. (2017) 'Moving the goalposts: 25 years of the Black/White achievement gap' *British Educational Research Journal* 43/5: 848–74.

Gilley, B. (2017) 'The case for colonialism' *Third World Quarterly* 15 August.

Gilroy, P. (1987) *There Ain't no Black in the Union Jack*. Hutchinson.

Gilroy, P. (2004) *After Empire: Melancholia or Convivial Culture*. Routledge.

Giordano, E. (2025) 'Trump claims leaders are "kissing my ass" to make trade deals as tariff onslaught begins' *Politico* 9 April.

Godwin, E. (2025) 'Riots fuelled by Guardian editors' *The Times* 31 March.

Gohil, M. and Vinter, A. (2024) 'I have night-mares: victims of far right talk of their lingering fears' *The Guardian* 28 September.

Goldberg, D.T. (2009) *The Threat of Race*. Wiley–Blackwell.

Goodhart, D. (2004) 'The discomfort of strangers' *The Guardian* 24 February.

Goodhart, D. (2017) *The Road to Somewhere: The Populist Revolt and the Future of Politics*. Hurst.

Gov.UK (2017) *Race Disparity Audit*. The Cabinet Office.

Gov.UK (2020) *Schools, Pupils and their Characteristics*. UK Government.

Gov.UK (2025) *PM Remarks at Immigration White Paper Press Conference*. 12 May. The Prime Minister's Office.

Gove, M. (2006) *Celsius 7/7:How the West's Policy of Appeasement Has Provoked More Fundamental Terror and What Is to Be Done*. Weidenfeld and Nicolson.

Gove, M. (2013a) *Speech to the Social Market Foundation*. Social Market Foundation. 23 August.

Gove, M. (2013b) 'I refuse to surrender to the Marxist teachers who are hell-bent on destroying our schools; Education Secretary berates "the new enemies of promise" for opposing his plans' *Mail Online* 23 March.

Graham, D. with Tytler, D. (1993) *A Lesson for Us All: The Making of the National Curriculum*. Routledge.

Green, F. and Kynaston, D. (2019) *Engines of Privilege: Britain's Private School Problem*. Bloomsbury.

Greenfield, P. (2018) 'National Geographic admits racist reports' *The Guardian* 14 March.

Guest, A. (1910) 'Social ideals: The Earl of Meath' *Court Journal* 16 February.

Hadow Report (1926) *The Education of the Adolescent*. HMSO.

Hall, S. (ed) (1978) *Policing the Crisis*. Macmillan.

Hall, S. (1991) 'Old and new identities: old and new ethnicities' in King, A. (ed) *Culture, Globalisation and the World System*. Macmillan.

Halliday, J. (2024) 'Wanting to belong to something: children sentenced for rioting' *The Guardian* 29 September.

Halliday, J. and Pidd, H. (2024) 'Southport attacks, the failures that allowed Axel Rudakubana to kill' *The Guardian* 24 January.

Hansard (1992) *Columns 149–202*. House of Commons.

Hansard (2022) *Vol 724*. House of Commons. 7 December.

Hare, D. (2016) 'Like all revolutions, it will eat its own' *The Guardian* 2 July.

Hargreaves, D. (1993) 'Preface' in King, S.A. and Reiss, M.J. (eds) *The Multicultural Dimension of the National Curriculum*. Falmer.

Harper Lee, N. (1960) *To Kill a Mocking Bird*. Harper Collins.

Harward, K. and Komarova, M. (2018) 'Brexit on the border' *QEB Institute for Peace, Security and Justice*. Queen Elizabeth University.

Hastings, M. (2007) 'Premiership of Tony Blair tainted with mendacity' *The Guardian* 12 April.

Hattenstone, S. (2018) 'Why was the scheme behind May's 'Go Home' vans called Operation Vaken' *The Guardian* 16 April.

Hattersley, R. (2005) 'Even Enoch Powell did not stoke fears like this' *The Guardian* 25 April.

Heath, E. (1970) *Letter to Bexley Community Relations Council*. Bexley, Kent. June.

Hechter, M. (1975) *Internal Colonialism: The Celtic Fringe in British National Development 1536–1966*. Routledge and Kegan Paul.

Helm, T. (2024) 'I will help working class pupils defy the odds to succeed – just as I did' *The Observer* 21 July.

Henig, B. and Dorling, D. (2016) 'The EU Referendum: political insights' *The Spectator* September.

Henry, L. and Ryder, M. (2021) *Black British Lives Matter*. Faber.

Herbertson, A.J. and Cossar, J. (1909) *Commercial Geography of the World*. A. and R. Chambers.

Herbertson, A.J. and Cossar, J. (2016) *Commercial Geography of the World Part 11. Outside the British Isles*. A. and R. Chambers.

Herrnstein, R. and Murray, C. (1994) *The Bell Curve: Intelligence and Class Structure in American Life*. The Free Press.

Higgins, C. (2025) 'Music is never fixed in me, cellist Sheku-Kanneh Mason surviving a volcano of racism' *The Guardian* 21 May.

Hirsch, A. (2018) *Brit(ish): On Race, Identity and Belonging*. Jonathan Cape.

HM Government (2018a) *Integrated Communities Strategy Green Paper: Building Stronger More United Communities*. Department for Communities and Local Government.

HM Government (2018b) *The Future Relationship Between the Government and the European Union*. Cabinet Office.

Hobsbawm, E. and Ranger, T. (1983) *The Invention of Tradition*. Cambridge University Press.

Holmwood, J. and O'Toole, T. (2014) *Countering Extremism in British Schools: The Truth about the Trojan Horse Affair*. Policy Press.

Home Affairs Committee (1981) *Racial Disadvantage* (cmd 6234). HMSO.

Home Office (1965) *Immigration from the Commonwealth* (cmd 2739). HMSO.

Home Office (1978) *Proposals for Replacing Section 11 of the Local Government Act*. HMSO.

Honeybone, R.C. and Robertson, B.S. (1971) *The Southern Continents* (3rd edn). Heinemann Educational Books.

Honeyford, R. (1982) 'Multiracial myths' *Times Educational Supplement* 19 November.

Hopkinson, J. (2017) *Interviews with Adults Bussed as Children in Huddersfield in the 1960s*. University of Huddersfield.

Hoque, A. (2015) *British – Islamic identity: Third Generation Bangladeshis From East London*. Institute of Education Press.

Hughes, K. (2015) 'Dorm feasts and red-hot pashes' *Guardian Online* 14 February.

Hughill, B. (1987) 'Dramatic steps that will carry Britain forward' *Times Educational Supplement* 16 October.

Humphries, S. (1981) *Hooligans or Rebels?*. Oxford University Press.

Hunter, A. (2017) 'Corry Evans apologises for wife's racist rant at Romanian footballer' *The Guardian* 10 November.

Hutton, Lord J. (2004) *Inquiry into the Circumstances Surrounding the Death of Dr David Kelly* (HC 247). HM Government.

Hymas, C. (2025) 'Albania snubs Starmer's plea to take asylum seekers' *The Telegraph* 15 May.

IAAM (1950) *The Teaching of History*. Incorporated Association of Assistant Masters in Secondary Schools.

Inclusive Britian (2024) *Second up-dated report*. UK Parliament.

Independent (1995) *'The sleaze list'* 22 July.

Inglis, F. (1985) *The Management of Ignorance*. Blackwell.

Instead Consultancy (2014) *The Trojan Horse Affair in Birmingham: Competing and Overlapping Narratives. March–May 2014* (www.instead.co.uk).

ITV (2017) *Victoria*. Independent Television Channel 3. Serial in six parts.

Jack, I. (2018) 'Hoarding food now seems the only sensible thing to do' *The Guardian* 28 July.

Jackson, B. and Marsden, D. (1962) *Education and the Working Class*. Routledge and Kegan Paul.

Jacques, M. (2003) 'Tennis racist – it's time we did something about it' *The Guardian* 25 June.

James, O. (1990) 'Crime and the American mind' *The Independent* 22 May.

Jay Gould, S. (1981) *The Mismeasure of Man*. Penguin Books.

Jebb, Lord, G. (1961) *Speech to the House of Lords*. London.

Jeffcoate, R. (1979) *Positive Image: Towards a Multicultural Curriculum*. Harper and Row.

Jenkins, R. (1966) *Address to a meeting of Voluntary Liaison Committees*. 23 May. National Council for Commonwealth Immigration.

Jenson, A. (1969) 'How much can we boost IQ and scholastic ability' *Harvard Education Review* 39: 1–23.

John, Gus (2010) 'The people of Grenada need answers' *The Guardian* 10 October.

Johnson, B. (2013) *The 2013 Annual Margaret Thatcher Lecture*. Centre for Policy Studies 27 November.

Johnson, B. (2017) 'Brexit mustn't leave us a "vassal state"' *Sunday Times* 17 December.

Johnston, J. (2020) 'Minister says No 10 must improve vetting process after Andrew Sabinski quits' *Civil Service Newsletter* 18 February.

Joseph, K. (1986) 'Without prejudice: education for an ethnically mixed society' *Multicultural Society* 4/3: 6–8.

Judt, T. (2010a) *Ill Fares the Land*. Allen Lane.

Judt, T. (2010b) *Postwar: A History of Europe since 1945*. Vintage Books.

Kaletsky, A. (2000) 'Who do these worthy idiots think they are?' *The Times* 21 October.

Kampner, J. (2003) *Blair's Wars*. The Free Press.

Kappal, B. (2017) 'Why Brexiteers need to update their colonial history' *New Statesman* 17 March.

Karaksoglu, Y. and Luchtenberg, S. (2002) 'Islamophobia in Germany' *Lifelong Learning in Germany* 3: 195–201.

Kelly, Sir C. (2009) 'MPs expenses scandal: a time-line' *Daily Telegraph* 4 November.

Kelly, E. and Cohen, T. (1988) *Racism in Schools: New Research Evidence*. Trentham Books.

Kelso, P. (2000) 'Prisoner killed in race hate attack' *The Guardian* 25 October.

Kennedy, C. (2000) *The Future of Politics*. Harper Collins.

Kennedy, D. (2024) 'Who are the far-right groups organizing the Southport protests?' *The Times* 2 August.

Kettle, M. (2025) 'The UK risks falling apart: can Starmer mend it now' *The Guardian* 22 May.

Khomami, N. and Watts, H. (2017) 'Coverage of call to decolonise the English curriculum mad student "target" for abuse' *The Guardian* 27 October.

Kiernan, V.G. (1969) *The Lords of Humankind*. Century Hutchinson.

King, A.S. and Reiss, M. (1993) *The Multicultural Dimension of the National Curriculum*. The Falmer Press.

Kingsley, C. (1863) *The Water-Babies: A Fairy Tale for a Lost Baby* (reprinted 2003 in Oxford Classics). Oxford University Press.

Kipling, R. (1899) *Stalky and Co.* Hodder and Stoughton.

Kipling, R. (1940) *The Definitive Edition of Kipling's Verse*. Hodder and Stoughton.

Kirp, D. (1979) *Doing Good by Doing Little*. University of California Press

Kurshi, H., Roy, A. and Shamsie, K. (2017) 'Open the doors and let these books in' *The Guardian Review* 11 November.

Kynaston, D. (2007) *Austerity Britain 1945–1951*. Bloomsbury.

Labour Party (1989) *Multicultural Education: Labour's Policy for Schools*. The Labour Party.

Langford, E. (2020) 'Top civil servant out after exam fiasco as Johnson demand fresh official leadership' *Politics Home* 20 August.

Lawrence, D. (2007) *And Still I Rise: A Mother's Search for Justice*. Faber and Faber (first published 2006).

Lawson, N. (2007) 'A decade of Blair has left the Labour party on its knees' *The Guardian* 19 April.

Lawson-Walton, J. (1899) 'Imperialism' *Contemporary Review*. LXXV: 306.

Lawton, D. (2005) *Education and Labour Party Ideologies 1900–2001 and Beyond*. Routledge-Falmer.

Levy, A. (2004) *Small Island*. Headline Publishing.

Lewis. P., Newburn, T., Taylor, M. and Ball, J. (2011) 'Blame the police: why the rioters say they took part' *The Guardian* 5 August.

Lloyd, T.O. (1984) *The British Empire 1558–1983*. Oxford University Press.

Loach, K. (2016) *I, Daniel Blake*. Film directed by Ken Loach, Written by Paul Laverty. (Winner of the Palme D'or. Film Festival de Cannes).

Maastricht Treaty (1992) *The Unseen Treaty: Treaty on European Union Maastricht 1992*. Foreign and Commonwealth Office.

MacCleod, D. (1996) 'Clampdown on Inner city schools' *The Guardian* 7 May.

MacDonald, I. Bhavani, T. Khan, L. and John, G. (1989) *Murder in the Playground*. Longsight Press.

MacFarlane, R.A. (2007) 'Historiography of selected works on Cecil John Rhodes' *History of Africa* 34: 437–46.

MacIntyre, D. (1991) 'Baker seeks extra police after riots' *The Independent* 15 September.

MacKenzie, J.M. (1984) *Propaganda and Empire: The Manipulation of British Public Opinion 1880–1984*. Manchester University Press.

MacKenzie, J.M. (ed) (1986) *Imperialism and Popular Culture*. Manchester University Press.

MacKenzie, J.M. (2015) 'Epilogue: analysing echoes of empire in contemporary context: a personal odyssey of an imperial historian' in Nicolaidis, K., Sebe, B. and Maas, G. (eds) *Echoes of Empire: Memory, Identity and Colonial Legacies*. L.B. Taurus.

Mackie, T. (2017) 'UK cannot become a colony of the EU for two years' *Daily Express* 16 December.

Macpherson, Sir W. (1999) *The Stephen Lawrence Inquiry* (cmd 4262). The Stationary Office.

Macshane, D. (2017) *Brexit, No Exit: Why (in the End) Britain Won't Leave Europe*. L.B. Tauris.

Magraw, B.I. (1919) *The Thrill of History* 4 vols. Collins.

Malik, N. (2018) 'My joy was followed by a nausea of fury' *The Guardian* 5 March.

Mandelson, P. and Liddle, R. (1996) *The Blair Revolution: Can New Labour Deliver?* Faber and Faber.

Mangan, J.A. (1980) 'Images of Empire in Edwardian-Victorian Public Schools' *Journal of Educational Administration and History* XII: 1–10.

Mangan, J.A. (1986) 'The grit of our forefathers: invented traditions, propaganda and imperialism' in MacKenzie, J.M. (ed) *Imperialism and Popular Culture*. Manchester University Press.

Manning, S. (2016) 'Boris Johnson is perfectly in tune with Britain's post-colonial lament' *The Guardian Online* 19 July.

Mansell, W. (2004) 'Make room for the Empire' *Times Educational Supplement* 9 July.

Manzoor, S. (2008) 'Black Britain's darkest hour' *The Observer* 24 February.

Marquand, D. (2009) The spirit of Thomas Paine could yet inspire Cameron' *The Guardian* 9 September.
Marshall, T.H. (1951) *Citizenship and Social Class*. Cambridge University Press.
Marx, K. (1870) Letter to Sigfried Meyor and Augustus Vogt in New York. 9 August, in Marx, K. and Engels, F. (eds) *Selected Correspondence*. Progress Press.
Mason, R. (2017) 'May calls for inquiry into abuse of politicians' *The Guardian* 13 July.
May, T. (2016) 'A country that works for everyone', in *The Conservative Election Manifesto*. The Conservative Party.
May, T. (2023) *The Abuse of Power*. Headline Publications.
McCulloch, G. (2009) 'Empires and education: the British Empire' in Cowen, R. and Kazamias, A.M. (eds) *International Handbook of Comparative Education*. Springer.
McGlade, H. and Kelly (2025) *Investigating Educational Disadvantage and Place-Based Approaches in the North East of England*. Education Policy Institute and Durham University.
McInch, A. (2018) *Only Schools and Courses: An Ethnography of Working-Class Schooling in South Wales*. PhD thesis. Cardiff Metropolitan University.
McInnery, L. (2016) 'What society lets families fear deportation for sending their children to school' *Education Guardian* 18 October.
McKann, K. (2018) 'Amber Rudd resigns as Home Secretary as she admits to misleading Parliament on migration' *The Daily Telegraph* 30 April.
McNeal, J. and Rogers, M. (1971) *The Multiracial School*. Penguin.
McVeigh, T. (2011) 'The message when youth clubs close: no-one cares' *The Observer* 14 August.
McVeigh, T. (2016) 'Deaths are not just happening in the US: why activists brought the Black Lives movement to the UK' *The Observer* 7 August.
Meath, Lord (1910) 'Duty and discipline in the education of children', in Meath, L. *Essays on Duty and Discipline no 9*, Cassell and Co.
Meyer, H.D. and Benavot, A. (2013) *Pisa, Power and Policy*. Symposium Books.
Miles, A. (2007) 'Sneaky, unfair, divisive: welcome to church schools' *The Times* 23 May.
Mills, C. (2007) 'White ignorance' in Sullivan, S. and Tuana, N. (eds) *Race and the Epistemologies of Ignorance*. University of New York Press.
Ministerial Working Group on Public Disorder and Community Cohesion (The Cantle Report) (2001) *Report to the Home Secretary*. The Home Office.
Ministry of Education (1946) *The Nation's Schools*. HMSO.
Mirza, H.S. (1998) 'Race gender and the social consequences of a pseudo-scientific discourse' *Race, Ethnicity and Education* 1/1: 111–28.
Mishra, P. (2017) *The Age of Anger: A History of Government of the Present*. Allen Lane.

Modood, T., Berthold, R., Lakey, J., Nazroo, J., Smith, P., Virdee, S. and Beishon, S. (1997) *Ethnic Minorities in Britain: Diversity and Disadvantage. The Fourth PSI Survey.* Policy Studies Institute.

Mohsin, M. (2016) 'Empire shaped the world: there is an abyss at the heart of dishonest history textbooks' *The Guardian* 31 October.

Monet, J. (1945) *'There will be no peace'. Speech to the French Committee of National Liberation.* Paris. 5 August.

Montgomerie, T. and Pancevski, B. (2017) 'May drafts Gove in to Brexit war cabinet' *The Sunday Times* 3 November.

Moore, M. and Ramsey, G. (2017) 'UK media coverage of the 2016 EU Referendum Campaign, and voting patterns' *Kings College, London (Study of Media and Communications)* May.

Moore, P. (2016) 'How Britain votes: Over 65s were more than twice as likely as the under 25s to have voted to leave the European Union'. YouGov 27 June.

Moorhouse, G. (1984) *India Britannica.* Paladin.

Morris, S. (2017) "'Cardiff medical school "blacking up" play led to feeling of segregation' *The Guardian* 25 January.

Motavali, A. (2018) 'Student who called out lad culture for what it really is' *The Observer* 25 March.

Mounk, Y. (2018) *The People vs Democracy: Why Our Freedom Is in Danger and How to Save It.* Harvard University Press.

Msimang, S. (2016) 'Boris Johnson is perfectly in tune with Britain's post-colonial lament' *The Guardian* 19 July.

Murray, C. (1990) *The Emerging British Underclass.* London Institute for Economic Affairs (IEA Health and Welfare Unit).

Murray, C. (1994) 'Underclass: the crisis deepens' *The Sunday Times* 22 May.

Murray, D. (2010) 'The Prevent Strategy, a textbook example of how alienate just about everybody' *Daily Telegraph* 31 March.

Murray, D. (2017) *The Strange Death of Europe: Immigration, Identity, Islam.* Bloomsbury.

Myers, K. (2015) *Struggles for the Past: Irish and Afro-Caribbean histories in England.* Manchester University Press.

Nagesh, A. (2016) '11 things Boris has said to make him the perfect foreign secretary' *Metro* 14 June.

National Centre for Social Research (2024) *British Social Attitude Survey.* NATCEN.

National Education Union (2025) *Thinking beyond the Box.* NEU.

Naylor, F. (1988) 'Political lessons of Dewsbury' *The Independent* 22 December.

NCC (1991) *National Curriculum Council Newsletter.* National Curriculum Council.

NEU (2024) *Thinking beyond the Box. Evidence to the Review of Curriculum and Assessment.* National Education Union.

Nevett, J. (2018) 'Britain s prefer tough immigration: Windrush crisis could benefit Tories in local elections' *The Daily Star* 2 May.

Newsinger, J. (2006) *The Blood Never Dried: A People's History of the British Empire*. Trentham Books.

Newsom Report (1963) *Half Our Future: A Report of the Central Advisory Committee on Education*. HMSO.

Nicolaidis, K., Sebe, B. and Maas, G. (eds) (2015) *Echoes of Empire: Memory, Identity and Colonial Legacies*. L.B. Taurus.

Norton-Taylor, R. and Milne, S. (1999) 'Racism: extremists led Powell's marches' *The Guardian* 1 January.

NUT (1993) *Union Response to the Proposals for the Reform of Initial Teacher Training*. National Union of Teachers.

O'Brien, E. (1960) *The Girl with Green Eyes*. Hutchinson (reissued by Penguin 1975).

O'Carroll, L. (2017) 'Gina Miller fears acid attack following months of threats' *The Guardian* 10 August.

O'Carroll, L. (2018) 'Dutch judge allows British expats to pursue EU citizenship rights' *The Guardian* 8 February.

O'Connor, M., Hales, E., Davies, J. and Tomlinson, S. (1999) *Hackney Downs: The School That Dared to Fight*. Cassell.

O'Dowd, N. (2013) 'The era of no Blacks, dogs or Irish is over but should not be forgotten' *Irish Central News* 4 October.

O'Hara, M. (2015) *Austerity Bites*. Policy Press.

Oakley, N. (2017) 'Brenda from Bristol sums up the mood of the nation again in just four words' *Daily Mail* 9 June.

Obioma, C. (2107) 'Africa has been failed by Westernisation: it must cast off its subservience' *The Guardian* 13 November.

Oborne, P. (2021) *The Assault on Truth*. Simon and Schuster.

Observer (2007) *Comment 29 The big issue; segregated schools. The Observer* 3 June.

Observer (2017) Editorial. 'Behind this disaster lies indifference to the lives of the poor' *The Observer* 18 June.

Ofsted (1993) *Access and Achievement in Urban Education: A Report from HMI*. Office for Standards in Education.

Okundaye, J. (2025) 'The fire of Black Lives Matter is out, but still its embers burn' *The Guardian* 24 May.

Olusoga, D. (2016) *Black and British: A Forgotten History*. Macmillan.

Olusoga, D. (2017) 'Empire 2.0 is dangerous nostalgia for something that never existed' *The Guardian* 19 March.

ONS (2021) *Covid-Related Deaths in England and Wales 2020*. Office for National Statistics.

Osler, A. and Starkey, H. (2005) *Changing citizenship: Democracy and Inclusion in Education*. Open University Press/McGraw-Hill.

Owen, G. (2018) 'Vile racist attack on Meghan by mistress of UKIP chief' *Daily Mail* 14 January.

Owen, J. (2016) 'British Empire: students should be taught colonialism was "not all good" say historians' *The Independent Online* 22 January.

Palmer, F. (ed) (1986) *Anti-Racism: An Assault on Education and Values.* Sherwood Press.

Parekh, Lord B. (2000) *The Future of Multi-Ethnic Britain (The Parekh Report).* Profile Books.

Patten, J. (1992) *Things to Come: The Tories in the Twentieth Century.* Sinclair-Stevenson.

Paxman, J. (2012) *Empire.* Penguin/Random House.

Pearce, S. (1986) 'Swann and the spirit of the age' in Palmer, F. (ed) *Anti-Racism: An Assault on Education and Value.* Sherwood Press.

Pettifor, A. (2018) 'A triumph for Osborne austerity plan? Not when our social fabric is in tatters' *The Observer* 4 March.

Phillips, R. (1998) *History Teaching, Nationhood and the State.* Cassell.

Pierce, A. (2008) 'Queen asks why no-one saw it coming' *Daily Telegraph* 5 November.

Plowden Report (1967) *Children and Their Primary Schools.* HMSO.

Porter, B. (2015) 'Epilogue: After images of Empire' in Nicolaidis, K., Sebe, B. and Maas, B.G. (eds) *Echoes of Empire.* L.B. Taurus.

Postman, N. and Weingartner, C. (1969) *Teaching as a Subversive Activity.* Delta.

Powell, J.E. (1959) Hola Camp speech. *House of Commons* 27 July.

Powell, J.E. (1961) *Speech on nationhood to the St George Society.* 22 April.

Powell, J.E. (1968) Speech to the Annual General Meeting of the West Midlands Area Conservative Political Centre, Birmingham. 20 April.

Powell, J.E. (1971) *Speech on European Union to Association de Chefs Enterprise Libre.* Paris.

Private Eye (2018) '*Prickly Heaton*' No. 145.

Pyke, N. (1994) 'Patten is forced to apologise' *Times Educational Supplement* 24 June.

QCA (2007) *The National Curriculum: Statutory Requirements for Key Stages 3 and 4.* Qualifications and Curriculum Authority.

Raab, D. (2012) (co-editor) *Britannia Unchained: Global Lessons for Growth and Prosperity.* Macmillan.

Ramesh, R. (2015) 'Prevent Programme spying on our young people' *The Guardian* 6 December.

Ramsey, A. (2013) 'My public school days and the building of upper-class solidarity' *Bright Green (Independent media for a radical democratic green movement)* 25 June.

Ranson, S. (1984) 'Towards a tertiary tripartism: new codes of control and a 17+' in Broadfoot, P. (ed) *Selection, Certification and Control.* Methuen.

Rawlinson, K. (2017) 'Viscount jailed for offering money for killing of Gina Miller' *The Guardian* 13 July.

Rawlinson, K. (2018) 'Two arrested after complaints of racist chants' *The Guardian* 9 March.

Rawnsley, A. (2010) *The End of the Party: The Rise and Fall of New Labour*. Viking Books.

Rawnsley, A. (2024) ' In all this election debate why is there a conspiracy of silence about Brexit' *The Observer* 9 May.

Rawnsley, A. (2025) 'It is mission critical that Labour repairs the contract between citizen and state' *The Guardian* 16 March.

RCCCFM (1908) *Report of the Royal Commission on the Care and Control of the Feeble-Minded* (8 vols). HM Government.

Reclaiming Schools. (2016) 'Brexit campaign leaves children scared' *Reclaiming Schools.org* 30 June.

Reed Langan (2024) 'Judgment day for democracy' *Project Syndicate* 28 February.

Rees-Mogg, J. (2017) *BBC News night*. 15 December.

Rex, J. (1973) *Race, Colonialism and the City*. Routledge and Kegan Paul.

Rex, J. (1986) *Race and Ethnicity*. Open University Press.

Rex, J. (1996) *Ethnic Minorities in the Modern Nation State*. Macmillan.

Rex, J. (2004) 'Multiculturalism and political integration in modern nation states' in Gorny, A. and Ruspini, P. (eds) *Migration in the New Europe*. Palgrave Macmillan.

Rex, J. and Moore, R. (1967) *Race, Community and Conflict*. Oxford University Press.

Rex, J. and Tomlinson, S. (1979) *Colonial Immigrants in a British City: A Class Analysis*. Routledge and Kegan Paul.

Rich, P.S. (1986) *Race and Empire in British Politics*. Cambridge University Press.

Richardson, B. (ed) (2005) *Tell It Like It Is: How Our Schools Fail Black Children*. Bookmark Publications/Trentham Books.

Rizzo, M. (2006) 'What was left of the Groundnut Scheme? Developmental disaster and Labour Market in Southern Tanganyika 1946–1952' *Journal of Agrarian Change* 6/2: 205–38.

Robbins, Lord A. (1963) *Higher Education, Report of the Prime Minister's Committee* (cmd 2154). HMSO.

Roberts, A. (2012) 'Enoch Powell and the Nation State' in Lord Howard of Rising (ed) *Enoch at 100*. Biteback.

Roberts, R. (1971) *The Classic Slum: Salford Life in the First Quarter of the Century*. Penguin.

Rodrigues, J. (2017) 'From the Archive: How the Guardian reported the partition of India 70 years ago' *Guardian Online*.

Rollock, N. (2022) *The Racial Code. Tales of Resistance and Survival*. Penguin.

Rollock, N., Gillborn, D., Vincent, C. and Ball, S.J. (2015) *The Colour of Class*. Routledge.

Rose, E.J.B. and Associates (1969) *Colour and Citizenship: A report on British Race relations*. Oxford University Press for Institute of Race Relations.

Rose, H. and Rose, S. (2012) *Genes, Cells and Brains*. Verso.

Rosebery, Lord (1900) *Inaugural Address on the Conferment of Title as Rector of Glasgow University*. Glasgow.

Roth, A. and Christou, W. (2025) 'Trump signs £107 billion deal with the Saudis as tour of Gulf begins' *Guardian* 14 May.

Roth, A. Smith, D. and Helmore, E. (2018) 'EU is my foe, says Trump as he heads for summit with Putin' *The Guardian* 16 July.

Roundtree, C. (2018) 'The new Windrush betrayal: Home office shredded documents that proved Caribbean migrants came to the UK decades ago' *Daily Mail* 17 April.

Runnymede Trust (1993) *Racist Attacks and Harassment: The Epidemic of the 1990s*. The Runnymede Trust.

Runnymede Trust (2021) *Statement Regarding the Report of the Commission on Racial and Ethnic Disparities*. The Runnymede Trust.

Rushdie, S. (1988) *The Satanic Verses*. Viking Books.

Rutter, M. and Madge, N. (1976) *Cycles of Disadvantage*. Heinemann.

Sabbagh, D., Stewart, H. and Elgot, J. (2018) 'May narrowly heads off defeat after caving in to the Brexit hard-liners' *The Guardian* 16 July.

Saini, A. (2019) *Superior: The Return of Race Science*. 4th Estate.

Sampson, S. (1992) *The Essential Anatomy of Britain: Democracy in Crisis*. Hodder and Stoughton.

Saunders, A. (2016) 'Jamaicans deported over four years: 9425 sent back to Jamaica, mainly from the UK' *Jamaican Gleaner* 8 September.

Saunders, B. (2023) *It's Okay to Be Angry about Capitalism*. Allen Lane.

Savage, M. and Ferguson, D. (2020) 'How ministers made a shambles of English schools' *The Guardian* 20 December.

Scarman, Lord (1982) *The Brixton Disorders 10–12th April 1982. (Report of an Inquiry by Lord Scarman)*. Penguin.

School Enquiry Commission (1868) *The Taunton Commission*. HM Government.

Scott Inquiry (1996) *Report on Arms Sales to Iraq by Lord Justice Scott*. HMSO.

Scruton, R. (1986) 'The myth of cultural relativism' in Palmer, F. (ed) *Anti-Racism: An Assault on Education and Value*. The Sherwood Press.

Scruton, R. (2017) 'Brexit will give us back pride in our island roots' *The Times* 18 November.

Seeley, J.E. (1883) *The Expansion of Empire*. Macmillan.

Seldon, A. and Newell, R. (2023) *Johnson at 10, The Inside Story*. Atlantic Books.

Select Committee on Race Relations and Immigration (1969) *The Problems of Coloured School Leavers*. HMSO.

Select Committee on Race Relations and Immigration (1973) *Education*. HMSO.

Select Committee on Race Relations (House of Commons) (1977) *The West Indian Community*. HMSO.

Sennett, R. (2006) *The Culture of the New Capitalism*. Yale University Press.

Sewell, T. (1997) *Black Masculinities and Schooling*. Trentham Books.

Shackle, S. (2017) 'What really happened in the Trojan Horse schools?' *The Guardian* 2 September.

Shain, Farzana (2013) 'Race, nation and education; an overview of British attempts to manage diversity since the 1950s' *Education Inquiry* 4/1: 63–85.

Sherman, A. (1979) 'Britain's urge to self-destruction' *The Daily Telegraph* 9 September.

Shindler, C. (2012) *National Service: From Aden to Aldershot: Tales from the Conscripts 1946–62*. Sphere.

Shipman, T. (2016) *All Out War: The Full Story of Brexit*. William Collins.

Shipman, T. (2017) *Fall Out: A year of Political Mayhem*. William Collins.

Shipman, T. (2024) *Out: How Brexit Got Done and the Tories Were Undone*. William Collins.

Shotte, G. (2002) *Education, Migration and Identities: Relocated Montserratian Students in London Schools*. PhD Study. Institute of Education.

Shukla, N. (ed) (2016) *The Good Immigrant*. Unbound.

Siddiqui, A. (2007) *Islam at Universities in England*. Department for Education and Skills.

Siedler, V. (2018) *Making Sense of Brexit*. Policy Press.

Simon, B. (1960) *Studies in the History of Education 1780–1870*. Lawrence and Wishart.

Simon, B. (1991) *Education and the Social Order 1940–1990*. Lawrence and Wishart.

Sky News (2024) 'Who is Frank Hester and what did he say about Diane Abbott?' 14 March.

Slack, J. (2016) 'Enemies of the people: fury over "out of touch" judges who have declared war on democracy by defying the 17.4 million British voters and who could trigger a constitutional crisis' *Daily Mail* 3 November.

Smith, D. (2013) 'Tony Blair plotted military intervention in Zimbabwe, claims Thabo Mbeki' *The Guardian Online* 27 November.

Smith, E. (2015) 'Communist attitudes towards Polish migration to post-war Britain' *Hateful of History* (Blog). 5 May.

Smith, M. (2017) 'Myths about the EU since 1992' *Daily Mirror* 9 October.

Speed, B. (2016) 'How different demographic groups voted in the EU Referendum' *(The Lord Ashcroft Poll) New Statesman* 24 June.

Standards and Publications Committee (2021) *Correspondance between the Committee Chair and Mr David Ross*. Appendix 4. 8 July. UK Parliament.

Stanley, J. (2022) 'Buffalo shooting: how white replacement theory keeps inspiring mass murder' *The Guardian* 15 May.

Stembridge, J. (1939) *The World: A General Regional Geography*. Oxford University Press.

Stembridge, J. (1951) *New World Geographies: Europe*. Oxford University Press.

Stephens, P. (2018) 'Nostalgia has stolen the future' *Financial Times* 27 July.

Stewart, H. (2017) 'Focus on students was a "stupid policy based on bad data"' *The Guardian* 25 August.

Stewart, H. (2024) '*Blocked Labour candidate Faiza Shaheen to challenge deselection*' *The Guardian* 30 May.

Stewart, H., Cregar, P. and Elgot, J. (2018) 'Johnson attacks "miserable" Brexit plan' *The Guardian* 19 July.

Summers, D. (2009) 'Brown sticks by British jobs for British workers remark' *The Guardian* 30 January.

Syal, R. (2013) 'Anger at "go home" message to illegal migrants' *The Guardian* 26 July.

Sylvester, R. (2000) 'The nine charmed lives of Stephen Norris' *The Telegraph* 26 August.

Sylvester, R. (2025) 'Starmer's "deep regret" for Island of strangers speech' *The Observer* 25 June.

Taylor, D. (2017) 'Curt, almost implausible email puts FA chairman in firing line' *The Guardian* 17 October.

Taylor, D. (2018) 'UK removed legal protection for Windrush immigrants in 2014' *The Guardian* 16 April.

Tax Justice (2024) '*A quarter of global tax dodging is enabled by the Uk and British overseas territories*' 21 November.

Thatcher, M. (1978) *Interview for Grenada Television* 30 January.

Thatcher, M. (1993) *The Downing Street Years*. Harper Collins.

The Times (1849) *Editorial*.

The Times (1919) *Letters* 14 June.

The Times (1919) *Letters* 19 June.

Tilly, C. (1976) 'Reflections on the history of European state-making' in Tilly, C. (ed) *The Formation of Nation States in Western Europe*. Princeton University Press.

Times Educational Supplement (1990) *Editorial* 23 June.

Times Higher Educational Supplement (2017) *Letter*. '*Pro-colonialism paper: how did it get published*' 28 September p 31.

Tinker, H. (1982) *A Message from the Falklands*. Junction Books.

Tiratsoo, N. (1997) *From Blitz to Blair: A New History of Britain since 1939*. Weidenfeld and Nicholson.

Tocci, N. (2025) 'The UK didn't leave Europe after all' *Prospect* June.

Tomlinson, S. (1981) *Educational Subnormality: A Study in Decision-Making* (reprinted 2018). Routledge and Kegan Paul.

Tomlinson, S. (1982) *A Sociology of Special Education* (reprinted 2012). Routledge and Kegan Paul.

Tomlinson, S. (1984) *Ethnic Minorities in British Schools.* Heinemann.

Tomlinson, S. (1990) *Multicultural Education in White Schools*. Batsford.

Tomlinson, S. (1992) 'Disadvantaging the disadvantaged: Bangladeshis and education in Tower Hamlets' *British Journal of the Sociology of Education* 13/4: 437–46.

Tomlinson, S. (1993) 'The multicultural task group: the group that never was' in King, A.S. and Reiss, M. (eds) *The Multicultural Dimension of the National Curriculum*. The Falmer Press.

Tomlinson, S. (1995) 'Hit Squad needs new set of rules' *Times Educational Supplement* 22 December.

Tomlinson, S. (1998) 'New inequalities? Educational markets and ethnic minorities' *Race Education and Ethnicity* 1/2: 20.

Tomlinson, S. (2005) *Education in a Post-welfare Society*. Open University Press/McGraw-Hill.

Tomlinson, S. (2008) *Race and Education: Policy and Politics in Britain*. Open University Press/McGraw-Hill.

Tomlinson, S. (2013) *Ignorant Yobs? Low Attainers in a Global Knowledge Economy*. Routledge.

Tomlinson, S. (2017) *A Sociology of Special and Inclusive education: Exploring the Manufacture of Inability*. Routledge.

Tomlinson, S. (2018) 'Enoch Powell, empires, immigrants and education' *Race Ethnicity and Education* 21/1: 1–14.

Tomlinson, S. (2022) *Ignorance: The Five Giants*. Agenda Publishing.

Tomlinson, S. and Dorling D. (2016) ' Brexit has its roots in the British Empire: so how do we explain it to the young'? *New Stateman (Staggers)* 10 May.

Tomlinson, S. and Johnston, C. (2024) 'Joining the dots? Special education and alternative provision' *Forum* 66/1: 91–100.

Touraine, A. (2000) *Can We Live Together?* (trans. D. Macey). Polity Press.

Townsend, H.E.R. and Brittan, E.M. (1973) *Multiracial Education: Need and Innovation*. Evans-Methuen.

Toynbee, P. (2017) 'The Irish question may yet save Britain from Brexit' *The Guardian* 28 December.

Toynbee, P. and Walker, D. (2015) *Cameron's Coup: How the Tories Took Britain to the Brink*. Guardian Books and Faber and Faber.

Travis, A. (2015) 'How Cameron advisor helped thwart plan to aid young Black people after 1985 riots' *The Guardian* 30 December.

Troyna, B. and Smith, D.I. (1982) *Racism School and the Labour Market*. National Youth Bureau.

Trump, D. (2025) 'I was saved by God to make America Great again' *Presidential Inaugural Address*, Washington DC, USA.

Van Rebrouk, D. (2024) *Revolusi: Indonesia and the Birth of the Modern World*. Bodley Head.

Verkaik, R. (2018) *Posh Boys: How the English Public Schools Run Britain*. One World.

Vincent, C. (2019) *Tea and the Queen: British Values, Education and Citizenship*. Policy Press.

Vine, D. (2011) *Island of Shame: The Secret History of the Military Base on Diego Garcia*. Princeton University Press.

Vinter, R. (2024) 'Boy, 17, remanded in custody over the murder of three girls in Southport' *The Guardian* 1 August.

Walker, P. Siddique, H. and Grierson, J (2020) 'Dismay as no. 10 adviser is chosen to set up race enquiry commission' *The Guardian* 15 June.

Wallace, W. (2004) 'History tells us we must nip it in the bud' *Times Educational Supplement* 4 June.

Walters, S. (2014) 'Tory bloodbath over Muslim schools fiasco' *The Mail on Sunday* 8 June.

Warmington, P. (2014) *Black British Intellectuals and Education*. Routledge.

Warsi, S. (2017) *The Enemy Within: A Tale of Muslim Britain*. Allen Lane.

Waterson, J. (2018) 'Data abuses and fake news a risk to democracy' *The Guardian* 28 July.

Watson, D. (1996) '*Research Note*' *Historical Studies in Industrial Relations*. March p157. Also in Hansard 8 June 1948 col 11851.

Watt, H. (2013) 'Cash for questions: a scandal that should have changed the face of British politics' *Daily Telegraph* 31 May.

Watt, N., Laville, S. and Dodd, V. (2011) 'Too few, too low, too timid, Tories attack police over riots' *The Guardian* 12 August.

Weale, S. (2015) 'Swedish Free schools: famed for success and a beacon for Britain. So what went wrong?' *The Guardian* 11 June.

Weaver, M. (2016) 'Polish ambassador calls for unity against xenophobia as he visits scene of killing' *The Guardian* 1 September.

Whitelaw. Lord W. (1976) *Speech to Leicester Conservative Party*. June.

Whittaker, F. (2018) 'Progress 8 forcing schools to ask for more PRU places' *Schools Week* (edition 132).

Whittaker, F. (2023) 'SEND system is "lose, lose, lose" admits Keegan' *Schools Week* 19 October.

Whitty, G., Power, S. and Halpin, D. (1998) *Devolution and Choice in Education*. Open University Press.

Wilby, P. (2011) 'Mad professor goes global' *The Guardian* 14 June.

Wilkinson, R. and Pickett, K. (2009) *The Spirit Level: Why More Equal Societies almost Always Do Better*. Allen Lane.

Williams, R. (1965) *The Long Revolution*. Pelican Books.

Williams, S. (1988) 'Foreword' in Verma, G.K. (ed) *Education for All: A Landmark for Pluralism.* Falmer.

Williams, S. (2011) *Who Killed Hammarskjold? The UN, the CIA, War, and White Supremacy in Africa.* Hurst and Company.

Williams, Z. (2024) 'It's clearer than ever that Brexit has failed let's not inflict it's misery on young people' *The Guardian* 23 April.

Williams, Z. (2025) 'Pack up all your cares and they'll be great on Truss Social' *The Guardian* 17 April.

Willis, P. (1977) *Learning to Labour: How Working Class Lads Get Working Class Jobs.* Saxon House.

Winder, R. (2004) *Bloody Foreigners.* Abacus.

Wolf, A. (2011) *Review of Vocational Education (The Wolf Report).* Department for Education.

Woodham-Smith, C. (1962) *The Great Hunger.* The Free Press.

Worsthorne, P. (1982) 'Editorial' *The Sunday Telegraph* 23 May.

Wrye Society (2011) 'The villa holiday' *Financial Times Magazine* 12 August.

Yaqoob, S. (2014) 'No need for ideology' *The Guardian* 23 July.

Younge, G. (2007) 'A decade of Blairism has left society more segregated, fearful and divided' *The Guardian* 28 May.

Zephaniah, B. (1996) 'I have a scheme' *Propa Propaganda.* Bloodaxe Books.

Zephaniah, B. (2005) 'Over and out' in Richardson B. (ed) *Tell It Like It Is: How Schools Fail Our Black Children.* Trentham Books.

Zimmern, A.E. (1926) *The Third British Empire Oxford.* Oxford University Press.

Index

A

Abbas, T. 154
Abbott, Diane 70, 153, 180
academies 93, 107–8, 114, 120–2, 137, 139–41, 178, 189–90
Academies Act 2010 140
Acheson, Dean 51
Action for Cities 70
Acts of Union 35, 36, 37, 39
Addai-Sebo, Akyaaba 72
Aden 48
Adonis, Andrew 107, 121
Afghanistan 101, 104, 113
Agnew, Lord 169
Ainley, P. 138
Aitkin, Jonathan 87
Akala 172
Akomaning, L. 110
Aliens Act 1905 21
Allen, Graham 132
Almond, H.H. 24–5
alternative provision 141, 166, 177, 178, 179, 189
anti-Irish racism 38–41, 42, 50
anti-Islamic racism 2, 82, 84–5, 105, 113, 117, 133–5, 154, 181
anti-Semitic racism 2, 30, 38–41, 50, 66
Apple, Michael 93
apprenticeships 122, 139, 184
arms trade 10, 48, 84, 87, 137, 150
Ashcroft, M. 128, 129
assimilation 52, 57, 58
Asylum and Immigration Act 1993 86
asylum seekers 2, 82, 85–6, 90, 105–6, 155, 181, 189
attainment gaps 75, 110, 139, 165, 178
Attlee, Clement 31, 47–8, 53, 148
austerity 119, 126, 128–30, 132, 148
autism and ADHD 166

B

Baden Powell, Lord 20, 25
Badenoch, Kemi 2, 161, 168, 173, 179
Bailey, Shaun 170
Baker, Kenneth 73, 79, 91, 96, 97
Bale, T. 168, 169, 170, 173
Balfour Declaration 21, 133
Balkan wars 86, 104
Balls, Ed 126
banking 119
Barber, Michael 92, 95, 106, 111, 170
beacon schools 106
Beck, Ulrich 109

behaviour in schools 141
Bell, Steve 108
Benn, Tony 53
Bermuda 6–7
Biggar, N. 9
bilingualism 98
Birmingham 51, 56, 59, 67, 126, 134
Birmingham Centre for Contemporary Cultural Studies 65
Black History Month 72
Black identity 67
Black Lives Matter 3, 145–6, 166–9, 183, 188
Black men and boys in education 85, 107, 124, 166, 178, 179
Black Papers 54, 71
Black Studies 59, 78
Blair, Tony 25, 37, 40, 95, 100, 104, 106, 108, 112, 113, 115, 120, 122, 131, 133, 134, 149
Blunkett, David 105, 106, 107, 140
Board of Education 4, 22, 25, 28
Boer war 20, 21
Bolton, Henry 153
book burnings 76
Booth, R. 160
border controls 86, 135, 145, 184
Botswana 49–50
Bourne, Sir Clive 95
Bousted, Mary 165
Boy Scouts 20, 25
Boyle, Frankie 143
Bradford 76, 89
Braithwaite, Eustace 55
Bratton, J.S. 31
Braverman, Suella 160, 176
Brazil, Angela 31
breakfast clubs 148
Breivik, Anders 134
Brendon, P. 8, 20, 49, 67
Brexit
age of leave voters 4
anti-European immigration sentiments 50
and British values 137
early Brexit years 143–7
exclusion politics 151–3
Irish border question 38, 41
Johnson, Boris 160
Leave campaign 11, 127, 130, 133, 149, 189
lies and wishful thinking 149–50, 152
May and Machiavelli 150–1
non-materialisation of benefits 4, 189

Index

precursors to 126
referendum 10–11, 130, 133, 144–5, 148–9
Scotland 36
self-interest politics 148–9
Windsor Framework 41, 43, 173, 176
'Britain First' 152
'Britannia' 23
British Brotherhood League 21
British citizenship 61, 76, 105, 155
British Empire Union (BEU) 25
British National Party (BNP) 90, 91, 104, 105
British Nationality Act 1948 44
British Trades Alphabet 56
British values 17, 23, 122–3, 126, 134, 136–7
Brown, Gordon 6, 45, 101, 113, 115, 116, 118–19, 120, 122, 124
Browne Review 122, 138
Building Schools for the Future 120
Bullock Report 75
Burma 28
Bush, George 104, 119

C

Cadet Corps 24
Callaghan, James 71, 78
Cambridge, University of 29, 69, 126, 138, 157
Cambridge Associates 108
Cameron, David 10, 69, 88, 125, 126, 128, 130, 132, 148, 150, 154, 154–5
Campaign against Racial Discrimination 57
Campaign for Real Education 78
Campbell, Alistair 100
Cantle, Ted 105, 154
Caribbean 7, 44, 58–9, 66, 75, 86
Carron, William 66
Casey, Louise 154
'cash for questions' 86
Catholic church 76, 122
censuses 85, 153, 167
centralisation of education 106–7
Centre for Policy Studies 88
Centre for Social Justice 132
Chagos islands 50, 188
Chakrabortty, Aditya 152
Chantiluke, R. 29
Cheltenham school 19–20, 25
childcare 107
Children Act 107
Children Plan 2007 122
Children's Centres 107
children's literature 29–31, 156
China 86, 150

choice, parental 78, 91–3, 95, 110, 124, 138, 139, 140
Christianity 56, 121–2
Churchill, Winston 24, 25, 47, 48, 167
citizenship, British 61, 76, 105, 155
citizenship education 112
citizenship tests 105
City Technology Colleges 107
civil rights protest movements 57, 67
Civitas 123
Clarendon Commission 19–20
Clark, A. 111
Clarke, Kenneth 10, 85, 89, 91, 92, 98, 129
classics 20
Clegg, Nick 128, 138
Cleverly, James 177
Climbié, Victoria 107
Clinton, Bill 103, 104
Clive, Lieutenant-General Robert 7
Coalition government 70, 89, 119, 123, 125–42
Coard, Bernard 58, 68
Cobain, I. 47, 49
COBRA 131, 160
Cohen, T. 90
Cold War 48
Colenso, J.W. 18
Collingham, L. 7, 8
Collins, P. 184
Collins, Sir Kevan 165
Colston, Edward 167
Comic Relief 143
comics 31, 55, 120
Commission for Racial Equality (CRE) 66, 91, 105, 117
Commission on Race and Ethnic Disparities 161, 167, 185
Commission on the Future of Multi-Ethnic Britain 103
commodification of education 72, 107–8, 114
Commonwealth 40, 61, 62, 67, 96, 130, 143, 150, 163, 172
Commonwealth Immigrants Advisory Council 57, 58
community cohesion 101, 105, 113, 116, 154
Community Studies courses 59
competition between schools 120, 126, 139
comprehensive schools 22, 54, 69, 70, 71, 72, 93, 94, 138
compulsory schooling 20
concrete 177
Conservative Education Association (CEA) 93
Conservative Party 48, 52, 70–1, 98, 106, 145, 184

Contest 117, 134
Controlling Migration Fund 154
Corbyn, Jeremy 119, 144, 160, 180
Coronavirus Act 2020 164
corporal punishment 72
Council for National Academic
 Awards 62–3
Counter-Terrorism and Security Act
 2015 134
Coupland, R. 37
COVID-19 3, 159, 160, 163–6, 169–70,
 179, 188
Cox, Brian 98
Cox, Jo 152
Crace, J. 184
Creoles 75
Crick, Bernard 112
cricket 9, 70
Critical Race Theory (CRT) 168
Crossman, Richard 51, 184
Crouch, Colin 114
Cummings, Dominic 11, 132, 149,
 159–60, 163, 169
curriculum
 2016–19 156
 2022–25 185–6
 absent curriculum 110–12
 British values 122–3, 136–7
 bureaucratic control of 78–9
 central control of 72
 de-colonisation 9, 145, 186
 ethnocentric curriculum 4, 16–32, 56,
  137, 146, 189
 Gove 141–2
 international outlook 74
 multicultural society 79
 national curriculum 73, 77, 92, 95–8,
  120, 123, 127, 141, 186, 190
 national identity 83
 Social Darwinism 55
Curriculum and Assessment
 Review 186, 190

D

Dalrymple, W. 7
D'Ancona, Matthew 123
Darling, Alistair 119
Darwin, Charles 20, 42
Davies, N. 130
Davis, David 151, 157
democracy 23, 57, 134, 136–7, 138, 149, 170
Democratic Unionist Party (DUP) 33, 38,
 40, 176
Department for Children, Schools and
 Families 122, 126
deportations 106, 135, 136, 155, 161
'deprivation' 88–90
 see also poverty

Derbyshire, H. 91
devolution 37, 103
Dewsbury 76, 78
dialect speech 75
'disadvantaged' children 74, 93, 126, 139
dispersal policies 58, 105–6, 154
documentary evidence, destruction of 47
Donelan, Michelle 177, 180
Dorling, Danny 4, 6, 125, 129, 148, 152,
 159, 187, 189
Dowden, Oliver 168
drug crime 131
Duke of Devonshire 21–2
Duncan Smith, Iain 104, 131, 132, 180
Dutch Empire 10
dysfunctional families 132–3

E

early years 107
East India Company 7
East London Mosque 84
Eastern European immigration 44–5, 82,
 113, 124
Eden, Anthony 48
Education Act 1870 20
Education Act 1902 22
Education Act 1944 52, 70
Education Act 2006 122
Education Acts 1979–1988 72
Education Acts 1988–1996 82, 93
Education Acts 1998–2005 106,
 109, 120
Education Association 95
Education Code 1892 27
Education Endowment Foundation 186
'Education for All' (DES 1985) 60, 96
Education Health and Care Plan
 (EHCP) 166, 179
Education in Schools (DES 1977) 71
education policies
 1945–60s 52
 1970–90 70–3
 1990–97 91–3
 2005–10 120–1
 2022–25 177–9
 New Labour 95
Education Recovery Plan 165
Education Reform Act 1988 73, 96
Education Support Grant (ESG) 105
Educational Excellence Everywhere (DfE
 2016) 142
'educationally subnormal' category 58, 74
Egerton, Lord 20
Elgot, J. 135
elite schools in colonial countries 19
Elkins, C. 8, 9
Ellis, Frank 118
Eminent Persons Group 130

Emotionally and Behaviourally Disturbed (EBD) 107
Empire Day 26
Empire Exhibition 1924 8
employability 53, 71
English as an Additional Language (EAL) 105
English Baccalaureate (EBacc) 141
English curriculum 97, 98, 141
Equalities Act 2010 121
Equality and Human Rights Commission 117
Ethnic Minorities Achievement grant 100, 107
ethnocentric curriculum 4, 16–32, 56, 137, 146, 189
Eton 25, 53, 69, 71, 148
EU (European Union)
  1990–97 82, 85
  2022–25 184–5
  Coalition government 130–2
  Euroscepticism 82
  Lisbon Treaty 119
  Major, John 81
  myths about regulations 87
  Powell on 66
  see also Brexit
eugenics 20, 25, 42, 53–4, 55, 109, 118, 132
Euro-myths 87
European Convention on Human Rights 103, 184
European Court of Justice (ECJ) 144, 176
European Economic Community (EEC) 10, 62, 66, 68
European Research Group 10, 157, 189
Euroscepticism 81, 82, 130, 144, 149, 152
examinations, public 18, 53, 73, 93–4, 110, 120, 178
'excellence' rhetoric 126
exclusion politics 151–3
exclusions from school 107, 166, 178
expense claims scandal 119, 166
extremism 126, 134
Eysenck, Hans 42–3, 59, 75

F

Fabian Society 25
'failing schools' 92, 93–5, 106, 120, 121
Faith in the City 1985 72
faith schools 107, 113–14, 120, 137, 140
Falkland Islands 17, 31, 62, 67, 68
Fallon, Michael 96–7
far right 3, 90, 145, 152, 184
Farage, Nigel 10, 130, 148, 152, 161, 173, 175, 180, 181
fascism 21, 52, 66, 90, 180
Ferguson, Niall 8, 141

Festival of Britain 55
Fettes school 25, 37, 108
films 55
Financial Times 131, 158, 183
Finnemore, J. 5, 7, 28
First World War 21
Floyd, George 3, 160–1, 167, 188
food banks 129
football 91, 153, 164, 168
Foreign and Commonwealth Office 49
foreign policy 104, 119
Fox, Liam 144, 150
Francis, Becky 186
Frayne, James 169
free markets 69, 71, 85, 92, 173
free movement 21, 85, 86
free school meals (FSM) 110, 138, 139
free school milk 70
free schools 140
'free speech' 168
free trade 7, 8, 125, 130
Fryer, P. 38
funding of schools
  1990–97 93, 94
  1997–2005 100–1, 106, 107
  2010–16 139, 140
  academies 140
  COVID-19 164, 165–6
  New Labour 120
  SEND and AP 166
  spending on education as proportion of GDP 106
Further and Higher Education Act 1992 92
further education (FE) colleges 92, 139

G

Gaitskell, Hugh 50, 53, 59
Galton, Francis 20, 42
gangs 131
Gardiner, J. 106
Gaskell, Elizabeth 41
GCSEs 73, 141, 165
Geddes, A. 152
genetic determinism 88, 132
geography 27, 29, 55, 97
Ghandi, Mahatma 22
Gibbons, E. 8
Gibraltar 145
Giddens, Anthony 118
Gill, Dawn 97
Gillborn, D. 75, 100, 110, 168, 178
Gilley, B. 9
Gilroy, Paul 69
Gladstone, William 39–40
global financial crisis 2008 113, 118, 129
globalisation 62, 68, 114, 125, 158
Goldberg, D.T. 17

Goldsmith, Zac 82, 171
Goodhart, David 116–17, 146
Gordon-Walker, Patrick 49
Gove, Michael 9, 37, 38, 93, 122, 123, 126, 132, 133, 134, 135, 138, 139, 140, 141–2, 144, 149, 150, 151, 152, 156, 169
Graham, Duncan 96, 97, 98
grammar schools 20, 22, 53, 54, 83, 93, 139
grant-maintained schools 71, 93, 106
Gray, Sue 170, 180
'Great Britain' 35
Grenada 62, 68
Grenfell Tower fire 153, 181–2
Guardian 42, 87, 181
Gulf wars 84

H

Hackney Downs School 94–5, 106, 121
Hadow Committee 22
Haileybury school 20, 25, 48
Hale, Lady 160
Hall, Stuart 65, 82
Hamilton, Neil 86
Hancock, Matt 163, 164, 165, 166
Hargreaves, D. 73
Harman, Harriet 121
Hastings, Max 81
Hattersley, Roy 91, 117
Headmasters' Conference (HMC) 53
Heath, Edward 65, 66
Heaton-Harris, Chris 146, 157, 173
Hechter, M. 38
Henry Jackson Society 134
Henty, G.A. 30
Herbertson, Professor 27, 29
Heseltine, Michael 69, 89
Hestor, Frank 180
higher education 108–9, 118
 see also universities
Hirsch, Afua 111, 151–2
history curriculum 9, 97, 111, 123, 141, 145, 156
history textbooks 28, 55, 112
Holmwood, J. 135
homosexuality 73
Honeyford, R. 76, 84
Hong Kong 8, 86
Hoque, A. 17
'hostile environment' 4, 126, 135–6, 155
House of Commons debates 91
House of Commons Select Committees 60, 67, 73, 149
Howard, Michael 117, 128
Hughes, Katherine 31
human rights 131
Humphries, S. 26

Hussein, Saddam 84, 87
Hutton report 115

I

immigration
 1990–97 84–6
 1997–2005 105
 2022–25 183–5
 Aliens Act 1905 21
 and the EU 2, 82, 130
 'hostile environment' 4, 126, 135–6, 155
 illegal immigration 135–6, 176
 immigration control 48, 50, 52, 66, 114, 116, 117, 173, 176
 'integration 105, 153–4
 internal colonialism 35
 Ireland 40
 Turkey 149, 152
 visas 149
Immigration Acts 50, 66, 136, 155
imperial values 16–32
Importance of Teaching (DfE 2010) 141
'inclusion' agenda 166
independence 48, 49, 80
Independent 86, 142
India 7, 8, 19, 22, 28, 48, 55, 150, 183
Indian Workers' Association 57
Individual Learning Accounts 108
individualism 71, 103
industrial revolution 7
inequality gaps 6, 89, 103, 113, 116, 125–6, 131, 139, 164, 189
inner city schools 89
Inner London Education Authority 72
inspection regimes 58, 72, 92, 109, 120, 178–9, 189
Insted Consultancy 135
Institute for Community Cohesion 154
Institute for Fiscal Studies 139
institutional racism 91, 167, 188
'integration 105, 153–4
intelligence 53–4, 58–9, 75, 88–9, 118, 132–3
internal colonialism 188
international students 136, 155
internationalism 97
IRA 86
Iraq 84, 101, 104, 113, 115, 133
Ireland 5–6, 33, 35, 38–41, 66, 76, 188
Islamic Studies 117
Islamism 133, 134
Islamophobia 84–5
 see also anti-Islamic racism
Israel 21, 133, 177

J

Javid, Sajid 149, 154, 156, 166
Jebb, Gladwyn 47

Jenkins, Roy 52
Jenson, A. 59
Jogia, Ameet 153
John, Gus 95
Johnson, Boris 5, 11, 28, 41, 53, 55, 77, 82, 87, 128, 133, 134, 143, 144, 145, 149, 150, 151, 152, 158, 159, 161, 163, 164, 167, 170, 172, 176, 185
Joseph, Keith 23, 77
Judt, T. 88, 125

K

Kannah-Mason, Sheku 173
Kappal, B. 5
Kaunda, Kenneth 67
Keegan, Gillian 168, 177, 179, 180
Kelly, E. 90
Kelly, Ruth 116, 189
Kelly, Sir Christopher 119
Kennedy, Charles 106
Kentridge, William 21
Kenya 21, 49, 67–8
Key Stages 73
Khama, Seretse 49–50
Khayani, Mahmoud 122
Kiernan, V.G. 33
King Charles III 151, 175
Kingsley, Charles 33, 35, 39
Kipling, Rudyard 26, 27, 28, 30
Kirp, D. 74
Kuwait 84
Kwarteng, Kwasi 175
Kynaston, D. 50, 52, 55

L

Labour 21, 45, 47–8, 51, 53, 54, 70, 87, 95, 140, 144, 173
labour shortages 52
Lammy, David 154, 167
languages 37, 39, 55, 75, 98, 105
Latin 53
Lawrence, Doreen 81, 91
Lawrence, Stephen 81, 82, 91, 100, 103, 169
Lawson, Neal 118
Lawson-Walton, J. 24
Lawton, D. 21–2, 71, 106, 111
league tables 91, 93
Learning and Skills Act 2000 107, 139
left-wing politics 72, 82, 92, 96–7, 104
Letwin, Oliver 69, 106
'levelling up' agenda 164
Levy, Andrea 18, 44, 56, 60
Liberal Democrats 124, 126, 128
liberalism 50–1, 54, 57, 61, 71, 103
Lisbon Treaty 119, 151
literacy 106, 111, 120
Livingstone, Ken 121

Lloyd, T.O. 16
Loach, Ken 125–6
local education authorities 72, 81, 92, 94, 95, 106, 107, 108
Local Government Act 1988 73
London bombings 7/7 113, 117, 133

M

Maastricht Treaty 81, 85, 88, 104, 144
Macauley, Lord 8, 18
MacFarlane, R.A. 28
Macgregor, John 91
MacKenzie, J.M. 28, 30
Mackinder, Halford 29
Macmillan, Harold 49, 175
Macpherson Inquiry 90–1, 103
Magraw, B.I. 28
Major, John 10, 81, 82, 83, 86, 87, 88, 91, 96
Malthouse, Kit 177
Mandelson, Peter 107, 116, 122, 128
Mangan, J.A. 24, 25
Manpower Services Commission 71
Manzoor, Sarfraz 52
maps 5, 9, 56
market ideologies in schools 92, 93, 100, 103, 113–14, 148
Markle, Meghan 153
Marlborough school 20
Marquand, D. 118
Marquis of Londonderry 22
Marx, Karl 41–2
mass education 18, 21–2
mathematical education 18–19
May, Theresa 4, 5, 41, 53, 55, 82, 87, 126, 131, 135, 136, 143, 144, 149, 150–1, 153, 154–5, 157–8, 159
McInnery, I. 136
McNeal, Julia 59
McSweeney, Morgan 180
Meath, Lord 25, 26
media 6, 67, 89, 90, 93, 117, 129–30, 178, 179, 184
Mellor, David 86
Men of Renown (Finnemore, 1902) 4–5, 7, 28
mental health 129, 179
middle classes 20, 26, 52–4, 56, 71, 72, 90, 130
Middle East 21, 84, 133, 137, 156, 173
Miliband, David 119, 124
Miliband, Ed 124, 132, 140
militarism 17, 24, 25, 30
military bases 50, 188
Miller, Gina 5, 151
miners' strike 62
Mirza, Munira 167
misinformation 149, 190

missionaries 20
'model minorities' 110, 120, 178
Modood, T. 85
Monday Club 66, 79
Mone, Baroness Michelle 169–70
Monet, Jean 145
Montserrat 86
Moore, M. 11
Moore, R. 51
Moorhouse, G. 18
Moral Instruction League 20
Morant, Robert 22
Morgan, Nicky 135
Mosley, Oswald 21, 52
Moss, W.H. 24
Mossbourne school 95, 121
motherhood 25
Mounk, Y. 137
MPs, Black 70
multi-academy trusts (MATs) 140, 178, 189
Multicultural Task Group 79, 98
Multiracial School (1971) 59
Murdoch, Richard 90, 113, 129, 134
Murray, Charles 88, 89
Murray, Douglas 134
Musk, Elon 6, 182
Muslim communities 70, 78, 105, 133
Muslim dress 85, 109, 120, 179
Muslim schools 70, 78, 100, 107, 134
Myers, K. 38

N

Napoleon 3, 17
National Council for Black Organisations 69
National Curriculum Council (NCC) 96, 98
National Education Union 165, 179
National Front 66, 67
National Geographic 157
national identity 51, 62, 63, 66, 68, 79, 96, 97, 101, 113, 122–3
national schools commissioner 140
National Service 25, 56, 61
National Tutoring Programme 165
National Union of Teachers 68–9, 74, 92
nationalism 17, 69, 85, 160, 172, 189
Nationality, Citizenship and Asylum Act 105
Navy 30–1, 68
neo-Nazis 66, 90, 152
New Cross fire 69
New Deal for Communities 116
'New IQism' 89
New Labour 95, 100–12
Newcastle 89
Newell, R. 168
Newsinger, J. 9
Newsom Report 54

Nolan Committee 87
Norman conquest 35
Northern Ireland 5–6, 33, 38, 40, 86, 103, 137, 145, 153, 173, 176
Northern Rock 119
numeracy 106, 111, 120

O

Oakeshotte, I. 128, 129
Oasis Christian Trust 122
O'Dowd, N. 42
Office for Fair Access (OFFA) 108
Ofsted 92, 95, 109, 135, 136, 140, 178–9
Olufemi, Lola 157
Olusoga, David 9
'Operation swamp' 69
Operation Vaken 135
Osborne, George 128, 148
Osler, A. 112
Oxford, University of 29, 48, 87, 121, 126, 128, 138, 148, 157

P

Palestine 21, 133, 177
Parekh, Lord B. 103, 104
Parental Alliance for Choice in Education 78
Paris Peace Conference 1946 48
Patel, Sir Hamid 178, 179
patriotism 17, 22, 25, 26, 27, 30–1, 56, 69, 104
Patten, John 87, 91–2, 157
Patterson, Owen 169
Paxman, J. 9
Peace Studies 79
Peach, Blair 67
Peel, Sir Robert 39
Percy, Lord Eustace 22
performance targets 106, 109, 120
Perry, Ruth 178–9
Peterloo Massacre 41
Pettifor, A. 148
Phillips, Rob 97
Phillips, Trevor 117
Phillipson, Bridget 179, 186, 190
phone-hacking scandal 129
Pincher, Chris 170
PISA (Programme for International Student Assessment) 110, 139, 140
Pitt, William 3, 17
Plowden Report 54
police relations 67, 69, 81, 89, 91, 103, 131, 167, 178
Policy Studies Institute 85
polytechnics 91, 92
Porter, B. 9, 45
poverty
  1970–90 74
  1990–97 88–90

2010–16 140
austerity 129
and continuing social division 189
COVID-19 164
cycles of deprivation 54
free school meals (FSM) 110
and intelligence 118
New Labour 116
Poor Laws 125
universities 138
see also inequality gaps
Powell, Enoch 17, 40, 44, 51, 52, 58, 62, 66, 75, 104, 112, 117, 146, 152, 184
Prescott, John 115
Prevent 113, 117, 134, 181
Price, Florence 18
primary schooling 20, 21, 53
prison populations 118, 131
Private Finance Initiative (PFI) 107, 120
private schooling
  1945–60s 53
  2010–16 138
  academies 121
  assisted places 71
  Cabinet ministers 71, 126, 128, 148
  Cameron government 126
  civil servants 56
  and the civil service 56
  Clarendon Commission 19–20
  curriculum 56
  influence of 18, 23–6, 189
  Scotland 25, 37
  training for Empire rulers 19–20
  VAT on fees 179
privatisation 71, 81, 87, 103, 107–8, 115, 126, 129, 138
Progress 8 141
propaganda, imperial 22, 23, 27, 28, 29
protectionism 7, 85
psychometric testing 58
Public Order and Community Cohesion Ministerial Review 105
public schools *see* private schooling
publishers 29, 156
Pupil Level Annual School Census (PLASC) 110
Pupil Premium 139
Putin, Vladimir 2, 3

R

Raab, Dominic 157
Race Disparities Unit 151
Race Relations Act 1976 66
Race Relations Amendment Act 2000 109
Race Relations Board 51, 58, 62
racial quotas 43
radicalisation 84, 113, 114, 133–4
Rampton Committee 75

Ramsey, A. 11, 37
Ranger, T. 36
Ranson, S. 72
Rashford, Marcus 164
rationing of education 72
Rawnsley, A. 116, 124, 159, 176
Raynor, Angela 169
'Reclaiming Schools' 152
Rees-Mogg, Jacob 53, 144, 180
Reeves, Rachel 184
Reform party 3, 161, 173, 176, 180, 181, 184
refugees 66, 81, 82, 90, 155
religion 16, 24–5, 36, 39, 40, 42, 70, 72
reparations 49, 121
repatriations 66
Rex, J. 51, 59, 65, 66, 84
Rhodes, Cecil 9, 28, 29, 157
Rice Burroughs, Edgar 30
right-wing politics 3, 6, 17, 52, 63, 160–1, 167, 183
riots 57, 67–9, 89–90, 117, 130–2, 154, 173, 181, 185
Robbins Report 54
Roberts, A. 51
Roberts, Robert 26, 30
Rollock, N. 130
Roma people 85, 105, 153
Roman Empire 34–6
Rose, E.J.B. 50–1
Rosebery, Lord 16, 172
Rosenburg, Dan 170
Royal Commissions 20
Rudd, Amber 155
'Rule Britannia' 35–6, 173
Runnymede Trust 90, 167–8
Rushdie, Salman 70, 76, 84
Russia 29, 177
Rwanda 106, 161, 176

S

Saudi Arabia 3, 49, 105, 137, 150
Saunders, Bernie 6
Savage, M. 165
Scarman, Lord 69
Schengen Agreement 86
School Boards 21
School Cuts Organisation 139
school-leaving age 22, 32, 70, 71, 116
Schools Inquiry Commission 20
Scotland 35, 36–7, 42, 103, 188
Scott Inquiry 87
Scruton, Roger 77, 146, 185
second generation immigrants 67
second language learners 94, 105
secondary education 18, 21, 22, 53, 106, 120
  see also comprehensive schools; grammar schools

secondary modern schools 22, 53
Seeley, J.E. 26
segregation, deliberate 117, 122, 154
Seldon, A. 168
selective education 54, 72, 94, 95, 100, 106, 108, 120, 139
self-interest politics 148–9
Sennet, Richard 6
Sewell, Tony 161, 167, 170, 171, 181, 185
sexism 26
Shaheen, Faiza 180
Shepherd, Gillian 92, 95
Sherman, Sir Alfred 65
Shindler, C. 56, 61
Shipman, Tim 1, 11, 149, 150, 163, 173, 176, 177
Shotte, G. 86
Shukla, N. 90
Sierra Leone 86, 104
Simon, B. 18, 20, 53, 70
Simon, David 67
single mothers 88, 89, 189
slave trade 7, 16, 28, 50, 121, 167, 168
sleaze 81, 86–8, 119, 169, 177
small boats 2, 161, 176
Smith, Tim 86
Social Darwinism 16, 20, 26, 42, 55
social democracy 45, 103, 125
Social Exclusion Unit 100, 107
social justice 100, 103
social media 149, 170, 172, 175
social mobility 89, 126, 138, 139
Social Mobility Commission 126
social services 107
socialism 45, 55, 61, 102–3
Somaliland 48, 85
South Africa 29, 49, 67
South Sudan 86
Southport 6, 173, 181–2
special educational needs 70, 74, 94, 166, 178, 179, 189
'special measures' 94
special schools 141, 177, 178
specialist schools 106
Spielman, Amanda 179
sponsorship of schools 106, 107, 121, 139–40
Standards and Effectiveness Unit 95, 106
Starkey, H. 112
Starmer, Keir 173, 176, 179–85, 188
statues 9, 29, 157, 160, 167
Stembridge, J. 16, 55
Straw, Jack 103, 120
strip search incident 178
student loans 89, 108, 138
Suez canal 10, 48
Sunak, Rishi 41, 161, 166, 173, 175–6, 177, 179, 180
supplementary schools 59, 79

Sure Start Centres 107, 133
'SUS' laws 67
Swann Report 63, 75, 78, 79, 96, 137
Sykes-Picot Agreement 21, 133

T

Tarzan 30
tax cuts 129–30
tax havens 4, 7, 67, 150, 188
Taylor, D. 136
Teacher Training Agency (TTA) 92, 108–9
teachers
  1990–97 92
  Black teachers 55
  British values 136
  from former colonies 55
  imperial values 25, 26
  modernising the profession 108
  national curriculum 73
  positive practices by teachers 59–60
  raising professional status of 141
  shortages of 56
  teacher training 62–3
  training 60, 63, 92, 108–9, 142
  unions 25, 165
Teaching and Higher Education Act 1997 108
Tebbit, Norman 70
technical schools 22, 53
terrorism 104, 113, 116, 117, 119, 134
textbooks 5, 16, 26, 27–8, 55, 79, 168, 183
Thatcher, Margaret 10, 61, 62, 65, 67–8, 69, 70–2, 73, 89, 94, 96, 98, 148
'Third Way' 100, 102
Thrill of History 28
Times 7, 38, 103, 120, 135
Times Educational Supplement 76, 79
Tinker, David 17, 68
Tinker, Hugh 68
Tiratsoo, N. 81, 87
Tomlinson, Mike 122
Tomlinson, S. 39, 42, 44, 51, 56, 58, 59, 63, 65, 71, 74, 75, 76, 77, 94, 98, 106, 108, 109, 117, 139, 148, 152, 159, 166, 169, 178, 179
Tower Hamlets 94
Toynbee, Polly 38–9, 148
trade 8, 55–6, 150–1, 182–3
trade unions 45, 66, 129
Trevelyan, Sir Charles 39
Trojan Horses 133, 134–5, 137
'Troubles' 40–1, 86
Trump, Donald 1, 2, 6, 112, 144, 150, 172, 173, 176, 182–3
Truss, Liz 161, 171, 173, 175, 176
tuition fees 89, 108, 116, 118, 122, 126, 138

U

Uganda 65
UK Independence Party 3, 10, 82, 130, 148
Ukraine 2, 3, 170, 173, 177
Ullah, Ahmed 78
Umunna, Chukku 154
UN Human Rights Council 183
unemployment 67, 69, 88, 89
Union Jack 30
United Learning Trust 121–2
United Nations 48, 49
universal credit 132
universities 29, 92, 94, 108–9, 118, 126, 138, 156–7
unskilled work 51
USA
  American Civil War 36
  Black Lives Matter movement 145–6, 167, 168
  civil rights protest movements 67
  Cold War 48
  George Floyd 3, 160–1, 167, 188
  global democratic leadership 2
  Grenada 68
  Headstart 54
  Iraq war 84
  military bases 50
  'model minorities' 110, 178
  'Third Way' 103
  trade with 144
  underclass 88
  see also Trump, Donald

V

Van Rebrouk, D. 9–10
Varadkar, Leo 40
Verkaik, R. 24, 26
Victoria, Queen 7, 16–17, 39, 85
Victorian values 16–17, 24, 27, 39, 71–2, 88, 96, 109, 129, 132
Villa Holiday 131
Vincent, Carol 136–7
Violence Crime and Reduction Act 117
violent crime 117–18
visas 149
Viscount St Davids 5
vocational education 92, 94, 122, 139, 164
voluntary-aided schools 100
vote influencing 11
'vulnerable' pupils 141

W

Wales 33, 35, 37, 42, 103
Water-Babies, The (Kingsley) 39
Watson, Commander Michael Saunders 98
Watson, D. 48
Weldon, J.E.C. 24
welfare state 45, 52, 89, 100, 125–6, 129, 131, 132, 138, 148, 156
West Indian Standing Conference 57
white collar jobs 56
white superiority 10, 17, 24, 26–31, 35, 44, 47, 55, 60
white supremacy 16, 17, 24, 169
Whitelaw, William 66, 69
Wilkinson, Ellen 48
Willetts, David 88, 138
Williams, Jenny 56
Williams, S. 49, 63
Williams, Shirley 71, 78
Williams, Sir Ralph 38
Williams, Venus and Serena 120–1
Williams, Z. 1
Williamson, Gavin 164, 165, 166
Willis, P. 26
Wilshaw, Michael 95
Wilson, Harold 50, 52, 66
Winder, R. 42, 44, 70
Windrush 4, 44, 135, 136, 154–6
'Winds of Change' 49
'woke' culture 161, 168, 173, 183, 184, 185
Wolf, Lord Justice 94
Woodhead, Chris 87, 92
working classes
  class-based expansion of mass education 18, 20
  and deprivation 88
  education policies 53
  elementary education 21
  eugenics 20
  higher education 108, 138
  imperial rule and class 22
  imperial values 26
  incorporation of immigrants 51–2, 76
  internal colonialism 33, 41
  miners' strike 62
  National Service League 25
  white working class boys 140, 179
World Studies 79
World Trade Centre attacks (9/11) 101, 105, 118, 154
World Trade Organization (WTO) 125
Wragg, Ted 121

Y

Yeo, Tim 86
Younge, Gary 112
youth training schemes 67, 69, 71

Z

Zahawi, Nadhim 166, 177
Zephaniah, Benjamin 73–4
Zimbabwe 67, 86, 104
Zimmern, A.E. 29

www.ingramcontent.com/pod-product-compliance
Lightning Source LLC
Chambersburg PA
CBHW071157070526
44584CB00019B/2821